The Practice of Human Resource Management in Canada

OPEL—Open Paths to Enriched Learning
Series editor: Connor Houlihan

Open Paths to Enriched Learning (OPEL) reflects the continued commitment of Athabasca University to removing the barriers—including the cost of course material—that restrict access to university-level study. The OPEL series offers introductory texts, on a broad array of topics, written especially with undergraduate students in mind. Although the books in the series are designed for course use, they also afford lifelong learners an opportunity to enrich their own knowledge. Like all AU Press publications, OPEL course texts are available for free download, as well as for purchase in both print and digital formats.

Series Titles

Open Data Structures: An Introduction
Pat Morin

Mind, Body, World: Foundations of Cognitive Science
Michael R. W. Dawson

Legal Literacy: An Introduction to Legal Studies
Archie Zariski

Health and Safety in Canadian Workplaces
Jason Foster and Bob Barnetson

Interrogating Motherhood
Lynda R. Ross

Canada's Labour Market Training System
Bob Barnetson

The Practice of Human Resource Management in Canada
Bob Barnetson and Jason Foster

The Practice of Human Resource Management in Canada

Bob Barnetson and Jason Foster

AU PRESS

Published by AU Press, Athabasca University
1 University Drive, Athabasca, AB T9S 3A3

https://doi.org/10.15215/aupress/9781771994255.01

Cover design by Martyn Schmoll
Cover image by wonry (iStock Images)
Printed and bound in Canada

Library and Archives Canada Cataloguing in Publication
Title: The practice of human resource management in Canada / Bob Barnetson and Jason Foster.
Names: Barnetson, Bob, 1970– author | Foster, Jason, author
Series: Open paths to enriched learning.
Description: Series statement: Open paths to enriched learning | Includes bibliographical references and index.
Identifiers: Canadiana (print) 20240427181 | Canadiana (ebook) 2024042722X | ISBN 9781771994255 (softcover) | ISBN 9781771994279 (EPUB) | ISBN 9781771994262 (PDF)
Subjects: LCSH: Personnel management—Canada—Textbooks. | LCGFT: Textbooks.
Classification: LCC HF5549 .B26 2024 | DDC 658.3—dc23

We acknowledge the financial support of the Government of Canada through the Canada Book Fund (CBF) for our publishing activities and the assistance provided by the Government of Alberta through the Alberta Media Fund.

Canadä Alberta Government

Contents

Acknowledgements

We would like to acknowledge the importance of the research leaves in the collective agreement negotiated by the Athabasca University Faculty Association. These leaves have given us the time to research, think through, and write this book. We would also like to thank Dr. Rupa Banerjee and Dr. Johanna Weststar, two anonymous reviewers, and the staff of Athabasca University Press for their assistance in improving this book and making it available as an open educational resource. Finally, we would like to thank our respective families for their support during the writing process.

Preface

This text is designed to introduce university- and college-level students to the practice of human resource management (HRM) in Canada. Its unique feature is that it combines a traditional introduction to the technical aspects of HRM with an ongoing exploration of the political economy of day-to-day HR practice. This mixed approach reflects our experience that good technical solutions to HR issues require practitioners to understand the interests of different actors, acknowledge that these interests sometimes conflict, and devise solutions that accommodate (or at least anticipate) these conflicts.

To this end, the 11 chapters introduce the major domains and techniques of contemporary human resource practice while also identifying and exploring how power, conflict, and intersectionality affect this practice. The last chapter contains six short case studies that draw together many of the concepts and techniques introduced in the book and illustrate their application to real-world problems.

1 Introduction to the Practice of Human Resource Management

Sometimes bad things happen at work. For example, organizations hire workers all the time. Usually, hiring goes well, in part because human resource (HR) practitioners work to minimize and manage the financial cost and reputational risk that it can entail. The case of Dr. Kim Barker, however, illustrates what can happen when organizations don't have strong HR practices for hiring.[1]

In 2013, Barker was CEO of Algoma Public Health in Sault Ste. Marie, Ontario. Prior to her arrival, a senior employee had been charged with breach of trust and theft, so when Barker arrived Algoma Public Health needed to hire a new chief financial officer (CFO). She hired Shaun Rothberg as CFO in late 2013. It was later revealed that Shaun Rothberg was an alias used by Shaun Rootenberg and that Barker was aware of this fact when he was hired. Rootenberg had been incarcerated for fraud. By allowing him to use an alias during the hiring process, she enabled Rootenberg to pass a required criminal record check.

Why would Barker help a candidate for the CFO job hide prior convictions for fraud? The short of it was that she had met Rootenberg on a dating site in July 2013. She did not tell the board about her personal relationship with Rootenberg and hoped that hiring him would lead to a more intimate relationship. He introduced her to Ron Hulse (who ran a Toronto-based consulting firm, Rhulse26). Barker engaged Rhulse26 to handle the hiring of Rootenberg. An investigation uncovered that she began discussing the hiring with Hulse months before the Algoma Public Health board began the hiring process.

Rootenberg left the position of interim CFO with the health unit on May 31, 2014, after 27 weeks of service. Rhulse26 billed the board for $120,514 for Rootenberg's services. Barker resigned as CEO in January 2015. As a result of this incident, recruitment and hiring practices have been standardized across the organization. Interestingly, in 2017, Rootenberg was charged with defrauding both Barker and another woman with whom he was romantically involved.

The Barker case is interesting for three reasons. First, it is a clear example of how poor hiring practices can cause both financial and reputational harm for an employer. Barker's behaviour clearly embarrassed the organization and imperilled its already shaky reputation as a competent steward of public funds. And hiring a convicted fraudster as the CFO exposed the organization to significant financial risks. It is the job of HR practitioners to minimize these risks. One way that they can do so is by creating organizational processes that eliminate opportunities for malfeasance or incompetence by organizational actors.

Second, the CEO of the organization was the bad actor in this case. Often it is assumed that misbehaviour is more likely to come from low-level employees. This bias—in favour of executives and against workers—is a recurring blind spot for many organizations and HR practitioners. Consider how many cashiers work with cameras pointed at them, and contrast that with the significant discretion that CEOs have using company credit cards. Although most employees follow most organizational rules most of the time, it is the job of HR personnel (in conjunction with line supervisors) to ensure that everyone follows the rules all of the time. Managing the (mis)behaviour of powerful organizational actors is one of the more challenging aspects of being an HR practitioner.

Third, it took a significant case of misbehaviour for a presumably sophisticated organization to standardize one of the most basic HR processes (recruitment and selection). This suggests that the real-world practice of human resource management (HRM) can diverge from the best practices that you will read about in this book. This gap between prescription (i.e., what should happen) and description (i.e., what actually happens) is a tension that HR practitioners often have to navigate. For example, organizations often say that workers are their most valuable resource, but then they turn around and squeeze their wages or sack them to increase the organization's profitability. This discrepancy between what is said and what is done can create organizational tensions and negative outcomes.

The Approach of This Book

We approach HRM in two complementary ways. First, we explain the major techniques used to manage workers in organizations. Then we consider how sometimes conflicting employer and worker interests can affect how HR practitioners apply these techniques. For example, HR practitioners often manage and deliver employee training and orientation. This usually requires them to develop a learning objective for a training session. The objective shapes what they teach, helps them to decide how to teach it, and guides how they evaluate whether the training was successful. In Chapter 7, you will learn about the three components of a learning objective and practice how to write one. This information is the kind of technical knowledge that HR practitioners must know and apply on a daily basis.

How this information is applied, however, is affected by the conflicting interests (sometimes called the "politics") found in employment relations. One of the most surprising things that new HR practitioners find is that workers might not be all that interested in the training offered. For example, an organization might wish to cross-train a group of workers so that they can do the others' jobs. That sounds great to most bosses because there's always someone around to cover sick leaves and such. Workers, however, might resist learning how to do more work because they fear that, once they are capable of doing more work, they will be compelled to do that work, possibly during what otherwise would be a period of rest.

Similarly, new HR practitioners often struggle with the conflicted nature of their job. On the one hand, they often assist workers to integrate into and operate within an organization. This can include advocating that a worker receive modified work duties following an injury or that the employer adopt name-blind hiring practices in order to reduce discrimination. In this way, HR practitioners sometimes appear to be there to help workers. On the other hand, though, practitioners are agents of employers. And they are expected to carry out the bosses' orders. This can include acting in ways that might be harmful to workers' interests or violate their rights. Bosses might not want to accommodate a disability because of the cost of doing so. And they might not want to adopt name-blind hiring because they want to hire their buddies' kids.

These conflicting interests play out across the various domains of human resource management. It is often a source of stress for HR practitioners as they navigate conflicting demands, often in high-pressure situations. Understanding, predicting, and managing such conflicts is a requirement of an effective HR practitioner. For this reason, in this book we pair a technical explanation of HRM with a political analysis. Incorporating this second approach means that you will be better able to understand the interests of different actors, acknowledge that these interests sometimes conflict, and devise solutions that accommodate (or at least anticipate) these conflicts.

To develop both your technical and your political understanding of HRM, we offer in this book a broader scope than that in most other HR textbooks. Where necessary, we step back from the "how-to" view of HR to consider the broader social context in which work and HRM take place. In the next few sections of this chapter, for example, we talk about the nature of employment and employment relationships before we turn to a more conventional discussion of how such relationships are managed. In other places, the narrative will interrupt an explanation of how some aspect of HR works to consider the degree to which commonly accepted ideas about HR are really true or useful. We think that this approach makes for a more interesting read and will make you a more effective HR practitioner. But it also requires some patience from you. If it is not clear why we are talking about a topic or how a point relates to the practice of HRM in Canada, just file your question for the time being. It will all come together in the end.

Human Resource Management

Human resource management comprises the practices and systems ensuring that an organization has the right number and mix of workers necessary to achieve its goals and, subsequently, that the workers achieve those goals. It is often useful to think of HRM as a continuum of activities designed to support an organization's strategy (see Figure 1.1). This includes analyzing work and designing jobs, determining how many workers are required, recruiting and selecting workers, setting their rates of compensation, orienting and training those workers, managing them, and then facilitating their departure from the organization. These HR activities are performed in a complex legal environment and a fluid labour market.

This textbook will introduce you to each of the major domains of HR practice set out in Figure 1.1. Each domain requires you to develop and use certain knowledge, skills, and abilities (KSAs). The application of these KSAs to achieve specific organizational outcomes reflects that HRM is a technical undertaking. As noted above, we will also introduce you to the idea that HRM is also a political undertaking. Recall that the purpose of HRM is to achieve organizational outcomes. These outcomes and how an organization pursues them might not always match up perfectly with the interests of an organization's workers. Using organizational power to require action that runs contrary to the wishes of other organizational actors (e.g., workers) is a political act.

For example, a company might wish to increase its profitability by lowering its labour costs. One option is to move staff to home-based

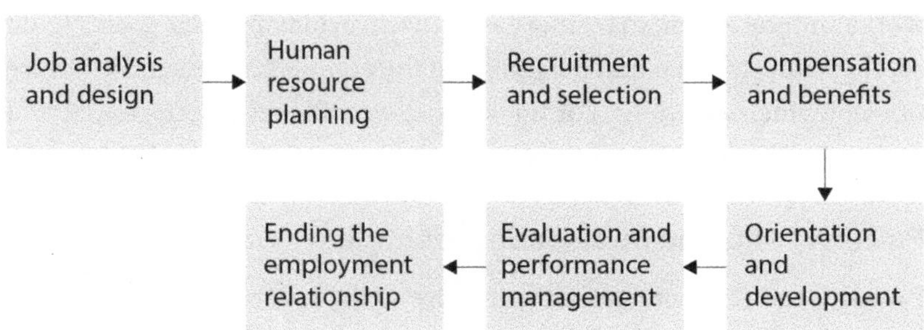

Figure 1.1 Human resource activities

offices. Doing so lowers costs because the employer no longer needs to rent workspace or provide office furnishings. The workers, who must now find their own desks and use parts of their homes for work, might be upset by this change. After all, it means that they are now subsidizing the employer's operating costs from their own pockets. Although the workers might be upset, the employer is likely to get its way because, as described below, it normally possesses greater legal and labour market power than do workers.

Understanding HRM as both a technical and a political function is often necessary to achieve organizational goals. For example, workers might be trained and required to report injuries so that supervisors can take actions to control workplace hazards (see Chapter 2). But, in practice, workers might be reluctant to report injuries. An HR practitioner might well diagnose non-reporting as worker irresponsibility or laziness. This diagnosis suggests that the issue should be treated as a disciplinary one, with penalties being applied to change workers' behaviour. But non-reporting might be more usefully understood when examined through a political lens that considers how workers' interests can drive their behaviour. Non-reporting might reflect, for example, workers' belief (perhaps well founded) that they will be punished for reporting injuries and that, even if they do report them, the employer will not control the hazards that caused them. Workers who believe this to be true will not report injuries because doing so is not in their interests. This political analysis of the problem can suggest non-disciplinary ways to improve reporting and thus make the workplace safer.

HR practitioners who can anticipate, recognize, and respond to worker interests tend to be more effective in achieving their goals. To do so, they must have an understanding of the complex and nuanced nature of employment relations. For this reason, we will focus on the impacts of power, profit, and intersecting identities on the practice of HRM.

Power, Profit, and Intersecting Identities

Power is the ability to get someone else to do or accept something that they do not want to do or accept. HR activities and techniques comprise an important way that employers exercise power over workers. Employers typically use their power to capture the profits generated by organizational work. Narrowly defined, **profit** is the excess of revenue after paying all expenses. Another way to understand profit is to see it as the allocation of the surplus value generated by workers' labour to employers. Surplus value is the additional price that can be charged for a product or service because of the efforts of workers. For example, a furniture company can sell an assembled bookshelf for more than the unassembled parts because a worker spent time and energy putting it together. By seeing profit in this way, it becomes possible to recognize that workers contribute to the value of a product or service through their labour and that who reaps the benefit of that extra value is a point of conflict between workers and employers.

Workers typically prefer to see the surplus value of their labour used to improve their salaries and working conditions. In contrast, employers want to keep that surplus value for themselves as profit. The struggle over who benefits from this surplus value drives much of the contestation in the workplace. HR practitioners must manage the resulting tensions. Public sector and non-profit organizations do not earn profits (although they might accumulate operating surpluses). Nevertheless, even in those workplaces, tension exists over how the surplus value is allocated (i.e., to workers or the organization), meaning that the same dynamic is at play.

Although it is convenient to talk about workers and their interests in generic ways, workers are not a monolithic group. Different workers might have different interests. For example, a cook and the manager at a fast-food restaurant are both workers because they trade their labour for compensation. But the manager might have an interest in pushing the cook to work faster, for example to secure a management bonus. The cook, whose salary is fixed, might not want to work faster and, indeed, might have a higher risk of being injured by working faster around grills and slicers.

Workers' experiences of work and the world can also shape their interests. These experiences, in turn, often differ significantly depending on workers' identity factors. For example, men and women often experience the world differently, and this can affect the employment benefits that they value. The compounding effect of our intersecting identity factors is often called intersectionality (see Feature Box 1.1).

Feature Box 1.1 Intersecting Identity Factors

Identity factors are characteristics ascribed by others to individuals. Some examples of identity factors include

- age,
- gender identity and expression,
- ethno-racial background (sometimes called ethnicity, race, ancestry, heritage, or culture),
- (dis)ability,
- social class,
- religion,
- sexual orientation,
- family status, and
- citizenship.

Some of these identity factors, such as one's age, are seemingly objective descriptors. But it is useful to speak about identity factors as ascribed because they typically entail someone else making assumptions about a person. For example, a worker might be 35 years old, but perhaps their hair has gone prematurely grey, so they appear to be older. Or perhaps they have a young-looking face. These differences affect the age that people ascribe to the worker and might not align with the worker's objective age.

These ascribed identity factors can significantly affect how workers are treated. For example, an employer might conclude that a young-looking 35 year old is too young for a promotion even though the employer's ability to estimate age is limited and age is a poor proxy for ability.

One's identity factors do not exist in isolation. Rather, they can interact in complex ways. For example,

- Men typically earn more than women for the same work. But workers who are men and also people of colour tend to earn less than workers who are men and white. And workers who are women and also people of colour tend to earn less than workers who are women and white.
- Whether a young-looking worker is deemed too young for a promotion might depend on the worker's ascribed gender. An employer might be more willing to give a young-looking man a

promotion (as a developmental opportunity) compared with a young-looking woman.

In this way, identity factors can be a source of both advantage and disadvantage. And they can have compounding effects on workers' experiences of work and, more broadly, the world.[2] The compounding impact of social identities on our experience of work and the world is called **intersectionality**. Intersecting identity factors help to explain why, even when researchers hold factors constant—such as education, experience, and skill—they still cannot fully explain significant differences observed in labour market outcomes, such as employment rates and income levels.

Workers, particularly those whose social identities result in disadvantages, are often well aware of how intersecting identify factors can affect them in the workplace. In contrast, organizational responses to concerns about the equitable treatment of all workers (regardless of their social identities) are typically limited to examining single identity factors (e.g., gender or disability) in isolation. Being mindful of the interactive and potentially compounding effects of identity factors can make HR practitioners better able to anticipate, recognize, and respond to these effects.

Employment Relationships in Capitalist Economies

Employers hire workers because they require help (in the form of labour) to achieve an organizational goal. Paying someone to do a job is the most common way for employers to access labour. Some organizations also utilize unpaid labour (e.g., interns, volunteers, prisoners), but such arrangements are beyond the scope of this book. Broadly speaking, employers can either pay an employee or pay a contractor to have work completed.

Employees work for someone else rather than for themselves. They trade their labour for wages and other forms of remuneration. By entering into a contract of employment, employees agree to do what the employer tells them to do. Typically, the employer directs how work is done and provides any required tools or equipment. A worker who agrees to such a **contract of service** generally has no opportunity to hire someone else to do the work (i.e., subcontract). The rights and obligations of employees are examined in detail in Chapter 2.

In contrast, **contractors** work for themselves. They can enter into a commercial relationship with an organization in which they agree to provide certain goods or services to that organization. With a **contract for service**, contractors retain the right to perform the work in the ways that they think best, typically supply their own equipment and tools, and can hire others to perform the work. A contractor also typically has the opportunity to make a profit but also risks taking a loss on the work.[3]

Both employees and contractors are subordinate to the organization that hires them. Although in this book we focus on the relationships between employees and employers, it is useful to remember that the world is more complex. There are different types (or classes) of workers and bosses. Feature Box 1.2 provides a more nuanced introduction to social class in Canada.

Feature Box 1.2 The Complexities of Social Class in Canada

In this book, we often talk about employers (sometimes called capitalists) and workers (sometimes called labour) as the only two types of participants in the labour market. This simple typology is useful because it is easy to understand. But the class structure in Canada is much more complicated than just labourers and capitalists. Table 1.1 considers ownership, specialized knowledge, and delegated authority to identify nine social classes in Canada today. (Delegated authority exists when a worker exercises managerial power on behalf of the actual owners of the company.)

Table 1.1 Social Classes in Canada

Capitalists	Intermediaries	Labourers
Self-employed	Managers	Industrial workers
Small employers	Supervisors	Service workers
Large employers	Professionals	Unemployed workers

Capitalists can be divided into the self-employed, small employers, and large employers. The self-employed sell their labour but own their own businesses. An example might be a small appliance repair person or a freelance writer. Small employers typically have a small number of employees with the owner(s) actively managing the business and perhaps working alongside their workers. Large employers possess or direct significant amounts of **capital** (i.e., money, land, equipment, and tools), often act through intermediaries (e.g., managers and supervisors), and employ significant numbers of workers.

There are also three categories of labourers. Industrial workers produce material goods, such as machinery and foodstuffs, and have relatively little autonomy or discretion in their work. Service workers provide a range of services but also lack autonomy. Some industrial or service workers can have significant specialized knowledge but lack discretion in its use. Finally, there are workers who, by choice or circumstance, are unemployed.

Between capitalists and labourers are workers who are intermediaries: managers, supervisors, and professionals. Professionals have specialized knowledge, which grants them significant discretion over how they do their work (e.g., lawyers, IT specialists, qualified tradespeople). That said, unless they are also employers or self-employed, they remain subordinate to employers. Employers also hire supervisors and, to manage them, managers. Both of these groups ensure that workers meet employers' goals.[4]

Although most workers are employees, many employers use contractors as well. Hiring a contractor might be a cost-effective way to meet short-term staffing needs, such as covering a parental leave or increasing staff to deal with a sudden surge in demand. Large employers can also contract out entire areas of work (e.g., payroll functions) in order to save money and/or focus on work that they consider to be their core business. Employers can also hire contractors to externalize (i.e., transfer) certain costs to contractors. For example, employers that operate almost entirely using independent contractors in sectors such as transportation (e.g., Uber) and food delivery (e.g., Skip the Dishes) might be able, in some jurisdictions, to avoid the costs associated with meeting statutory deductions for employment insurance, paying benefits, or providing tools (e.g., vehicles and gas).

The use of contractors is an example of employers that structure work to minimize the cost of labour. Private sector employers seek to minimize labour costs to increase the profitability of their organizations. Unprofitable organizations go out of business, so the **profit imperative** is a powerful influence on organizational behaviour. The need for public sector and non-profit organizations to work within budgets creates a similar dynamic regarding labour costs. The profit imperative reflects that work in Canada occurs in a capitalist economy. A **capitalist economy** is a system of production and exchange characterized by the private ownership of capital. Capitalists combine their capital with the efforts of workers (often called **labour**) to produce goods and services sold in a marketplace both to cover the cost of production and to generate a profit for the capitalists.[5]

In a capitalist economy, those who own the **means of production** (i.e., equipment, land, and money) are generally allowed to operate their businesses as they see fit, including directing how work will be performed. The rationale for giving capitalists such authority is that they are risking their capital, so they must be able to operate as they think best. Over time, governments (sometimes called *the state*) have imposed some limits on employers' discretion. Important limits include statutory and common law rights and obligations (presented in Chapter 2). The rules to which employers are subject still give them significant power and, importantly, much more power than workers.

HRM typically focuses on how best to deploy labour to achieve organizational goals. Not surprisingly, the majority of an HR practitioner's work entails hiring and managing workers. That said, workers do not just magically appear, resumés in hand. Rather, the workforce is created and continually recreated through complex social processes. These processes are often referred to as **social reproduction** (see Feature Box 1.3). The nature of these processes means that HR practitioners often must grapple with their demands, such as child care and elder care.

Feature Box 1.3 Social Reproduction

Human resource management focuses on helping organizations to produce goods and services. But the production process is dependent on social reproduction. Broadly speaking, that is the process of recreating the circumstances that allow for production to occur. It includes creating new workers (i.e., having and raising children, maintaining a home) as well as maintaining workers' acceptance of capitalism and their role within it.[6]

Social reproductive activity associated with raising children and maintaining a home tends to be unpaid or poorly paid. For example, most homemaking activity tends to be performed without remuneration by workers or their family members. Where these activities are purchased as services from others (e.g., child care, cleaning), the workers who perform the services tend to be poorly paid and often employed precariously (i.e., receiving low wages, limited benefits, and little job security). Social reproduction is also usually gendered in that it is performed (with or without pay) mostly by women.

Social reproduction activity associated with maintaining workers' acceptance of capitalism and their role within it is performed primarily in the school system. In addition to teaching literacy and numeracy, schooling inculcates certain behaviours and beliefs into future workers. For example, schools train children to obey authority (under threat of punishment) and perform tasks for arbitrary periods of time. They also reward students based on their performance, which reinforces the idea that society is a meritocracy. These teaching jobs (also heavily feminized) tend to pay slightly better than other forms of domestic work, in large part because they are heavily unionized (see Chapter 10).

Although it might seem strange to discuss social reproduction in a textbook about human resource management, it is important for HR practitioners to recognize how dependent organizational production is on social reproduction. For example, consider the recent COVID-19 pandemic. The closure of daycares and schools (functionally a form of child care) downloaded these responsibilities onto parents. This meant, in turn, that many workers were suddenly unavailable for work or available only if they could work from home around their parenting responsibilities. Even before COVID-19, though, workers required leaves to address their own or dependents' illnesses. For this reason, many workplaces provide paid sick leave (see Chapter 8).

Organizations are often forced to address issues related to social reproduction. As discussed in Chapter 2, employers have long been prohibited from discriminating on the basis of pregnancy. More recently, employers have been compelled to accommodate child-care obligations in certain circumstances under human rights legislation. That the state has had to compel employers to address these issues reflects the operation of the profit imperative. Essentially, employers often seek to minimize their labour costs by externalizing (i.e., offloading) costs onto workers (e.g., the costs of having and raising the next generation of workers). Not every employer adopts this approach. As will be discussed in Chapter 8, some organizations choose to offer assistance with social reproduction in the form of leave and child-care subsidies in the expectation that doing so will improve productivity.

Labour Market Power and Dynamics

Employment relationships are formed in a labour market. Historically, labour markets were physical places where employers inspected workers and haggled with them over wages. Wages were set based on the supply of and demand for labour. If there was a **tight labour market** (i.e., greater demand for workers than supply), then wages would go up as employers competed for workers. If there was a **loose labour market** (i.e., greater supply of workers than demand), then wages would decline as workers underbid one another to secure scarce jobs.

A contemporary **labour market** is a metaphorical place where employers and workers negotiate the price of labour.[7] There are actually many labour markets, often segmented by both geography and skill. For example, although many people could probably perform the work of a cashier or barista, the pool of workers available to take these low-wage jobs is likely to be limited geographically. Only those workers who live within a reasonable commuting distance will be interested in such a job, and no one is going to uproot their family and move to take such a job. The labour market for jobs for which specific credentials are required (e.g., nursing, gas fitting) is limited by skill. Only adequately qualified workers are able to perform these jobs. However, if jobs also entail high-enough wages, then workers might well move or commute to another locale to perform the work.

Typically, there are more workers seeking work than there are jobs available. Exceptions to this general rule typically occur in highly skilled occupations or during periods of significant economic growth, when the demand for workers can temporarily exceed the supply. This routine oversupply of workers means that employers can easily replace workers whom they find unacceptable or troublesome. This gives employers **labour market power**, which bolsters the greater power that they already possess because of their control over the workplace. Furthermore, workers need jobs to purchase the necessities of life for themselves and their families. In contrast, employers do not face any significant repercussions if they are short an employee or two. The threat of unemployment (sometimes called the **whip of hunger**) weighs heavily on workers and further buttresses employers' labour market power. Over time, employers have used their power to increase the precarity of employment for some workers (see Feature Box 1.4).

Feature Box 1.4 Precarious Work

An important trend in the past 30 years has been the growth of precarious forms of employment. **Precarious employment** is work that entails low wages, limited job security, and/or limited access to employment protections and benefits.[8] Precarious work deviates from the standard employment relationship (i.e., full-time, permanent employment with a single employer). The growth in precarious employment is one way that employers reduce their labour costs in pursuit of greater profitability.

Precarious employment is difficult to define and quantify. This difficulty reflects that context matters, and not every individual whose employment exhibits some features associated with precarious employment is a precarious worker. For example, most people would likely agree that a recent graduate hired to work part time on a nine-month contract with no benefits is precariously employed. An NHL player hired on the same terms would likely not be considered to be precariously employed. The differences between these superficially similar situations centre on the economic vulnerability of the workers. This vulnerability, in turn, might reflect their relative power (i.e., their financial security and labour mobility).

A 2018 analysis by the Chartered Professional Accountants of Canada attempted to tease out the levels and trends of various kinds of precarious employment.[9] This study suggested that, between 1996 and 2016, there was significant growth in part-time and temporary employment in educational services; information, culture, and recreation; and food services and accommodations. Workers in the latter two sectors were already paid among the lowest wages.

The impacts of these changes were not equally distributed among all workers. The prevalence of part-time employment increased sharply between 1993 and 2016 for women between the ages of 15 and 24 and slightly for men in all age groups (particularly 20- to 24-year-old men). Workers without a university degree also saw sharp increases in part-time employment. Temporary work has increased significantly for women (especially those under 24 and over 65). These patterns suggest that intersecting identity factors—such as gender, education, and age—are compounding the employment precarity faced by young women without a university education.

In addition to lower income and less job security, employment precarity is often associated with the absence of employment benefits (e.g., dental benefits, retirement plans) and limited access to statutory protections. As discussed in Chapter 2, Canada's employment laws mainly operate on a model of complaint-based enforcement. Workers who are economically vulnerable are less likely to complain about **wage theft** (i.e., when an employer fails to pay owed wages) and unsafe workplaces. This dynamic reflects that most public policy continues to assume that workers have full-time, permanent jobs.

When workers and employers enter into a contract of service, typically two bargains are being struck. Most obviously, the parties are striking a **wage-rate bargain**. It sets out the compensation that workers will receive while employed. In exchange, workers agree to make themselves available for work. Whether any work actually gets done is up to the employer, which has to convert the workers' **capacity to work** into productive work. As discussed later, employers convert workers' capacity to work into actual work primarily through job design (Chapter 3) and performance management (Chapter 9).

The less obvious bargain being struck by workers and employers is the **wage-effort bargain**. It is hard to see because it is often based on an implicit understanding of how hard and in what ways workers are prepared to work given what they are being paid. Employers might be highly motivated to alter the wage-effort bargain (e.g., getting workers to work faster or harder). But altering that bargain can trigger significant worker resistance. In this way, the wage-effort bargain can act as a limiting factor on the ability of employers to increase their profitability through intensifying work.

For example, an employer might notice that individual workers have a certain amount of down time in their jobs (i.e., time when they are not performing productive tasks). An employer might seek to increase the tempo of work or add tasks to fill up the time. Employers often frame such efforts as multi-tasking or job enrichment (see Chapter 3). Although some workers might welcome greater diversity in their jobs or the chance to learn new skills, others might be concerned about the increase in work or the loss of recovery time between tasks. For this reason, workers might cooperate informally to work at a fixed pace and be reluctant to provide their employers with a clear understanding of how hard they could work if absolutely necessary in order to avoid the employers making such changes.

Human Resource Management and Strategy

Modern human resource management has its roots in 19th-century factories. Concentrating workers in large numbers required (and allowed for) the development of centralized personnel management functions to address hiring, pay, discipline, and worker welfare. In the late 19th century, employers sought to increase their control over production in order to increase profitability via scientific management (see Chapter 3). By the 1930s, employers also began to explore more deeply how the behaviour of people in groups, working conditions, and compensation could be leveraged to increase productivity further.

Over time, **human resource management** has replaced **personnel management** as the general term for the task of ensuring that an organization has the right number and mix of workers necessary to achieve its goals. Organizations carry out HR functions in many different ways. In a small organization, a manager or an owner can perform some or all of these functions, possibly in addition to directing the operation of the business. A large organization can have a dedicated HR practitioner or department. Organizations can also contract out certain HR functions, such as payroll administration.

Many HR practitioners continue to perform the routine administrative tasks that were the purview of personnel administration, such as recruiting and terminating staff or administering payroll and benefits. But in HRM these tasks are intended to be performed with a greater degree of integration among HR functions. For example, annual performance assessments occurred historically in isolation from other functions. In modern HRM, performance assessments are often linked to the training and compensation that workers subsequently receive. The expected result is a more systematic administration of workers that better meets employers' needs. When thinking about the operation of HR systems, it is important to remain mindful of possible gaps between prescription (i.e., what should happen) and description (i.e., what does happen).

Although it can be useful to discuss human resource management as if it is a widely accepted and understood practice, it is operationalized differently in every organization. These differences can sometimes reflect different organizational strategies. A strategy is a plan designed to achieve organizational goals. Organizational strategies often differ in their depth and sophistication. It can be useful to distinguish among three levels of strategy.

1. Corporate: A corporate strategy sets out the purpose and approach of the entire organization. It answers questions such as "which business(es) should this organization be in?" and "how can one aspect of our business help another?"
2. Business: A business strategy identifies how a specific activity or area of business will be carried out. It answers questions such as "how should this organization compete in this specific business area?"
3. Functional: A functional strategy identifies how each department (e.g., human resources, finance) supports the overall business strategy and tends to be most detailed.

Broadly speaking, there are three main business strategies that organizations can adopt.

1. Cost leader: Organizations can emphasize minimizing the costs of their products or services by standardizing their products, developing economies of scale, and/or attaining control over all steps in production and distribution.

2. Differentiation: Organizations can emphasize unique aspects of their products or services (e.g., quality or expertise) and customer loyalty, thereby reducing the impact of price competition.
3. Focus: Organizations can provide a specific service targeted at a selected (i.e., niche) audience ideally in a market with few or no competitors.[10]

HR strategies are functional strategies designed to ensure the success of an organization's business strategy. Not surprisingly, organizational HR strategies differ depending on an organization's business strategy as well as other factors, such as organizational size and labour market. For example, a meat-processing plant might adopt a cost-leader business strategy reflecting that meat processing is a crowded marketplace, meat is a fungible (i.e., easily interchangeable) commodity, and therefore retailers buy meat based largely on price. Furthermore, the nature of meat packing is that jobs can be designed to require little pre-existing skill. Consequently, the company might adopt an HR strategy based on paying low wages for difficult work and accepting that there will be a high level of worker turnover. The viability of this functional strategy turns on the availability of an adequate labour force, and the meat-packing plant will need to have a plan to address this. For example, the plant might rely heavily on migrant workers from other countries whose work visas make it difficult for them to quit their jobs at the plant.

In contrast, an organization that operates five high-priced artisanal charcuterie shops might adopt a business strategy of differentiation. It would emphasize the quality of its products and the expertise of its staff, thereby avoiding competing on prices. Furthermore, it requires highly qualified workers and a stable workforce able to develop personal relationships with customers. This organization's human resource strategy will likely emphasize more careful staff recruitment and selection, pay higher wages, and seek to retain staff for as long as possible. The viability of this business strategy turns on the continued demand for fancy meats with high-end service and, to a lesser degree, the absence of a similar competitor.

Both of these organizations will likely perform the full range of HR functions. But the emphasis and tone of each will be different (see Feature

Box 1.5). Consider their likely approaches to employee training. The meat-packing plant will be required to train workers frequently how to do basic job functions (e.g., killing, dismembering, and packaging a chicken). Because of high staff turnover, there will likely be little emphasis on further worker development. In contrast, the charcuterie shop might choose to hire trained staff because doing so will be less costly than training new workers to butcher and prepare the meats. Additional staff development might focus on deepening the workers' skills and be used as part of a worker-retention strategy.

Feature Box 1.5 Control versus High-Performance HR Strategies

The meat-packing plant and artisanal charcuterie shops discussed above illustrate two contrasting approaches to developing an HR strategy. The meat-packing plant adopts a traditional, control-based HR strategy. Power and authority are centralized. This allows managers to minimize labour costs through prescriptive job design and precarious work. A contrasting HR strategy, one likely appropriate for the charcuterie shops, is to develop a high-performance work system (HPWS).

An HPWS distributes decision-making power more broadly within the organization. Essentially, workers have more say in the development of organizational goals and how these goals will be achieved. This devolution of authority is intended to leverage workers' knowledge as well as increase their buy-in and thus effort. The degree to which power is distributed varies among organizations.

To facilitate greater worker decision making and buy-in, key organizational information about goals, processes, and outcomes tends to be more broadly distributed than in control strategies. Some degree of self-management of teams is common. Selection processes might be more rigorous (to ensure a good fit), and evaluation metrics must be consistent with the behaviours expected of workers. Workers might also have greater access to training programs as well as greater compensation and job security. In an HPWS, workers (and their skills and knowledge) are an organizational asset that creates a competitive advantage, and they are not seen primarily as a cost.

Implementing these HR practices as coherent bundles is expected to have a synergistic effect. In short, these practices are expected to reinforce and intensify each other's effect and generate a higher level of organizational performance than would implementing them individually. There is evidence that an HPWS improves the financial performance of organizations. The impact of an HPWS on individual workers is more mixed, with some evidence emerging that such a system entails greater physical and psychological stress. These outcomes make a certain amount of intuitive sense. An HPWS is designed by organizations to extract additional effort from workers in order to improve organizational performance, including profitability. It is not surprising that, in at least some cases, this approach imposes additional burdens on workers.[11]

An HPWS is not an optimal HR strategy for every organization. Organizations facing extreme price sensitivity might find a cost-leader business strategy combined with a more traditional control-based HR strategy the best way to maximize profitability. In this way, we see how the utility of different HR strategies is shaped by an organization's business strategy.

Sometimes people unconsciously conflate human resource management with **strategic human resource management** (SHRM). As noted above, **human resource management** is a general term for the practices and systems that ensure an organization has the right number and mix of workers necessary to achieve its goals and, subsequently, that the workers achieve these goals. Strategic human resource management is a specific approach to (or perspective on) HRM asserting that organizational performance can be improved by linking human resource management with an organization's business strategies (see Feature Box 1.6). This approach heightens the organizational importance of human resource management, but the degree to which SHRM delivers on its promise of improved performance is unclear.

Feature Box 1.6 Strategic Human Resource Management

The terms *human resource management* and *strategic human resource management* are often used interchangeably. These terms, however, are not synonymous. Strategic human resource management is one approach to HRM. SHRM asserts that human resource policies must be integrated into and inform organizational strategy and that this vertical integration will improve organizational performance.[12] This approach also requires horizontal integration of the specific HR functions set out in Figure 1.1 to shape organizational culture. In SHRM, line managers play a greater role in delivering HR services.[13]

The prevalence of the term *strategic human resource management* suggests that there is wide agreement about what SHRM is, how to implement it, and what it does to and for an organization. This, however, is not the case. Once one gets beyond the high-level description above (which emphasizes the vertical and horizontal integration of human resources), SHRM becomes a contested and amorphous concept that can mean any number of things. Some of the challenges associated with nailing down what it is and whether it delivers on its promise include the following.

- Conceptual: There is no complete agreement about what SHRM entails in terms of concrete practices, and it is often operationalized quite differently in different organizations. Even among researchers, there are different approaches to studying it. Some researchers have adopted a universalist position (i.e., SHRM is always better), others suggest that it can be effective in certain situations (and thus not in others), and others suggest that certain factors or configurations of HR practices can make SHRM effective.[14]
- Context: The outcome of practices consistent with human resource management can depend on the organizational context, such as size, industry, stage of organizational life cycle, and unionization.[15] Furthermore, there can be factors that mediate the relationship between SHRM and organizational performance. For example, an organization's performance can be determined by its market orientation (i.e., how well it meets market demand). SHRM can be useful in helping a market-oriented organization to meet this demand (i.e., SHRM indirectly improves performance), but implementing it alone will not improve performance.[16]
- Methodological: It can be difficult to link specific SHRM practices (e.g., offering training, promoting from within the organization) to organizational outcomes (e.g., financial performance). Often specific practices can be related to intermediate performance measures (e.g., changes in absenteeism, turnover,

satisfaction), but these outcomes are sometimes ambiguous. For example, what level of employee turnover is good (or bad)? Turnover entails costs but can also mean that underperforming employees leave the organization and that new talent is acquired. Furthermore, the relationship between these intermediate outcomes and organizational outcomes (e.g., financial returns) can be tenuous and difficult to establish and objectively measure.

- Impact: Practices often seen as a part of SHRM can have synergistic or conflicting organizational impacts. For example, there is some evidence that promoting from within reduces employee turnover, whereas increased training can increase turnover.[17] This complexity suggests that practices need to be studied in different configurations to understand their effects. Overall, the evidence that strategic human resource management improves organizational performance is mixed and weak.

Given these complexities and uncertainties, it is interesting that SHRM enjoys the popularity and reputation that it does. One explanation of this dynamic might be in the aspirations of HR practitioners and managers. SHRM heightens the profile and importance of HRM, involving HR practitioners in making organizational decisions rather than just carrying out decisions (a task delegated to line managers). It also suggests that HRM is a core organizational business that should not be contracted out. This analysis draws our attention to how, even within organizational management, there can be diverging interests that shape actors' behaviours and decisions.

Social Construction of Human Resource Management

It is axiomatic that different people view the world and work differently. Individuals' views reflect their personal experiences of work as well as the experiences of their friends and family members. Their views also reflect information received in school, from the media, and from their employers. **Social construction** is the process by which an individual combines personal experiences with the information provided by institutions to develop an understanding of how the world works and what certain objects, behaviours, and events mean.

Social construction is based on the belief that there is effectively an infinite amount of stimulus in the world and that what certain things mean is open to interpretation. In deciding what stimulus to pay attention to and how to interpret it, individuals draw from their existing knowledge, beliefs, and values. The understandings that they develop through this process can be shared by others in similar circumstances but not necessarily by those in different circumstances. For example, one's lived experience (which can be affected by one's gender and ethno-racial background) can influence one's view about whether it is safe to walk down a particular street at a particular time. Or whether contacting a police officer is an effective way to resolve an issue or even a safe thing to do.

Workers use the understandings that they develop to guide their behaviour in the workplace. For example, on the one hand, if workers' experience is that a 15-minute coffee break can be safely stretched out to 20 minutes, then those workers might sometimes do so. If, on the other hand, their experience is that the boss watches the clock and docks pay accordingly, then they will probably be careful to get back to work on time every day. Workers, and specifically HR practitioners, have a variety of understandings about the nature of employment relationships and the nature and degree of conflict in these relationships. Although every individual's understanding is likely unique in some way, it is possible to discern broad schools of thought about employment and conflict: **unitarism** and **pluralism**.

Unitarism, as its name suggests, asserts that there are no fundamental conflicts of interest between workers and employers. Rather, both groups are united in the pursuit of shared workplace objectives. Their different roles in the workplace mean that employers and managers determine what these objectives are and how they will be achieved, and workers carry out the tasks that they are assigned. Despite the unitarist expectation of a unity of purpose in the workplace, conflict does occur. It is explained as being caused by some combination of miscommunication, poor leadership, the influence of outside actors (e.g., unions), and/or a lack of commitment or work ethic among workers. What these explanations of conflict have in common is that they avoid discussing the potential for the interests of workers and employers to conflict. Rather, they assert that conflict stems from error, outside interference, or poor character.

Consequently, unitarism seeks to manage conflict via emphasizing shared interests, excluding outside actors, and rooting out discontented or disruptive workers.

Pluralism, in contrast, accepts that the interests of workers and employers can both converge and diverge. In this view, conflict stems from a contest over who will capture the surplus value generated by workers. Employers typically want to maximize their profits (or, in the public and non-profit sectors, to minimize their expenditures). Workers typically want better wages and working conditions. Because pluralism accepts that the conflict arises from conflicting interests, it seeks to manage it through some combination of repressing and accommodating workers' interests.

The unitarist perspective on employment and conflict often resonates with HR practitioners more than the pluralist perspective. This preference for a unitarist view reflects, in part, that many employers and HR practitioners believe that a culture of cooperation and mutual commitment benefits both parties. And many HR practices seek to encourage and reward worker commitment to organizational goals. These personal and institutional experiences of HR practitioners tend socially to construct work as unitarist.

Before adopting a unitarist perspective, however, it is worth probing a bit deeper. A useful place to start is to recall the difference between prescription (i.e., how things should be) and description (i.e., how things are). HRM exists to ensure that organizations have the right number and mix of workers necessary to achieve their goals as well as to ensure that workers achieve these organizational goals. The HR practices associated with this goal (e.g., developing incentive structures, performance management processes, discipline, and termination) recognize that, absent such structures, workers might not actually achieve the goals of the organization. This recognition implicitly acknowledges that workers and employers can have conflicting interests that must be managed. If workers and employers fully shared interests, then it would be largely unnecessary to link performance to pay, for example. In this way, the working perspective of HRM is pluralist (i.e., there are diverging interests) rather than unitarist.

This disconnect in HRM—between its unitarist prescription (i.e., we are all here to work together) and its pluralist description (i.e., workers must be managed)—is rarely acknowledged or examined. There are likely multiple reasons that HRM is framed as a cooperative activity rather than one underlaid with conflict. Emphasizing that work is a cooperative endeavour exerts normative pressure on workers to do what the employer asks (e.g., work harder), even if doing so is not necessarily in the workers' interests. Emphasizing cooperation delegitimizes the notion that the interests of workers and employers might conflict. This, in turn, impedes workers' ability to articulate their interests as distinct from those of employers and to mobilize other workers to pursue them, thereby making it easier for employers to secure the surplus value of labour as profit.

This analysis of how employment is framed is useful because it helps to explain how power, profit, and intersecting identity factors play out in HRM. Employers seeking profits use their social power to frame employment as a cooperative undertaking. This framing obscures how the interests of labour and capital conflict and how the employment relationship helps employers to shift production costs onto workers (in the form of low pay and poor working conditions). Workers, by virtue of their identity factors (specifically being legally subservient to employers), have a limited ability to challenge this framing or outcome. And, of course, some workers are even less able to challenge this framing because of their other social identities related to gender, ethno-racial background, citizenship status, or disability.

Conclusion

In this chapter, we introduced human resource management and placed it in its political, economic, and legal contexts. The broad purpose of HRM is straightforward. It ensures that employers have the right staff and that those staff achieve organizational goals. HR practitioners achieve these outcomes by applying sets of organizational practices within the organization's environmental context. In the following chapters, we introduce the contexts and the functional areas of HRM.

Chapter 2 examines the legal environment in which HRM occurs. Common and statutory law delineate the range of permissible employment arrangements and behaviours for HR practitioners. That the government has enacted employment laws suggests that, absent such laws, employment relationships can result in outcomes not in the public interest. Specifically, state intervention in employment law is required because the conflicting interests of labour and capital in the surplus value of labour can result in social instability.

Key HR tasks include workflow analysis, job analysis, and job design. Chapter 3 examines how job analysis helps an organization to identify the number and qualities of the workers whom it needs to employ. Chapter 4 explores how organizations use this information to ensure that they have the right number of appropriately skilled workers, both now and in the future, through HR planning. Job analyses and HR plans are then used to inform the recruitment of prospective employees (Chapter 5) as well as the selection of which candidates to hire (Chapter 6).

When workers are hired, organizations typically provide them with an orientation. Some workers might also be provided with further training opportunities. Chapter 7 explores orientation and training. The compensation provided to workers (in the form of wages and benefits) is examined in Chapter 8. Chapter 9 considers how employers convert workers' potential to work into actual work through performance management. This chapter also examines how employers discipline workers as well as bring employment relationships to an end. Chapter 10 considers one way that workers seek to increase their power in the workplace: forming unions and collectively bargaining their terms and conditions of work. Chapter 11 shows how HR techniques and analyses can be integrated and applied through a series of real-world case studies.

Although these chapters provide an introduction to the technical nature of HRM, they also give due consideration to its political nature. Specifically, each chapter considers how the converging and conflicting interests of workers and employers affect (and are affected by) human resource management practices. For example, Chapter 3 explores how workers can be both a valuable and a problematic source of information about job duties during a job analysis. Workers can be valuable sources because they often have the best understanding of how a job is done and how it might be redesigned to be performed more efficiently. But it might be problematic for HR practitioners to get this information from workers because it is not in the workers' interest to tell their employers how to speed up work or shed jobs.

Thinking back to the opening vignette, it is clear that Dr. Kim Barker acted in a way that advanced her own interests at the expense of the organization's interests. She was able to do so because the organization did not have effective hiring practices. This case is particularly striking because Barker was also the CEO and, presumably, the most trustworthy employee of Algoma Public Health. This case highlights that one of the tasks of HR practitioners is to minimize organizational liability by constraining workers' scope of action through the creation of standardized policies and processes.

This case is also notable because a relatively sophisticated employer did not have standardized recruitment and selection processes. This draws our attention back to how important it is to distinguish between prescription and description in HRM. HR practitioners must grapple with what is actually happening in a workplace rather than what is an ideal or expected situation or process. Complicating matters is that other organizational actors (e.g., senior executives) might struggle to grasp how reality (description) diverges from their expectations (prescription). This gap can cause stress and conflict as well as negatively affect decision making.

EXERCISES

KEY TERMS

Define the following terms.

- Capital
- Capacity to work
- Capitalist economy
- Contract for service
- Contract of service
- Contractor
- Employee
- Employer
- Human resource management
- Intersectionality
- Labour
- Labour market
- Labour market power

- Loose labour market
- Means of production
- Pluralism
- Power
- Precarious employment
- Profit
- Profit imperative
- Social construction
- Social reproduction
- Strategic human resource management
- Tight labour market
- Unitarism
- Wage-effort bargain
- Wage-rate bargain
- Whip of hunger

DISCUSSION QUESTIONS

Discuss the following topics.

- What is the purpose of human resource management?
- What is power, and how is it relevant to human resource management?
- How is human resource management both a technical and a political undertaking?
- What is the difference between prescription and description, and how can it affect HRM?
- Why would an employer want to make jobs more precarious?
- What is intersectionality, and how is it relevant to human resource management?
- How do the interests of workers and employers converge and diverge?
- How do the wage-rate and wage-effort bargains relate to one another?

SELF-REFLECTION QUESTIONS

Write self-reflections of between 200 and 500 words on the following topics.

- Think about an organizational decision on employment or working conditions that you experienced or witnessed in which the profit imperative appeared to play a factor in the decision. Summarize the decision and explain how the profit imperative affected the decision.
- Briefly summarize a time when you experienced or witnessed a boss telling a worker to do something that the worker was not keen to do. Explain why you think that the worker obeyed the boss.
- Name four identity characteristics that you possess. Then explain how they are likely to affect your experience in the labour market. Give some thought to how these characteristics can interact and whether that interaction is positive, negative, or neutral.
- Imagine that you are employed but dissatisfied with your current wage rate. Your employer declines your request for a 15% wage increase. Identify three ways in which you might increase your wage and identify the pros and cons of each option.
- Decide whether you have a unitarist or a pluralist perspective on employment and conflict. Explain why you choose to adopt this perspective. How would you go about convincing someone who holds the opposite view that your perspective is the correct one?

2 Employment Law

Rules are an important feature of organizational life. We can all think of some basic ones. Show up on time. Pay your workers what they are owed. Do not sexually harass anyone. An important source of these rules are laws passed by a legislature that require or prohibit certain behaviours. Organizations may also develop their own rules to guide their behaviour and decision making or to enter into contracts that include certain rules. This complex web of rules can sometimes be difficult for human resource practitioners to navigate.

For example, in 1992, Tawney Meiorin was hired by the British Columbia Ministry of Forests as a firefighter. After she was on the job for three years, the employer implemented a series of new fitness tests for firefighters. These tests were developed in response to a coroner's inquest report that recommended only physically fit employees be assigned front-line firefighting duties. Meiorin passed all of the new tests except an aerobic test. This test required her to run 2.5 kilometres in 11 minutes. Her best time in four attempts was 11 minutes and 49.4 seconds. She was subsequently fired.

Through her union, Meiorin contested the termination. The union argued that there was no evidence that passing the aerobic test was necessary to perform the work of a firefighter. It also argued that the aerobic test discriminated against women. As a group, women have lower aerobic capacity than men and thus are less likely than men to pass the test. The union said that adopting this aerobic standard effectively barred most women from forest firefighting jobs and thus constituted discrimination on the basis of gender. Gender discrimination was prohibited by British Columbia's *Human Rights Code*. Employers seeking to impose discriminatory standards were required to demonstrate that the standard was a **bona fide occupational requirement** (BFOR). A BFOR is a qualification necessary to do the job and thus a basis on which discrimination is justified.

The arbitrator hearing the case found that there was no credible evidence that Meiorin's inability to meet the aerobic standard created any sort of safety risk and ordered Meiorin reinstated. A complex set of legal appeals followed. In 1999, the Supreme Court of Canada upheld her reinstatement and established a new test to determine when an employer can legally discriminate against a worker on the basis of a BFOR. A BFOR exists when the standard

- is rationally connected to the performance of the job,
- is adopted in an honest and good faith belief that it is necessary to the fulfillment of the job, and
- is reasonably necessary to accomplish a legitimate work-related purpose such that the worker cannot be accommodated without imposing undue hardship on the employer.[1]

The court held that the Ministry of Forests had failed to demonstrate that the aerobic test was reasonably necessary to identify those individuals who could safely perform the job. Indeed, that Meiorin had successfully performed the work of a firefighter for three years before the aerobic standard was established suggested that it was not a valid test. Because the employer could not demonstrate that the aerobic test was reasonably necessary to accomplish a work-related purpose, it was not a BFOR. Firing Meiorin for failing to meet a test that discriminated against women was therefore contrary to the *Human Rights Code*. The government was directed to rehire Meiorin and compensate her for lost wages.

Meiorin's case illustrates several important points. First, establishment of the rule (i.e., a fitness standard) was well intentioned. It was, after all, designed to protect the employer's workers. Unfortunately, it contravened the *Human Rights Act*. Both sides ended up with hefty legal bills. Meiorin lost her job and never returned to work as a firefighter because of the delays caused as the employer appealed the original arbitration decision.[2] The employer also experienced reputational and financial consequences because it violated the *Human Rights Act*. The difficulty that this relatively sophisticated employer had in effectively navigating the employment law when responding to a legitimate workplace concern (worker safety) illustrates how legally complex and risky the practice of human resource management can be.

Second, this case is a good example of how the social identities of workers can shape how employer policies affect them. The aerobic standard appears, on the surface, to be an objective one (i.e., run X distance in Y time). It is only after examining physiological differences between men and women that the discriminatory nature of the standard becomes apparent. This standard is an example of an insidious "male norm" that often underlies HR practices. Many aspects of the workplace—from hours of work to equipment and job design—are unconsciously based on the assumption that a worker is an averaged-sized, able-bodied man with a partner at home.

Third, this case illustrates how employment laws limit employer behaviour by either requiring employers to take action or prohibiting their behaviour. That these laws limit the power of the employer tells us that employer behaviour often has profoundly negative consequences for workers (such that laws are required to protect them). After all, employers are in the business of making money, not protecting workers. These laws also tell us that workers are often unable to resist such behaviours effectively on their own (thus, the state must act to protect workers from employer behaviour). On the surface, this dynamic suggests that governments use laws to balance (at least somewhat) the power of employers and that of workers. As explored below, though, the idea that the state operates as a neutral referee can be difficult to reconcile with the often weak government enforcement of employment laws that the state enacts.

The rest of this chapter introduces the common and statutory law relevant to employment. These sources of law form part of the web of rules that regulates employment relationships (see Figure 2.1). HR practitioners

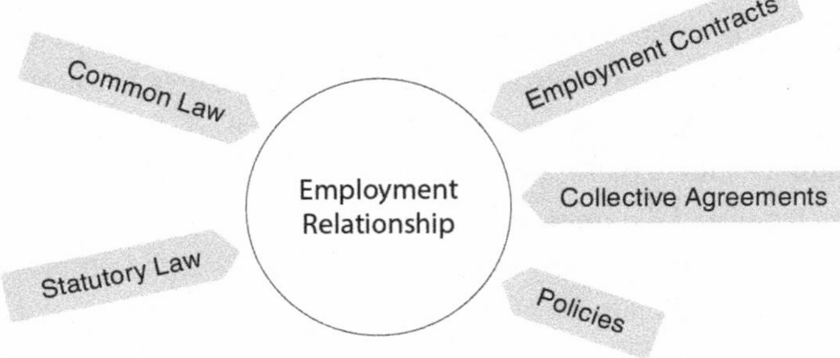

Figure 2.1. The web of rules

must understand the rights and obligations of both employers and workers to avoid running afoul of the common or statutory law. Subsequent chapters build upon this introduction to employment law and flesh out how the law applies to each of the main human resource functions. Special attention is paid to the law affecting hiring in Chapters 4 and 5 as well as discipline and termination in Chapter 9. A third source of worker employment rights (collective agreements negotiated by unions) is addressed in Chapter 10.

Common Law of Employment

Employment is a contractual relationship. As discussed in Chapter 1, workers agree to make their capacity to work available to their employer in exchange for some combination of wages and benefits. Sometimes the details of the employment contract are recorded in a comprehensive, written form. Other times the contract is entirely verbal. More often, though, the contract is a combination of written and unwritten agreements. For example, an employer might provide a written employment offer that includes a job title, a start date, and a wage (e.g., $25 per hour). There might be a job description (probably outdated and incomplete) supplemented by some verbal promises. There might also be an employee handbook or a set of policies (which might or might not be provided to the worker at the time of hiring) that sets out things such as hours of work. All of the other details, from the dress code to how the employment relationship can be terminated, are left unwritten.

Given the converging and diverging interests of workers and employers, it is not surprising that disputes can arise about the exact terms and conditions of employment. For example, a worker might be hired to work full time (which, in practice, might be 35 hours per week). Later the employer might decide that business is slow and thus offer the worker only 16 hours of work in a week, with a commensurate reduction in wages. The employment contract might be silent on whether and how the employer can reduce the number of hours of work. If the worker and the employer cannot land on a mutually agreeable solution to the dispute, then what happens? Well, the employer can terminate the employment contract (termination is discussed in Chapter 9). But, more typically, the employer will simply impose its preference on the worker (by scheduling and paying the worker for only 16 hours of work). The worker can either accept this or quit and sue the employer for violating (in the worker's view) the verbal agreement on the hours of work.

When faced with a claim in a matter about which the contract is silent, the courts rely on the **common law** to reach a decision. The **common law** is a series of rules about employment that originates from past legal decisions (i.e., it operates on the principle of precedent). These rules give guidance on which rights and obligations exist in the absence of explicit contractual or statutory provisions that say otherwise. Basically, the common law lets judges fill in the blanks when adjudicating a claim in the absence of explicit rules. Given that the common law arises from precedent, interpretation of it can shift over time and in different contexts. Nevertheless, some core obligations are generally accepted to exist.

In the absence of a clear agreement to the contrary (e.g., language in a written contract), employers' common law obligations include the following.

- **Work and remuneration**: An employer must provide a worker with the wages that the two parties negotiated. An employer must provide the worker with the opportunity to work as per their agreement. If the employer significantly alters a worker's job duties or reduces a worker's hours, then this is a repudiatory breach of the employment contract. That is, the employer has effectively terminated the worker's employment.

- **Consideration**: An employer that wishes to alter the terms of a contract must gain the consent of the worker and provide that worker with something of value (called consideration) in exchange for the new terms. If a worker does not consent to the change, then the employer can choose to provide the worker with notice that it is terminating the employment contract.
- **Notice of termination**: Unless otherwise specified (e.g., a temporary job with a fixed termination date), employment relationships are normally considered to continue for an indefinite period of time. An employer that wishes to terminate an indefinite employment relationship must normally give the worker reasonable notice of termination (or pay in lieu of the notice). An exception is when the employer has just cause (i.e., an acceptable reason) to terminate the employment immediately, such as when the employer catches the worker stealing. Notice and just cause is explored further in Chapter 9.
- **A safe worksite**: Under common law, employers are required to provide a reasonably safe system of work. This obligation generally has been usurped by statutory occupational health and safety laws (see Workplace Injury Prevention and Compensation below).

Employers are also vicariously liable for their workers' actions. That means that employers are responsible for negligent acts or omissions by workers while they carry out job-related duties. This reflects the fact that the employer has the right, ability, and duty to control the worker in the execution of the worker's job.[3]

Workers' common law obligations include the following.

- **The obligations of good faith and fidelity**: A worker must act in a manner consistent with advancing the employer's business interests. For example, a worker cannot normally operate a business on the side that competes with the employer's business. Workers are also prohibited from behaving in a way that undermines the fundamental relationship of trust that exists, for example by stealing from or bad-mouthing the employer.
- **The duty to obey**: Once employed, the worker is the employer's to command. Although there are common law and statutory limits

on what an employer can demand of a worker, generally speaking a worker must obey lawful commands of the employer in the workplace context. Refusing to follow an employer's lawful orders is considered a form of insubordination and can give an employer just cause to terminate a worker's employment.

- **The obligation to perform work competently**: A worker must normally be able to perform competently the duties assigned by the employer. Gross incompetence or repeated failure to perform work in a satisfactory manner will void the employment contract.
- **The requirement to provide notice of resignation**: A worker is required to provide the employer with notice of intention to terminate the employment contract. This requirement is rarely enforced because an employer is usually happy to be rid of a departing worker as quickly as possible.[4]

These common law rights and obligations are clearly asymmetrical. An employer's obligations are significantly less expansive than a worker's obligations. Basically, an employer is required to pay what it has agreed to pay and not to change the terms of the contract without the worker's agreement. In contrast, workers must do pretty much whatever their employers tell them to do. Indeed, the obligation of good faith and fidelity requires workers to subordinate their own interests (even when they are not working for the employer) to the employer's interests.

The common law rights and obligations regarding employment were informed by the **master and servant tradition**, which subordinated workers to employers. The assumption of the subservience of workers to employers remains evident in today's common law. This legal asymmetry reinforces the labour market power that employers wield over workers. This means, first, that workers must take jobs in order to purchase food, shelter, and other necessities of life, and employers can use the usual surplus of workers looking for jobs to drive hard bargains, and, second, that when workers take jobs they must legally subordinate themselves to their employers.

Sophisticated employers can include language in their employment contracts that reduces their common law requirements. Consider the earlier example of a worker whose boss has reduced the hours of work from

35 to 16. Under the common law, the employer would be in breach of its duty to provide work and remuneration. The employer could offer the worker some consideration to reduce the worker's hours. A sophisticated employer, however, might have anticipated that it would need one day to vary workers' hours and included provisions for doing so (perhaps with one week of notice) in the original contract. This explicit contract language would stand in place of the common law and allow the employer to do this.

Any employer that did not have this foresight, but also did not want to offer consideration or pay reasonable termination notice (because that would cut into its profit), could just ignore the common law. That is, it could reduce the worker's hours and see what the worker does. The worker (who needs a job) might just accept the change or might quit and perhaps sue for breach of contract. But a lawsuit is a slow and expensive process that few workers can afford. The relative inaccessibility of a legal remedy for workers suggests that there is sometimes a difference between the rights that a worker has and the rights that a worker can realize.

This is not to say that workers are without recourse or power. Workers whose bosses change the wage-effort bargain can sometimes force their employers to accommodate their interests. For example, if an employer adds steps to a work process (so that the worker has to work harder to achieve the same output), then the affected worker might just ignore the extra steps or do the job less well. Workers can ignore many employer directives if they are prepared to risk the potential consequences (i.e., discipline or termination). This kind of resistance, whether individual or collective, can pressure an employer to negotiate mutually acceptable terms, such as a different work process, lower production targets, or higher wages.

Statutory Employment Law

Governments sometimes enact laws (also called legislation) that extend or usurp the rights and obligations that workers and employers have under the common law. This **statutory law** often sets certain minimum terms and conditions of employment and/or empowers government agencies to enforce the law. For example, few workers will sue their employers for stolen wages since it usually costs more than the value of the wages that they would recover and takes years. To prevent rampant wage theft, governments have enacted employment (or labour) standards that require at least monthly wage payments and allow government inspectors to recover stolen wages.

There are 14 different sets of statutory employment laws in Canada: one for each of the 10 provinces and three territories as well as one in the federal jurisdiction. Although that sounds confusing, 90% of workers are subject to the laws enacted by the **jurisdiction** (i.e., the province or territory) in which they work. Federal employment law affects federal government employees as well as workers in interprovincial industries, such as banking, interprovincial rail and trucking, telecommunications, air travel, and uranium mining.

Typically, a jurisdiction enacts laws addressing

- minimum terms of employment,
- unionization and collective bargaining,
- work-related injury prevention and compensation,
- discrimination, harassment, and pay equity, and
- information privacy.

This chapter considers all of these statutory laws except unionization and collective bargaining, which are dealt with in Chapter 10. A sometimes-confusing topic is the role of the **Charter of Rights and Freedoms** in employment law. Feature Box 2.1 provides a brief overview of how the **Charter** shapes the content of employment law as well as the behaviour of governments when they act as employers.

Feature Box 2.1 The *Charter of Rights and Freedoms*

The *Charter of Rights and Freedoms* plays an important but sometimes confusing role in employment law. The *Charter* is part of Canada's Constitution. It sets limits on the power of the government by identifying certain fundamental rights and freedoms that all individuals in Canada are deemed to possess, including political rights (applicable to Canadian citizens) and civil rights (applicable to anyone in Canada). The *Charter* has two main implications for employment relationships.

First, it indirectly affects all employment relationships by limiting the content and application of statutory employment laws. For example,

Section 15(1) of the *Charter* says that "every individual is equal before and under the law and has the right to the equal protection and equal benefit without discrimination and, in particular, without discrimination based on race, national or ethnic origin, colour, religion, sex, age or mental or physical disability."[5] This requirement means that statutory laws must not be discriminatory. The case of Delwin Vriend illustrates how this can affect employment law. Vriend was a lab coordinator at a religious college in Alberta fired for being gay. At that time, Alberta's human rights law did not prohibit discrimination on the basis of sexual orientation, so Vriend was unable to file a human rights complaint against the college. The Supreme Court eventually found that the omission of sexual orientation from Alberta's law was contrary to Section 15 of the *Charter* and ordered sexual orientation read into the law.[6] Sexual orientation was eventually added to Alberta's *Human Rights Code* as an enumerated ground on which discrimination is prohibited.

Second, the *Charter* can directly affect public sector employment relationships by limiting the behaviour of the government when it acts as an employer. For example, in 2008, the government of Saskatchewan enacted laws that allowed public sector employers to deem employees "essential workers" and bar them from participating in strikes. The Saskatchewan Federation of Labour asserted that this law interfered with workers' freedom of association (as set out in s. 2(d) of the *Charter*). In 2015, the Supreme Court agreed with the federation, finding that the right to strike was a fundamental part of collective bargaining, and struck down the law.[7]

Governments have two ways to "get around" *Charter* limits when acting as legislators or employers. The first is to demonstrate that any limitation on a *Charter* right or freedom is "demonstrably justified in a free and democratic society" (s. 1). The second is for a government to use the "notwithstanding clause" (s. 33), which allows it temporarily to override some *Charter* rights and freedoms (ss. 2, 7–15).

When an individual worker or a group of workers thinks that the government has violated their *Charter* rights, they can challenge the law or government action in court. Such challenges are usually both expensive and lengthy. Normally, the worker(s) must live with the consequences of the law or action in the meantime. The *Charter* is further discussed in Chapter 10 because it has significant implications for the laws governing unionization and collective bargaining.

It is important to reiterate that the *Charter* applies only to the content of laws and government actions. The actions of private sector employers (and individuals) are regulated by provincial and territorial laws. These laws must comply with the *Charter*. In the Vriend case, it was Alberta's human rights law, and therefore the Alberta government, and not the actions of the private college, which were subject to the *Charter* challenge.

Minimum Terms of Employment

All Canadian jurisdictions have enacted laws setting out minimum terms and conditions of employment. These laws are often called labour standards or **employment standards** and comprise some combination of acts, regulations, and other forms of rules (see Feature Box 2.2). These laws establish certain minimums that most employers must meet related to wages, hours of work, vacations, and other types of leaves. Although this **floor of rights** is often discussed as universal, some groups of employers and workers are excluded from some or all of the minimums set out in these acts (e.g., professionals such as doctors and industries such as agriculture).

Feature Box 2.2 Acts, Regulations, and Codes

The structure of employment laws can be a bit confusing. Each jurisdiction has its own amalgam of acts, regulations, policies, codes, and guidelines.

- An **act** is a federal, provincial, or territorial law that sets out the broad legal framework around an area of employment law. This legislation is passed by the legislature that has the authority to regulate work in the jurisdiction.
- A **regulation** typically sets out how the general principles of the act will be applied in specific circumstances. A regulation is authorized by the government cabinet and is easier to change than an act. Several regulations can flow from an act, each addressing a different facet of the act.
- **Guidelines, codes, and policies** are more specific rules about an area of law. They might or might not be legally enforceable,

depending on what the act or regulation(s) of the jurisdiction permit, and are usually the easiest kind of rule for the government to amend.

The exact arrangement within each jurisdiction differs and can often be complicated. For example, in Alberta, the **Employment Standards Code** (which, confusingly, is an act) sets out most of the minimum entitlements and rules about employment, including a prohibition on employing children under the age of 15 during normal school hours. The **Employment Standards Regulation** contains additional rules that further restrict when and in which occupations individuals under 18 may be employed. The director of employment standards can also use powers granted under Subsections 52 and 54 of the *Regulation* to make policies further restricting which restaurant tasks a 13 or 14 year old is permitted to perform.

It is often necessary for HR practitioners to sort through fairly complex and cascading sets of statutory rules to understand fully what is permissible or required under what circumstances. Most governments have developed topic-specific fact sheets to address common questions. These sheets often provide a useful overview that can guide further research.

Employment standards legislation also establishes a process by which workers can enforce their rights against employers. This usually involves filing a complaint with the government department charged with enforcing the relevant law. A complaint typically triggers an investigation. This process is intended to resolve disputes more quickly and at lower cost to the worker than a lawsuit.

The rights and obligations set out by each jurisdiction vary, but typically they include setting a minimum wage that employers must pay. This minimum is usually expressed as an hourly rate (e.g., $15 per hour). Some jurisdictions stipulate different minimum wages based on workers' age or industry. Governments typically also make rules that limit the deductions that employers can make from workers' salaries (e.g., for cash register shortages or work uniform costs). Finally, governments typically stipulate the maximum duration of a pay period and set out requirements for employer record keeping. Collectively, these requirements are designed to limit economic exploitation and wage theft by employers (see Feature Box 2.3).

Feature Box 2.3 Wage Theft and State Enforcement

Wage theft occurs when employers fail to pay workers the compensation that they have earned. Overt wage theft includes employers not paying some or all of the wages owed (including overtime premiums) and failing to provide required rest breaks or paid leaves. There are also subtler forms of wage theft. Employers can make illegal deductions or utilize confusing or misleading bookkeeping structures to minimize their labour costs.[8] For example, 22-year-old Brampton, Ontario, student Satinder Kaur Grewal recently won more than $16,000 in unpaid wages from her former restaurant employer, Chat Hut.[9] The exact level of wage theft across Canada is unknown, but the practice appears to be widespread.

When workers are not paid what they are owed, they can file a complaint with the government. A complaint typically triggers an investigation by a government inspector. (Some jurisdictions also do random or targeted investigations to assess employer compliance, but they are much less common than complaint-driven investigations.) Sometimes an employer might voluntarily pay the stolen wages during an investigation. Other times an inspector might order the wages paid and, if still unpaid, engage the services of a collections company to get some or all of the money owed by the employer. In practice, inspectors sometimes negotiate a partial payment to resolve the issue, even if the worker is owed the full amount. It is unclear what proportion of owed wages is eventually recovered when a worker files a complaint.

One of the problems with complaint-driven enforcement of employment laws is that many workers are reluctant to complain for fear of (illegal) retaliation by their employers. Retaliation can be overt (e.g., firing a worker) or more subtle (e.g., assigning undesirable job tasks or shifts). The majority of wage theft complaints come from workers who have already quit their jobs. Workers whose employment is precarious or whose right to work in Canada is limited by their work permits are among the least likely to complain because of the potential consequences of doing so.

This analysis suggests a disconnection between the intention and the effect of Canada's labour standards laws. The intention of these laws is to prevent and remedy wage theft. But operation of the system is such that relatively few complaints are made (because of the risks associated with doing so), and only a few valid complaints result in full restitution. Some critics of this system suggest that this enforcement gap incentivizes employers to engage in wage theft. That is, wage theft might be an intentional strategy that employers adopt to increase profits because they know that most workers will not report the wage theft and that the worst-case scenario for an employer is simply having to pay the owed wages.

The ineffectiveness of employment standards in preventing and remedying wage theft also raises the question of whether the state is truly a neutral referee. On the one hand, the government enacts laws that make employer wage theft illegal. On the other hand, the government enforcement system does not work well. One explanation of this discrepancy is that the government is interested in limiting class conflict. It does so by passing laws that say wage theft is bad and create the appearance that the government is on top of the issue, which keeps most workers happy and docile. In practice, though, the laws have many loopholes and are poorly enforced, which keeps employers happy. Keep this discrepancy in government behaviour and this possible explanation of it in mind as you read the rest of this chapter.

Governments also seek to set standards for hours of work. This can include setting a daily or weekly limit to the maximum hours of work, identifying minimum rest breaks during the working day and rest periods between shifts, and placing limits on changes to work schedules. These limits serve both to provide workers with adequate time to perform necessary social reproductive tasks (e.g., eating, going to the washroom, resting, managing a household) and to reduce the incidence of fatigue-related injuries.

Some jurisdictions allow employers to schedule workers to work longer than a normal work day or work week. When workers work **overtime**, employers must pay them an overtime premium. Overtime is often calculated as some multiple of regular pay (e.g., one and a half times the regular wage rate). The purpose of an overtime premium is to encourage employers to hire more workers (rather than just making their existing employees work harder) by attaching additional costs to overtime. Some jurisdictions allow employers and workers to agree to paid time off in lieu of overtime pay.

Labour standards legislation also normally outlines time that workers can be away from work, either with or without pay. This includes identifying statutory holidays (e.g., Canada Day, Labour Day) and annual paid vacations from work. Workers might also be entitled to other forms of job-protected paid or unpaid leave to attend to civic duties (e.g., jury duty, military leave) and personal or family obligations (e.g., parental, sick, compassionate care, and bereavement leaves). These laws can also limit the employment of minors.

Finally, employment standards laws can provide for temporary layoffs and set minimum notice periods for termination. As noted above, when an employer fails to provide a worker with the work promised, it is considered a termination under the common law. Employment standards laws allow employers to lay off workers temporarily. Temporary layoffs usually have a fixed maximum period, after which the layoff is deemed a termination. Employment standards also set out the minimum period of termination notice that an employer is required to provide. (Employers may also choose to provide pay in lieu of notice.) This **minimum termination notice** is not the same thing as reasonable notice under the common law. This difference and its implications are considered in detail in Chapter 9.

Work-Related Injury Prevention

All governments have enacted laws designed to prevent workplace injuries. Occupational health and safety (OHS) laws assume that injuries are preventable when employers identify and control workplace hazards. A workplace **hazard** is any source of potential injury or illness. This can include an object, process, context, person, or set of circumstances (see Feature Box 2.4). OHS laws can also set out specific rules for the control of certain hazards, require reporting of some kinds of workplace incidents, and empower government staff to inspect workplaces and respond to complaints. Finally, OHS laws also grant workers three safety rights.

- **Right to know**: Workers have a right to know about the hazards in their workplaces as well as about hazard control strategies.
- **Right to participate**: Workers have a right to participate in making their workplaces safer. This right is usually operationalized through joint health and safety committees, comprising an equal number of worker and employer representatives.
- **Right to refuse**: Workers can refuse work that they think is unsafe without fear of losing their jobs.

The existence of a right to refuse unsafe work tells us that, sometimes, employers choose not to control hazards. Relatively few workers exercise their right to refuse unsafe work, in part because of fear of retaliation from their employers.[10]

Feature Box 2.4 Categories of Workplace Hazards

Workplace hazards are generally divided into five broad categories.

- **Physical hazards**: A physical hazard involves a transfer of energy that results in an injury. For example, a worker who is struck by an object or falls off a ladder entails a transfer of energy causing an injury. Other examples include noise, vibration, temperature, electricity, atmospheric condition, and radiation.
- **Ergonomic hazards**: An ergonomic hazard arises when the physical arrangement of work causes strain on workers' bodies. Poor desk fit and lighting as well as jobs that require repetitive motions or holding a single position for a long time are examples of ergonomic hazards.
- **Chemical hazards**: A chemical hazard causes harm to human tissue or interferes with normal physiological functioning. Such a hazard enters the body through respiration, skin absorption, ingestion, or cuts in the skin. Cleaning solutions are common chemical hazards. Fumes from building materials are a less obvious chemical hazard.
- **Biological hazards**: A biological hazard is an organism or a product of an organism (e.g., tissue, blood, feces) that harms human health. The three main types of organisms that give rise to biological hazards are bacteria, viruses, and fungi. Biological

hazards enter our bodies through respiration, skin absorption, ingestion, and cuts in our skin.

- **Psychosocial hazards**: A psychosocial hazard is a social or psychological hazard that negatively affects a worker's health. Harassment, bullying, and violence are easily visible psychosocial hazards in the workplace. Stress, fatigue, and overwork are less visible psychosocial hazards. Often the design of work tasks and processes can cause or intensify the stress and fatigue experienced by workers.[11]

Some hazards do not fit neatly into this typology. Working alone, for example, can increase exposure to workplace violence (because lone workers are easier targets). It can also intensify the consequences of other hazards because no one might be available to assist a worker who is injured or experiences a medical emergency.

Once a hazard has been identified, it must be controlled. Employers control a hazard when they take steps to eliminate or reduce the chance that it can result in an injury or illness. The hazards in a workplace can be identified through a process of **hazard recognition, assessment, and control**. Hazard recognition involves comprehensively identifying all of the hazards in a workplace. Typically, hazard recognition begins by considering the broad context of work (e.g., is it in a remote location? is it outdoors?). It then considers the specific context and tasks associated with the work. This process might include inspecting the workplace, talking with or observing workers, examining job descriptions and workplace records, and perhaps measuring or testing. In identifying hazards, it is useful to specify the hazard in detail (e.g., "benzene" rather than "workplace chemicals"), the type of hazard (e.g., chemical), and the injury or illness that it could cause (e.g., neurological problems, anemia, leukemia). In considering hazards, it is important to be mindful of how the male norm can influence what employers and workers identify as hazardous (see Feature Box 2.5).

Feature Box 2.5 Safety and the Male Norm

The **male norm** refers to often unconscious assumptions about workers' behaviour or physiology based on the expectation that workers are average-sized, able-bodied men with a partner at home to handle social reproductive tasks. This assumption can be found through human resource management functions, including job design, performance management, and health and safety. One implication of the male norm is that HR decisions and policies can disadvantage workers who do not fit the implicit norm. The application of a seemingly neutral aerobic test that effectively precluded women from being firefighters in the opening vignette of this chapter is a good example of the male norm and its effect.

The male norm is present in health and safety. For example, **occupational exposure limits**—the level of exposure to chemical or biological or noise hazards considered safe—historically were set based on research on healthy, young men. This approach ignores physiological differences associated with gender, age, and health. Similarly, the design of industrial equipment and work processes historically was based on assumptions about the height and strength of an average (i.e., five-foot-nine, able-bodied, male) worker. Ignoring the systematic anatomical differences between men and women leads to women being exposed to hazardous lifting requirements or being provided with safety equipment (e.g., harnesses and respirators) or tools unsuited for their size and shape.[12]

The presence of the male norm argues for an intersectional analysis of workplace safety. Such an analysis can draw our attention not only to health and safety hazards but also to the differential health effects caused by job-design decisions. For example, precarious employment practices are more often experienced by workers who are women, of colour, or disabled. Since their employment is less subject to government regulation, these workers can experience greater levels of exposure to hazardous working conditions. And, if they are injured, then they are likely to have less access to employer-paid benefits to treat work-related injuries or to workers' compensation to provide financial support when work-related injury or illness makes them unable to work.

This analysis suggests that organizations' HR strategies can create or intensify workplace hazards. Furthermore, these hazards do not necessarily affect all employees equally. Identifying and controlling such hazards require HR practitioners to think about hazard identification more broadly than simply a quarterly workplace inspection for loose electrical cords, slippery floors, and rickety ladders.

Once hazards have been identified, it is useful to consider the risk posed by each hazard. Doing so allows us to understand the hazard better as well as to prioritize which hazard to control first. Risk is a function of three factors: probability, consequence, and exposure. Probability is the likelihood that a hazard will cause an incident. Consequence refers to the severity of injury or ill health that will result from an incident. Exposure refers to how frequently a worker is exposed to the hazard. Figure 2.2 shows a sample hazard assessment form that allows you roughly to quantify the risk of a hazard.

Finally, it is necessary to control a hazard. There are different ways to control hazards. As outlined in Feature Box 2.6, it is useful to think about these different controls as a hierarchy, with those controls at the top of the hierarchy being both the most effective and the most expensive. OHS legislation generally requires employers to adopt the most effective control (i.e., the highest control in the hierarchy) reasonably practicable to implement. The **reasonably practicable** test is met by taking suitable or rational precautions given the circumstances.

Probability: Likelihood hazard will result in incident.

☐ Rare (1) ☐ Possible (2) ☐ Probable (3) ☐ Likely (4)

Consequence: Severity of injury/ill health caused by injury.

☐ Negligible (1) ☐ Marginal (2) ☐ Significant (3) ☐ Catastrophic (4)

Exposure: Frequency workers contact the hazard.

☐ Rare (1) ☐ Occasional (2) ☐ Frequent (3) ☐ Continuous (4)

Risk = Probability x Consequences x Exposure

Figure 2.2 Simplified risk assessment tool

Feature Box 2.6 The Hierarchy of Controls

There are often several ways to control a hazard. For example, loose carpeting can pose a tripping hazard. An employer might control the hazard by placing an orange cone beside the loose carpet to alert workers to the hazard. Or the employer might glue the carpet back down or replace it. Placing a cone takes little effort but is not very effective since the hazard remains, and a worker could still trip over it. Regluing or replacing the carpet eliminates the hazard but comes at a higher cost. The effectiveness of various control strategies is outlined in the **hierarchy of controls** (see Figure 2.3).

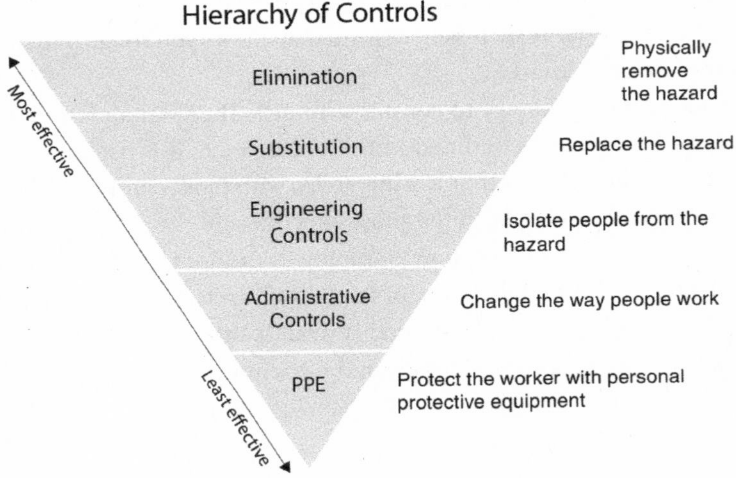

Figure 2.3 The hierarchy of controls

The controls at the top of the hierarchy are both the most effective and typically the most expensive to implement. This reflects that elimination, substitution, and engineering controls often involve making significant changes to workplace processes. These controls also tend to increase employer costs by slowing or otherwise altering production methods.

In contrast, the controls at the bottom are both inexpensive and often ineffective. They are ineffective because the hazard remains in the workplace, and it is up to the worker to avoid it by following rules or wearing **personal protective equipment** (PPE). They are cheaper, though, because they require little change to how production is organized.

In Canada, workers, employers, and the government all play a role in injury prevention. All Canadian jurisdictions use the **internal responsibility system** (IRS) to structure their OHS laws. The IRS makes employers and workers jointly responsible for workplace safety and is premised on the beliefs that workers and employers have the most knowledge of hazards in their workplaces and that they share an interest in making those workplaces safer. Under the IRS, workers have an obligation to report hazards to their employers. The employers must then control the hazards, and the workers must comply with whatever controls the employer has put in place. This might entail complying with safe working procedures and wearing required PPE. Some workplaces will be required to have a **joint health and safety committee** in which employer and worker representatives meet to discuss OHS issues and recommend control strategies.

Workers can turn to the government to adjudicate disputes about whether a hazard has been adequately controlled or whether workers' safety rights have been violated. The government also typically investigates serious injuries and fatalities and conducts inspections of workplaces to ensure compliance. Where unsafe working conditions are found, government inspectors can issue stop-work orders until the hazard is controlled. In some jurisdictions, inspectors can also issue financial penalties, and all jurisdictions provide for the prosecution of violators, although prosecution usually occurs only when there has been a serious injury or fatality.

Although OHS laws and practices undoubtedly mean that today's workplaces are safer than they were 100 years ago, OHS is often criticized for being unsuccessful in preventing large numbers of injuries and fatalities. Each year in Canada, the workers' compensation board (WCB) reports approximately 1,000 work-related fatalities and 264,000 serious injuries.[13] Although significant, these numbers include only injuries reported to and accepted for compensation by WCB systems. If you add unreported injuries and injuries that do not have to be reported, then the true number is about 10 times the number of serious injuries reported.[14] Ten thousand work-related deaths and millions of work-related injuries provide strong evidence that contemporary OHS is not particularly effective at preventing workplace deaths and injuries. An important factor in high injury rates is low employer compliance with even the most basic OHS obligations.[15]

Governments acknowledge that non-compliance occurs. They grant workers the right to refuse unsafe work, and they hire inspectors precisely because they know that employers sometimes fail to control hazards. One explanation of high rates of non-compliance and injury is that employers and workers do not actually share an interest in safer workplaces. Rather, employers seek to prevent injuries to the degree that doing so is cost effective (which reflects the operation of the profit imperative). In contrast, workers usually seek the highest level of safety possible (although sometimes they disregard safety measures because of forgetfulness, time pressure, or convenience). This dispute over how safe work should be reflects the broader divergence of worker and employer interests in capitalist economies over who will capture the surplus value of labour.

In theory, the state is supposed to step in and ensure that employers comply with legislative minimums. In practice, inspection programs are underfunded and often have intervals (the time between inspections of any one workplace) measured in decades. And the consequences of non-compliance are low (generally a stop-work order is issued until a hazard is remedied). Even employers who seriously injure or kill a worker are unlikely to receive a financial penalty.

Work-Related Injury Compensation

All jurisdictions operate **workers' compensation** systems that provide workers or their families with wage-loss and other benefits when they are injured or killed on the job. Each jurisdiction's system is operated by an independent government agency called a **workers' compensation board**, although the exact name varies among provinces and territories. Workers' compensation legislation typically empowers WCBs to set policies addressing claims acceptance and benefit levels. Although these policies vary among jurisdictions, all WCBs operate according to the Meredith principles (see Feature Box 2.7).

Feature Box 2.7 The Meredith Principles

William Meredith was an Ontario politician and judge appointed in 1910 to investigate the compensation of workplace injuries. This inquiry was designed in part to address the growing social instability caused by high rates of injury and the difficulty that workers had in securing compensation. In 1913, he tabled his report and proposed a system of workers' compensation based on five **Meredith principles**.

- No fault compensation: Compensation is due without regard for who was at fault for the injury. Workers cannot sue their employers for damages.
- Security of benefits: An "accident fund" is established by the WCB to ensure that compensation is paid.
- Collective liability: Employers pay for the cost of operating the system.
- Independent administration: Compensation is administered by an independent agency.
- Exclusive jurisdiction: All compensation claims are directed to the WCB, the final adjudicator of the system.[16]

In short, workers' compensation offered workers immediate, predictable, and stable wage-loss benefits. In exchange, workers gave up their right to sue employers for their injuries. Over time, the range of workers covered by workers' compensation, the types of injuries eligible for compensation, and the range of benefits offered have all increased.[17]

Workers, employers, and doctors are required to report certain injuries to the WCB, including those that require time away from work, modified duties, or medical treatment and those that resulted in fatalities. The WCB then applies the **arises and occurs test** to whether the injury arose from and occurred during the course of employment. If so, then the worker is entitled to access a range of benefits, including the following.

- *Wage loss and fatality benefits*: Workers can receive financial compensation for wages lost because of injuries. WCBs may limit the rate or total level of compensation. Dependants can also receive pensions when workers die on the job.

- *Health-care costs*: WCBs pay for the costs of treating injuries, including reimbursing the public health system or private providers for treatment costs.
- *Vocational rehabilitation*: Workers can receive assistance preparing for or finding post-injury employment as well as modifications to workplaces and homes.

In keeping with the Meredith principles, workers' compensation is funded by employer **premiums**. They are normally calculated based on an employer's payroll (e.g., a premium of $1.15 for every $100 of wages paid). These premiums can vary between industry sectors. Industries with higher claim costs have a higher premium rate than do industries with lower claim costs. Some jurisdictions have also established experience-rating systems. **Experience rating** adjusts an organization's premiums up or down based on the organization's injury claim costs. Experience rating is intended to incentivize employers to operate more safely. In practice, some organizations reduce claim costs by (illegally) pressuring workers not to report injuries.[18]

WCBs also encourage employers to return injured workers to work as soon as possible. This might require an employer to provide a worker with **modified duties** consistent with any injury-related job restrictions. Return-to-work programs assume that work can be rehabilitative and that returning to work quickly reduces the chance that workers will become permanently unable to work. The evidence supporting these beliefs is mixed. Furthermore, there is evidence that employers sometimes fail to provide a meaningful or safe return to work.[19]

Discrimination, Harassment, and Equity

All jurisdictions have established **human rights** laws that prohibit discrimination based on personal characteristics irrelevant to a worker's ability to perform a job. This prohibition on discrimination operates throughout the employment process, including pre-employment activities such as recruitment and selection. Workers who believe that they have been discriminated against can file a complaint with their jurisdiction's human rights tribunal or commission. Human rights commissions have broad remedial powers, including awarding damages and directing reinstatement.

There are two main types of discrimination. **Direct discrimination** occurs when an organization applies different rules or standards to workers. Historically, direct discrimination was common (e.g., barring women or non-white applicants or paying them lower wages). Over time, social approbation of discrimination has reduced (but not eliminated) direct discrimination. **Indirect discrimination** occurs when a seemingly neutral rule has an adverse effect on some workers based on a personal attribute. The fitness rule applied to Tawney Meiorin in the opening vignette is an example of indirect discrimination: a seemingly neutral rule reduced the chances of women becoming forest firefighters because of innate physiological differences.

When a human rights complaint is filed, an investigator typically asks two questions.

1. Does the behaviour discriminate against a worker on a prohibited ground?
2. If so, then is the discrimination permitted through a statutory exemption or defence?

Not all discrimination is unlawful. The list of grounds on which discrimination is prohibited differs among jurisdictions and has expanded over time as different bases of discrimination have become regarded as wrongful (see Feature Box 2.1). That said, not all forms of discrimination are prohibited. Some jurisdictions specifically allow workers under the age of 18 to be paid less than other workers. In this case, though paying a minor is discriminatory, it is permissible discrimination specifically allowed by a legislature.

Discrimination can also be permissible in certain circumstances. As noted in the opening vignette, a bona fide occupational requirement is rationally connected to the job, adopted in good faith, and reasonably necessary to accomplish a legitimate work-related purpose. For example, requiring a delivery driver to possess a driver's licence indirectly discriminates against workers who cannot get a licence because of a visual impairment. Such a requirement, though discriminatory, is permissible because being legally able to drive is a BFOR for a delivery driver.

Human rights legislation also places on employers a **duty to accommodate**. It is a requirement to remove discriminatory barriers to employment.

This duty can require employers to modify work duties, schedules, and the physical environment to allow workers to participate equally in work. The duty to accommodate is often invoked when health issues or disabilities limit workers' abilities to perform some or all of their job duties. But the duty to accommodate is broad and can include accommodating religious observances, addictions, and family responsibilities (see Feature Box 2.8).

Feature Box 2.8 Accommodating Child-Care Obligations

Many workers are responsible for the care of children. Sometimes child-care demands can conflict with work obligations. Although family status has long been a protected ground, employers historically had little duty to accommodate the child-care needs of their workers. Juggling employment and child care is one factor that disproportionately affects the careers and lifetime earnings of women.

In 2015, the Federal Court of Appeal found that Canadian Border Services was obligated to accommodate the child-care needs of an employee. The court set out a fourfold test to determine when an employer was obligated to accommodate child care.

- The child must be under the care and supervision of the worker.
- The child-care obligation must engage a legal responsibility for the child (it cannot simply be a matter of personal choice).
- The employee must make a reasonable effort to find child care.
- The workplace rule must meaningfully interfere with the fulfillment of the child-care obligation.[20]

If these conditions are met, then the employer must accommodate up to the point of undue hardship. Subsequently, some provincial human rights tribunals have adopted different tests for when an organization must accommodate workers' child-care obligations. Commissions in Alberta and Ontario, for example, assert that employees do not need to exhaust child-care options (the third test in the federal case) to trigger a duty to accommodate. Rather, that duty is triggered simply by a worker who has protected status and is meaningfully and adversely affected by a workplace rule.

A request by a worker to accommodate child-care needs can bring together some of the key tensions that exist in an employment relationship. For example, accommodating child-care requirements can entail additional costs for an employer, thereby lowering profitability. Refusing accommodation shifts costs onto the worker (most likely a woman) in terms of forgone income. Other factors—such as the location of work and thus the availability of informal (e.g., family and community) and formal (i.e., paid) child care—will influence how significant the resulting impact will be on the worker. Factors such as employment precarity will affect a worker's capacity to resist this employer behaviour.

Organizational responses to the COVID-19 pandemic, whereby large numbers of employees were moved into home offices and provided with alternative working hours, suggest that, when suitably motivated, some organizations are much more able to accommodate working from home than they previously have been. HR practitioners should be mindful of how organizations can accommodate workers coupled with the general trend in the case law toward an increasing expectation of accommodation. Even when an organization does not face legal and financial consequences for failing to accommodate child-care needs, it can face profound reputational harm.

An organization's duty to accommodate ends when the required accommodation meets the threshold of **undue hardship**, a variable and multi-faceted standard that assesses the point at which further accommodation would pose an unnecessarily demanding level of hardship on an employer. Factors that can influence when further accommodation constitutes undue hardship include organizational size (bigger employers have a greater capacity to accommodate than smaller employers), safety, organizational structure, cost, and morale.

Human rights legislation (and sometimes OHS legislation) also place an obligation on an employer to ensure that workers do not experience harassment, including sexual harassment. **Harassment** is generally defined as a course of vexatious comments or conduct that a reasonable person would find unwelcome. In this context, vexatious means words or actions that are annoying, distressing, or irritating to the recipient. Although a course of conduct or comments usually requires multiple incidents to have occurred, a single serious incident can be enough to constitute harassment.[21] Harassment with a sexual element is often called **sexual harassment**, which denigrates someone on the basis of their sex and includes sexual comments, leering, invading one's space, requirements to dress in a sexualized way, and demands for sexual favours. Sexual harassment can overlap with or be distinct from gender-based harassment, which targets an individual based upon traditional gender norms.

Employers can also be subject to legislated employment and **pay equity** requirements. Employment equity laws require employers in the federal jurisdiction to take proactive steps to increase the representation of women, persons with disabilities, visible minorities, and Indigenous persons (although the act uses the dated and narrower term *Aboriginal persons*). Employers in all jurisdictions have an obligation under legislation to avoid discrimination in wages on the basis of gender. This requirement mandates **pay equality** (i.e., that men and women be paid the same for performing the same job in the same organization). Some jurisdictions have also enacted pay equity legislation. Pay equity requires that men and women be paid the same for performing jobs of comparable value in the same organization. This requirement is not uniform across the provinces and territories. Pay equity also requires decisions about which jobs are comparable, and such subjectivity often arouses controversy and resistance.

As an example, the federal **Pay Equity Act** requires federally regulated employers with more than 10 employees to develop and maintain a pay equity plan. To develop the plan, they must identify job classes for positions in the workplace and determine whether a job class is predominantly male, female, or gender neutral. They then must determine the value of the work performed by each predominantly male or female class, calculate the compensation in each class, and compare compensation between the classes doing work of equal value. This process identifies female-dominated job classes that are paid inequitably. Most importantly, the law requires that the employer increase compensation for those classes over a three- to five-year period to eliminate the inequity. A pay equity commissioner administers and enforces the act.

Information Privacy

HR practitioners are often required to collect, store, use, and share personal information on workers. **Personal information** is any information about an identifiable individual. An organization possesses personal information about a worker in order to administer the employment relationship, such as a worker's legal name, address, phone number, social insurance number, dependants, and qualifications or credentials. Organizations can also collect information on a worker through various forms of electronic surveillance in the workplace (e.g., video cameras, keystroke logs) and as part of the performance assessment process. Organizations can also possess information on job applicants in the form of resumés and interview notes.

Broadly speaking, organizations are permitted to collect, store, and disclose personal information when that information is necessary to establish, manage, or terminate an employment relationship. It is difficult to be more specific because the law on workplace privacy is highly variable among the 14 jurisdictions. The common law on privacy is evolving, and only some jurisdictions have enacted privacy legislation relevant to the workplace. Where there are laws, the specifics can differ between public sector and private sector employers. Furthermore, issues of information privacy can spill over into human rights issues, such as when an organization collects seemingly necessary demographic information and that information is then used to discriminate against an employee on a protected ground.[22]

It is important for HR practitioners to ensure that the collection, storage, and disclosure of personal information is compliant with the rules in their jurisdiction. Managing how an organization handles personal information tends to be particularly important when recruiting and selecting new employees, when a worker requires a workplace accommodation, and when an employment relationship comes to an end. It is also important to be mindful of the collection, storage, and disclosure of personal information on non-employees (e.g., customers, clients, business partners) when an organization is designing jobs. The chapters that follow take up relevant aspects of information privacy.

Conclusion

An important role played by human resource practitioners is ensuring that organizations are compliant with the many rules to which they are subject. The laws regulating employment are an important set of rules imposed on organizations by the state. These rules exist, in part, to make employment relationships more predictable for workers and employers. But these rules also exist to address employers' profit-driven tendency, in the absence of rules, to organize work in ways that result in social problems, such as injury, economic exploitation, and discrimination. These problems can be politically and socially destabilizing enough to warrant government intervention.

Although it is tempting to frame governments as referees between the interests of labour and those of capital, this might overstate the neutrality of the state and the effectiveness of the system. Enforcing the common law requires expensive litigation out of reach of most workers (particularly low-wage workers). Government enforcement of statutory laws is generally weak and can even incentivize employers to break those laws. This suggests that the state is interested in benefiting from the appearance of being a neutral party, but in fact it allows employers significant latitude to operate until and unless their behaviour generates social disruption.

In theory, non-compliance with these laws can generate legal consequences for employers. In practice, the real risks of non-compliance flow from the possibility of reputational harm. Consider the 2013 case of Strange City, a tattoo parlour in Edmonton. The owner had been paying workers their wages with cheques that it had insufficient funds to cover (thus, the cheques "bounced"). The staff responded by seeking employment elsewhere and then picketing walk-in traffic at Strange City. They would tell potential customers about the poor treatment of staff and hand out discount coupons for other local tattoo parlours. Strange City went out of business in a few months.

The effectiveness of this worker pushback reflects that laws also serve a normative function. That is, they set out which employer conduct is considered acceptable and which is considered unacceptable. Organizations that violate the law might well evade legal consequences. But workers might still be able to apply powerful pressure on employers, particularly if the workers are prepared to risk discipline or termination. It often falls to human resource practitioners to help organizational leaders see the full range of potential consequences that employment decisions entail.

EXERCISES

KEY TERMS

Define the following terms.

- Act
- Arises and occurs test
- Bona fide occupational requirement
- *Charter of Rights and Freedoms*
- Common law
- Control
- Direct discrimination
- Duty to accommodate
- Employment standards
- Experience rating
- Floor of rights
- Harassment
- Hazard
- Hazard recognition, assessment, and control
- Hierarchy of controls
- Human rights
- Indirect discrimination
- Internal responsibility system
- Joint health and safety committee
- Master and servant tradition
- Meredith principles
- Minimum termination notice
- Modified duties
- Occupational exposure limit
- Overtime
- Pay equality

- Pay equity
- Personal information
- Personal protective equipment
- Premiums
- Reasonably practicable
- Regulation
- Sexual harassment
- Statutory law
- Undue hardship
- Wage theft
- Workers' compensation
- Workers' compensation board

ACTIVITY

Locate your jurisdiction's laws and answer the following questions.

- What are the minimum wage(s) and overtime premiums?
- What are prohibited grounds for discrimination?
- What requirement is there for pay equity?
- In which circumstances can a worker refuse unsafe work?
- To what degree are wages lost because of injury replaced by the WCB?

DISCUSSION QUESTIONS

Discuss the following topics.

- How does common law both benefit and harm workers?
- Why have governments enacted statutory laws?
- Which factors explain the high level of workplace injury in Canada?
- Why would governments not effectively enforce statutory laws?
- Why is discrimination sometimes permissible in the workplace?

SELF-REFLECTION QUESTIONS

Write self-reflections of 200 to 500 words on the following topics.

- Think about a time when you or someone you know was underpaid by an employer. How did you (or that person) seek to resolve the situation, and why did you choose that option? Which other options existed, and why did you not select them?
- If your employer is temporarily unable to provide you with work, would you want to be permanently terminated or temporarily laid off? Why would you choose this option, and which costs does it entail for you and your employer? How might your answer differ if you were the employer in this situation?
- Think about an uncontrolled hazard that you have seen in a workplace. How did this hazard endanger the workers? Which controls could the employer have implemented to address the situation? Why might the employer not have controlled the hazard?
- Imagine that you are an employer and that one of your workers is frequently off work because child care is unreliable. What are the likely impacts of this absenteeism? How might you try to resolve this problem? Why did you choose the strategies that you did?

3 Workflow, Job Analysis, and Job Design

Most people have held jobs of some kind. Jobs are the result of decisions made by organizations about how they are going to turn workers' capacity to work into actual work. At a high level, designing a job requires a human resource practitioner to understand an organization's workflow—the tasks that must be accomplished to produce a good or service. These tasks must then be grouped together to create jobs, and the knowledge, skills, and abilities required of workers in each job must be identified. Workflow analysis, job analysis, and job design are highly technical undertakings. But they are also political acts in the sense that organizations exercise their managerial power to maximize the value that they can extract from workers' labour by designing jobs in certain ways.

The changes seen in the job of grocery store cashier provide an interesting example of how job (re)design can operate across multiple HR domains. Historically, cashiers manually calculated the cost of groceries (using mechanical tills), took money, and made change. Beginning in the 1980s, barcode scanners were introduced at grocery store checkouts. Over time, this technology has radically deskilled cashiers' work by eliminating most memory and computational tasks. Effectively, cashiers now just scan and, perhaps, bag items. Reducing the skill level and required number of cashiers saved employers approximately 4.5% in wage costs.[1] Scanners have also allowed for real-time inventory tracking and automated reordering (thereby reducing the amount of clerical work and non-retail space required in each store). Combined with reward cards, scanners also produce detailed consumer consumption data that can be used for marketing.[2]

The effect of redesigning cashiers' jobs around scanning technology has been clearly harmful to workers. In addition to reducing the number of jobs and lowering wages, scanners have negatively affected workers' health. Janice Williams was a long-time grocery cashier who went two decades without a workplace injury. The introduction of scanners in 1993 resulted in physical injuries to up to half of the cashiers in her store, making a previously safe occupation much more dangerous. The increased rate of injury was caused by the increased number of items that workers handled in a shift (i.e., more motions and greater aggregate weight), a narrower range of motions and tasks, and more stressful postures. "On the older machines, you could rest your hands," she noted. "But with the scanner, your hands were totally suspended, with the constant motion of pulling groceries across it." Williams was eventually diagnosed with carpal tunnel syndrome and nerve damage in her neck.[3]

Some stores seek to reduce injuries by reintroducing task variety via in-shift job rotation. Other stores have introduced even greater automation via self-checkout lines. Self-checkout further reduces wage costs because customers are invited to do a cashier's job for free.[4] This innovation has received mixed reviews. Some customers like the convenience of self-checkouts. Other customers dislike the technology, including the extra work, the lack of interaction, and the resulting job losses. Some retailers, such as three Canadian Tire locations in Toronto, have decided to remove self-checkouts because of maintenance problems and greater levels of shoplifting. These retailers have found that replacing self-checkouts with customer queues for cashiers can result in shorter wait times.[5]

In this chapter, we explore workflow analysis, job analysis, and job design. A **job** is a group of related activities, tasks, and duties (i.e., what you do at work). For example, you might be a carpenter or an educational assistant. Jobs are sometimes confused with positions. A **position** is a specific instance of a job held by an individual. For example, imagine a fast-food kiosk in a mall that employs one manager, four cashiers, and six cooks. This restaurant has three jobs (manager, cashier, and cook) but 11 positions.

A job exists because the activities and duties associated with it are necessary for the organization to accomplish a piece of work. Work often involves workers who perform a series of tasks, either alone or in cooperation with others. The way that specific tasks are arranged to complete a piece of work is called **workflow**. To understand a job, it is necessary to understand the organizational workflow(s) to which the job contributes. For this reason, the first section of this chapter deals with workflows and workflow mapping.

Once HR practitioners understand the context of a job, they can then analyze it. **Job analysis** is the systematic study of a job to determine its duties, responsibilities, and working conditions as well as the requisite knowledge, skills, and abilities—or KSAs—of workers in the job. Job analyses inform HR tasks such as recruiting and selecting new workers as well as identifying the training needs of workers and performance standards of a job.

The last section of this chapter examines **job design**, the process of (re)structuring work and assigning specific tasks and duties to jobs and positions. Job design can result in the creation of entirely new workflows. More often, though, workflows already exist. In these instances, job (re)design techniques can be applied to improve workflows to achieve a broader organizational goal, such as improving worker satisfaction, increasing product quality, or reducing labour costs.

Workflow Analysis

Workflow is the way that people get work done. Every organization has at least one workflow (or business process). Often workflow entails a series of steps through which a piece of work passes, from initiation to completion. Workflows are often stable and broadly understood as "how we do things here." A **workflow map** is a visual representation of this process. Workflows can be examined at different levels of granularity. Feature Box 3.1 provides a simple example of workflow at a family restaurant, expressed both as a narrative and as a map.

Feature Box 3.1 Sample Workflow Analysis and Map

A workflow analysis typically results in a workflow map. The granularity of the analysis and map can vary. For example, an HR practitioner might map the high-level customer workflow of a family-style restaurant as having six steps. First, customers are welcomed and seated in the restaurant. Second, their food and drink order is taken. Third, the food and drink are then prepared, and, fourth, they are delivered, with any errors corrected. Fifth, the staff collect payment and, sixth, reset the table for the next customers. Figure 3.1 shows how this workflow might be expressed visually.

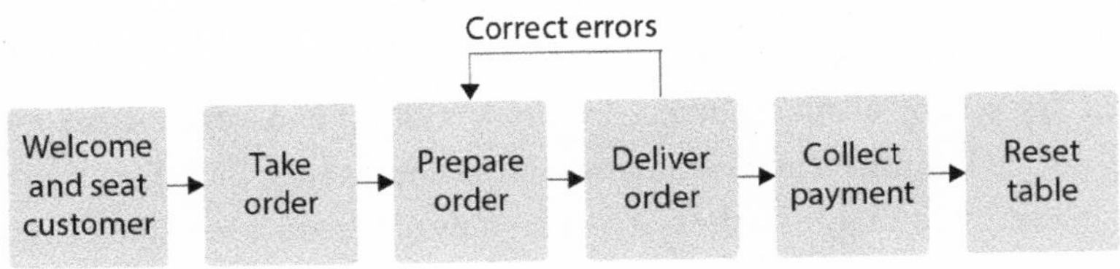

Figure 3.1 Sample restaurant workflow map

It is possible to break any of these high-level steps down into a more granular workflow. Consider step 2 in Figure 3.1, when the customer's food and drink order is taken. As suggested in Figure 3.2, drink and food orders are usually taken separately. This gives the customers time to peruse the food menu while the drinks are prepared and delivered. That said, a regular customer or a customer in a hurry might well place both orders at once. Documenting this sort of nuance can be helpful in training new staff members to understand their roles in the workflow, how their roles interact with jobs done by other employees, and common variations in the process.

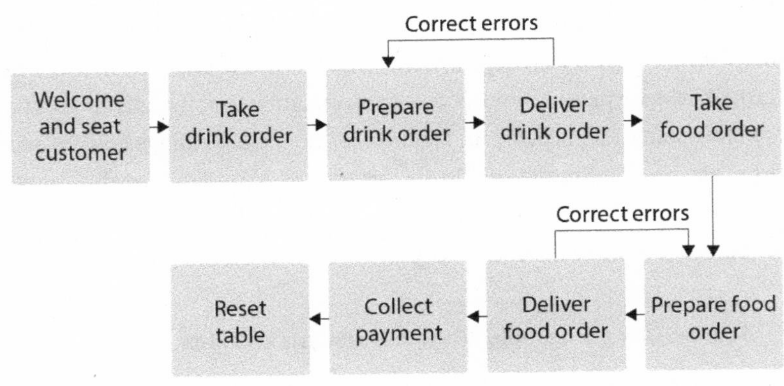

Figure 3.2 Food and drink order workflow

It is also possible to diagram the workflow such that it identifies who is responsible for each step. In this restaurant, the analysis might reveal that there are three main jobs: greeter/cashier, server, and cook. The workflow in Figure 3.3 is the same as the workflow in Figure 3.1, but the diagram has been stratified such that each row identifies which job is primarily responsible for each step.

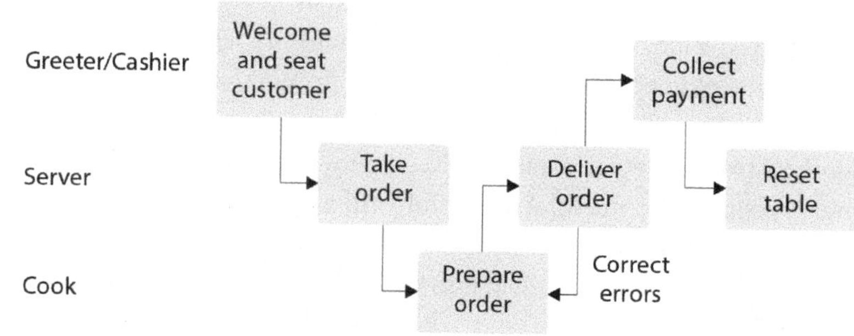

Figure 3.3 Restaurant workflow stratified by responsibility

Organizations map workflows for several reasons. A clear workflow map is very useful for identifying the kinds of jobs that must be performed. For example, the stratified restaurant workflow in Figure 3.3 immediately tells us that three jobs must be done (greeter/cashier, server/table busser, and cook). Workflow can also be a useful training tool for new staff (e.g., "this is how work is done, and here's how your job fits in") and help supervisors and HR practitioners to determine how to assess worker performance. In the restaurant example, an employer might decide to monitor employee performance by tracking cash register shortfalls, customer complaints, and kitchen errors (performance standards are discussed in depth in Chapter 9).

Workflow mapping also makes explicit how work gets done. Making the process of work visible helps employers to exert greater control over the workplace, resulting in both reduced worker power and lower labour costs. For example, in the early part of the 20th century, Frederick Taylor pioneered the use of time-and-motion studies to determine the steps needed to produce items. He observed and measured where workers moved, how long it took them to perform a task, and in what order they performed them. Using this information, he redesigned the workflow to break down production into a series of discrete, sequenced steps. This process, today called Taylorism (or sometimes scientific management), captured workers' knowledge and made it available to employers.

Scientific management also reduced the ability of workers to use their knowledge to control the pace of production. Once employers understood the workflow, they could rearrange it to their advantage. For example, knowing how long it takes to do each step allowed them to set and enforce production targets. Knowing the process of production also allowed them to resequence and simplify the steps in production and to hire less-skilled workers to complete some tasks (thereby lowering labour costs). Today's highly regimented manufacturing jobs (in which a worker does a single task over and over) are the outcome of this workflow mapping and job (re)design. This has also spilled into service industry jobs, most obviously fast-food restaurants.

This historical example reveals that workflow analysis is not an entirely technical activity. Employers and HR practitioners make decisions (if implicitly) during workflow analysis about what sort of workforce they will have and the conditions that the workers will face. For example, Taylorism allowed employers to hire fewer skilled workers (at lower wages). The introduction of a moving assembly line by Henry Ford allowed employers to increase the pace of repetitive jobs by speeding up the line, in turn increasing the rate of injuries. Workflow decisions shape subsequent HR decisions, such as which KSAs must be sought during recruitment and what workers will be paid. They also affect the quality of workers' lives. As shown in the opening vignette, all of these techniques and effects are evident in the implementation of scanners in grocery stores.

Although almost all organizations have established workflows, they are not always mapped or mapped accurately. Often the workflow exists only in the heads of those involved. Sometimes inaccurate or unmapped workflows reflect that the organization has simply not bothered to codify or maintain its workflow. For example, inaccurate written workflows can result from a long-term, incremental drift in processes, such as gradual changes in technology that make some steps redundant. Inaccurate workflows can also result from sudden, large changes that are not codified, such as jerry-rigged processes created in response to the COVID-19 pandemic. Inaccuracies can also be caused by employees who adjust processes on their own, such as deciding to skip steps to manage workload increases, change processes to make a job more enjoyable, or circumvent surveillance, such as by communicating via texts instead of through company email systems.

In other cases, the HR strategy adopted by an employer or the nature of the work can impede workflow analysis. For example, in a high-performance work system, jobs or tasks in which workers can (or must) exercise significant discretion can be challenging to map in a meaningful way. Consider the process of writing this textbook, a regular task for a university professor. Figure 3.4 maps this workflow at a high level.

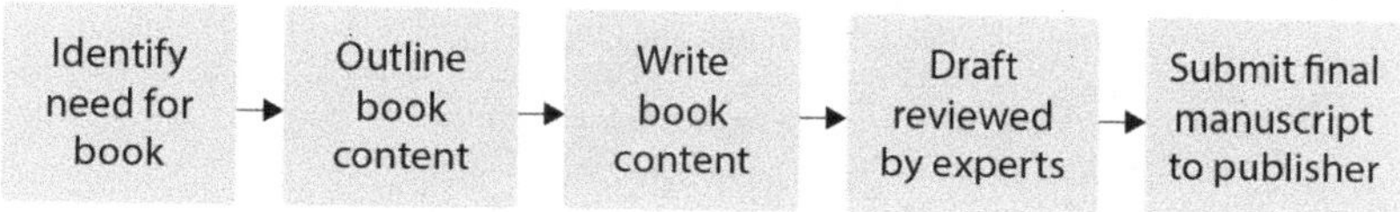

Figure 3.4 Textbook writing workflow

It is not really possible to break down each high-level step further to create a step-by-step process that someone without our KSAs could easily follow. This reflects that the overall process is highly iterative. That is, we moved back and forth among steps 2 and 4 right up to the minute that the final manuscript was sent to the publisher. And, within each step, the exact process that we used was idiosyncratic, and if mapped it would appear to be chaotic. For example, portions of chapters were written piecemeal, often months apart, out of order, and by different authors. Ideas, examples, and concepts were continuously added, cut, altered, and moved around in response to our own evolving understanding of what worked, comments from reviewers, and random thoughts and ideas that we had or encountered. The appearance of a chaotic process, however, is misleading. We have decades of experience with this book's content and teaching it to others. This expertise means that we can manage the complicated and demanding process of writing and revising a huge book (containing many interrelated parts) without losing track of either the details or the final goal. (A good editor also helps!)

Typically, workflow analysis entails performing three steps that can be broken into seven tasks. This process is set out in Table 3.1. Workflow analysis begins with answering the question of why it is necessary to analyze workflow. The purpose of the analysis will shape the focus and degree of granularity in the map. For example, mapping the workflow in a restaurant (e.g., Feature Box 3.1) to train new workers to do the job will likely require less detail than would mapping workflow to ensure that workplace hazards are identified and controlled. Consequently, the first step in a workflow analysis is to determine the reason(s) for it. This might require discussion among key stakeholders to ensure that this purpose is shared and understood.

Table 3.1 Workflow analysis phases and tasks

Phase	Tasks
1. Preparation	Determine purpose Identify workflow
2. Data collection	Identify information Design data Collect data
3. Data analysis and use	Create or revise Inform job analysis

The reason for analyzing workflow usually determines which workflow is analyzed, and more than one might be analyzed. For example, a quality control problem or a desire to contract out work (which requires a clear understanding of what is currently happening) can trigger a workflow analysis. Absent a compelling issue to trigger mapping, organizations tend to focus their resources on mapping only operationally essential business processes. This is because errors in these processes entail the greatest potential organizational risk.

Workflow requires information sources and a clear process for collecting the information. Many of the data collection techniques described below for job analysis (e.g., observation, interviews, questionnaires) can be used to gather data for a workflow analysis. The process of collecting and analyzing workflow data, however, tends to be a bit more iterative and visual than is typical of a job analysis.

Creating a new workflow map often begins with developing an initial sketch of the workflow by an HR practitioner. This process can be as simple as writing steps on sticky notes and then putting them in a sensible sequence, or it can involve using process-mapping software. This initial workflow can then be presented to a group of informants (e.g., workers, supervisors, clients) for review. This review can identify previously unrecognized tasks or sequences as well as interdependencies, contingencies, and feedback loops. If there is an existing workflow map, then it can be subjected to a similar process of reviewing and modifying the workflow. Eventually, the group will agree on a workflow map.

That map can be verified by observing the work process and comparing the actual practice to the map to identify differences or other errors. A map can also be refined by identifying which job is responsible for each task (see Figure 3.3) or what the inputs to the step are, how they are transformed, and what the outputs of the step are. For example, if an HR practitioner is mapping the process by which a university admits students to a degree program, then the process will include a step in which someone (likely a clerk in the registrar's office) actually decides whether each applicant should be admitted or rejected. The inputs to this decision are student applications and admission criteria. For the sake of simplicity, we can assume that the criteria include a simple grade cutoff, such as 75%, based on five named high school courses. With this criterion applied, the applications are then transformed into two outputs (accepted or rejected applications). These outputs then move into separate processes at the next stage of the workflow. Identifying inputs, processes of transformation, and outputs can make clear how this workflow relates to other organizational processes.

At some point, a reasonably accurate workflow map will be produced. If the workflow is complicated, then it might take several rounds of revision and validation for an HR practitioner to be confident that the map is accurate. At this point, the map can be used to inform other HR activities, such as job analysis or (re)design. For example, a workflow map might identify that five jobs are related to a particular task. The workflow analysis might identify that this number of handoffs results in errors (e.g., incomplete tasks or dropped handoffs). Redesigning the workflow to reduce the number of handoffs might be desirable. This can entail redesigning jobs (so that one person completes the entire task) or applying technology to prevent and/or detect errors in handoffs.

Job Analysis

Job analysis is the process by which an HR practitioner determines a job's duties, responsibilities, and working conditions as well as the requisite KSAs of workers in the job. The results of job analyses inform other HR tasks. For example, job analysis typically informs job descriptions and specifications used to help recruit and select the right worker for the job. Job analyses can also help to identify training needs among current staff, the best method and rate of compensation, and which standards should be used to assess worker performance.

As stated above, a job comprises a group of related activities and duties. When an organization has several distinct jobs with similar duties and responsibilities, those jobs can be assigned to a **job family**. They might have similar KSAs and training needs, have similar compensation structures, and provide pathways for career advancement. For example, a car dealership might have three job families: sales, administration, and servicing. The specific jobs in each job family are set out in Table 3.2. As you review these job families, assess whether they make sense from the perspective of the KSAs that they likely require and the potential job advancement within a job family. You might also wish to consider the best way to compensate work in each job family, such as commission, salary, or piecework.

Table 3.2 Example of job families at ABC car dealership

Sales family	Sales manager Senior salesperson Junior salesperson
Administration family	Dealership manager Financing officer Financing assistant Accounting officer Accounting assistant Human resource officer Receptionist
Service family	Service manager Mechanic Apprentice mechanic

The job analysis process has three main phases: preparation, data collection, and data analysis and use. Within each phase are specific steps as set out in Table 3.3. The first (preparatory) step is to determine the purpose(s) of the job analysis. For example, is the purpose simply to document the status quo in order to create accurate job descriptions and job specifications? Or is the purpose to identify areas where a job could be redesigned to streamline a work process? Understanding the purpose of the job analysis ensures that the right information is collected.

Table 3.3. Job analysis phases and tasks

Phase	Tasks
1. Preparation	Determine purpose(s) Identify jobs to analyze
2. Data collection	Identify information sources Design data collection process Collect data
3. Data analysis and use	Create or revise job description and specification Inform other HR tasks Inform job redesign

The purpose of the job analysis will also shape which jobs will be analyzed. Job analysis can entail a significant investment of organizational resources, particularly staff time. Using these resources to perform job analysis means that they cannot be used for another purpose. The forgone benefit that would have been derived from using these organizational resources for some other purpose is called the **opportunity cost.** The opportunity cost of performing job analysis suggests that HR practitioners should focus job analysis where there is a clear organizational need. Areas of need might include the following.

- Jobs that have changed because of environmental or technological factors can benefit from analysis to ensure that job descriptions, specifications, and compensation remain correct.
- Jobs that are difficult to fill or have high turnover might have structural problems such as requiring an uncommon set of KSAs, being too difficult to perform, or being undercompensated.
- Jobs that are key to organizational success because of the tasks that they perform; a workflow analysis that breaks down workflow by

job (e.g., Figure 3.3) can be helpful in identifying jobs key to organizational success.

- Jobs that pose organizational risk; for example, if a government requires contractors to demonstrate gender parity in their workforces, and a particular job family is male dominated, then a job analysis can suggest ways to address gender parity and attenuate the risk of non-compliance.

Once a job has been selected for analysis, an HR practitioner can identify the available sources of information about the job. Such information can be derived either from people or from documents. Table 3.4 summarizes the main sources of information about jobs: either people or documents. Feature Box 3.2 identifies that the potential for workers to provide inaccurate information exists, suggesting in turn that it is sometimes necessary to use multiple and independent sources of information. Designing the data collection process entails selecting which data sources to use, determining how best to get the data from each source, and deciding how the information will be recorded.

Table 3.4 Sources of information

People	Workers and co-workers Supervisors and subordinates Clients or customers Experts
Documents	Job descriptions and specifications Workflow maps Training and equipment manuals HR records (e.g., performance improvement plans, absenteeism rates, turnover rates)

Feature Box 3.2 Employees as a Source of Information

Employers often turn to workers for information when conducting a job analysis. This choice reflects that workers are the most likely to know which tasks and processes a job actually entails. Workers are also generally readily available to employers and can be compelled to provide the information sought. That said, it is important to remember that workers might not be entirely forthcoming about what they do and can do.

Workers' reluctance to be fully transparent about their work reflects that their knowledge of how a job is done is a form of power. Workers can use that knowledge to make their working lives better, for example by controlling the pace of work or how tasks are completed. Workers might worry that, if they reveal that they could work faster, their employers will restructure their jobs to make them do so. For example, an employer might change the wage-effort bargain by raising production targets or reducing staff while maintaining production.

Most workers know, at least intuitively, that job analysis is part of an employer's broad strategy to maximize its return on each worker hired (i.e., it is an exercise of employer power in the pursuit of profit). Consequently, workers might choose to obfuscate what they do (or can do) to maintain the existing wage-effort bargain. Workers might also choose to overstate their duties in order to increase their compensation. Or they might mislead their employers through earnest misreporting. These sources of error in workers' reports can reduce the **validity** or **reliability** of their information.

Valid information is accurate. For example, if a worker says that the job requires the ability to lift 50 pounds, and indeed the job requires lifting 50-pound boxes, then the worker's information is valid. Reliable information does not change over time. For example, workers and supervisors might say repeatedly that a job requires lifting 75 pounds (perhaps because they are sure that the boxes weigh 75 pounds). That information is reliable (because the interviewees say the same thing every time). But it might not be valid (i.e., correct) if, for example, the boxes actually weigh only 50 pounds. Ideally, information should be both valid and reliable. It is possible, however, for information to be valid only (and not reliable), reliable only (and not valid), or neither.

To control for the possibility of misreporting—whether innocent or intentional—HR practitioners can use **triangulation**. That means verifying facts using different data sources and methods to ensure that important information is accurate. Continuing with the lifting example, if the accuracy of the lifting requirement is important, then an HR practitioner might ask the workers how much they lift and how often. Then the practitioner might weigh boxes to confirm their weight and observe the workers to see how often they lift them. This verification ensures that important facts in the job analysis are correct. Although triangulation increases accuracy, it also entails extra work and thereby increases the opportunity cost of the data collection.

Selecting which data source to use entails trade-offs. For example, an HR practitioner might get a thorough job analysis if three workers, a supervisor, and three customers are interviewed and then a worker is observed for a week. But the opportunity cost of this approach would be high. The practitioner might get almost the same information by interviewing one worker and one supervisor and reviewing an existing job description or training manual. Whether the extra accuracy of the first approach is worth the additional cost is context dependent. It might be worth spending more organizational resources if there is a significant organizational risk attached to error in the job analysis. The practice of HRM is rife with these sorts of cost-benefit decisions. These trade-offs help to explain the difference between prescription (what a textbook says should happen) and description (what actually happens).

Data collected during a job analysis is typically recorded on a job analysis form (sometimes called a job analysis questionnaire). Forms ensure consistent data collection. A form typically includes the following information.

- *Job identification*: This section sets out which job is being analyzed (title, organizational unit), when the analysis took place, and who was involved.
- *Purpose, duties, and responsibilities*: This section identifies the major purpose(s) of the job as well as the major duties (and perhaps the frequency and importance of each). This section determines the job's key responsibilities (e.g., equipment operation, supervision of others) and whether they are major or minor responsibilities.
- *KSAs and working conditions*: This section identifies specific knowledge, skills, and abilities required by the job. It might also identify notable working conditions, hazards, or demands of the job.
- *Performance standards*: This section sets out how performance or success is measured.

Feature Box 3.3 provides an example of a job analysis form. The exact content of a form will vary among organizations and depending on the purpose of the job analysis.

Feature Box 3.3 Sample Job Analysis Form

Employee information

Position title

Department

Supervisor

Position purpose

In one or two sentences, indicate the main purpose of this job.

Responsibilities

List important job responsibilities in order of importance and estimate percentage of working time spent on each duty.

Education

List the minimum and specific educational qualifications required to perform this job.

Experience

List the minimum and specific experience required to perform this job.

Skills and certifications

List specific skills or certifications/licences required to perform this job.

Supervision

List any direct or indirect supervisory duties performed in this job.

Physical demands

Using a scale of 1–5, where 1 is never and 5 is constant, rate how often this job requires the following physical activities.

• Balancing	1___	2___	3___	4___	5___
• Carrying	1___	2___	3___	4___	5___
• Climbing	1___	2___	3___	4___	5___
• Crawling	1___	2___	3___	4___	5___
• Crouching	1___	2___	3___	4___	5___
• Feeling	1___	2___	3___	4___	5___
• Grasping	1___	2___	3___	4___	5___
• Hand-Eye Coordination	1___	2___	3___	4___	5___
• Handling	1___	2___	3___	4___	5___
• Hearing	1___	2___	3___	4___	5___
• Kneeling	1___	2___	3___	4___	5___
• Lifting	1___	2___	3___	4___	5___
• Pulling	1___	2___	3___	4___	5___

- Pushing 1___ 2___ 3___ 4___ 5___
- Reaching 1___ 2___ 3___ 4___ 5___
- Repetitive Motions 1___ 2___ 3___ 4___ 5___
- Sitting 1___ 2___ 3___ 4___ 5___
- Standing 1___ 2___ 3___ 4___ 5___
- Stooping 1___ 2___ 3___ 4___ 5___
- Talking 1___ 2___ 3___ 4___ 5___
- Walking 1___ 2___ 3___ 4___ 5___

List any notable environmental conditions associated with this job (weather, noise, other hazards).

List any specific physical abilities required by this job (e.g., maximum lift weight, speed and distance requirements).

Mental demands

Using a scale of 1–5, where 1 is never and 5 is constant, rate how often this job requires the following mental activities.

- Analyzing 1___ 2___ 3___ 4___ 5___
- Calculating 1___ 2___ 3___ 4___ 5___
- Comprehending 1___ 2___ 3___ 4___ 5___
- Coordinating 1___ 2___ 3___ 4___ 5___
- Diagnosing 1___ 2___ 3___ 4___ 5___
- Deciding 1___ 2___ 3___ 4___ 5___
- Learning 1___ 2___ 3___ 4___ 5___
- Negotiating 1___ 2___ 3___ 4___ 5___
- Persuading 1___ 2___ 3___ 4___ 5___
- Planning 1___ 2___ 3___ 4___ 5___
- Organizing 1___ 2___ 3___ 4___ 5___
- Problem Solving 1___ 2___ 3___ 4___ 5___
- Reading 1___ 2___ 3___ 4___ 5___
- Reasoning 1___ 2___ 3___ 4___ 5___

Other comments

Please list any other information required to understand this job.

When documentary evidence is used, typically an HR practitioner reads the documents, extracts the information relevant to the job analysis, and enters it on the form. It can be useful to indicate the source of the information in case it is ever necessary to go back to the original source.

There are four main ways to collect data from people (e.g., workers, supervisors, customers).

- *Questionnaire*: A written or electronic questionnaire is an inexpensive way to collect data. The main risk of questionnaires is that respondents might misunderstand written questions (even carefully written ones). It can also be necessary to follow up on questionnaires to generate or clarify responses. It is often useful to supplement questionnaires with interviews.
- *Interviews*: Asking questions of knowledgeable sources, either individually or in a group, can elicit useful information. Semi-structured interviews use a questionnaire to guide them but also give the job analyst latitude to explore unclear or unexpected answers. Separately interviewing people allows an interviewer to cross-check facts.
- *Diary*: Workers can be asked to track their activities using a diary (sometimes called a work log). Typically, they record their activities at regular intervals (e.g., every 20 minutes) over a long enough period (e.g., two weeks) to provide a representative picture of their jobs.
- *Observation*: Job analysts might be able to observe or shadow a worker. Doing so allows them to record which job duties and activities are performed and how frequently. Such observation can also reveal some of the KSAs that a worker must use on the job. Observation can be time consuming. It can also trigger an **observer effect**, by which the presence of an observer can affect the behaviour that the subject exhibits. This can undermine the validity of the information gathered by the observer.

Once data for a job analysis have been collected, they can be analyzed. Typically, this entails creating a job description and a job specification. A **job description** is a written statement of the duties of a job. It typically contains a job title, a job identification section, and a list of job duties. It can also contain information about the job's compensation. A job description can also identify important working conditions as well as contain a job specification. A **job specification** is the list of qualifications required to perform the job. Feature Box 3.4 contains a sample job description for a construction labourer on a road crew.

Feature Box 3.4 Sample Job Description and Job Specification

Job identity

Job title:	Construction labourer (road work)
Department:	Road Construction
Job analyst:	Bob Barnetson, Human Resources
Date analyzed:	August 17, 2020
Report to:	Worksite lead hand
Verified:	Zoe Murthy, lead hand
Compensation:	Pay band 4

Job summary

The construction labourer (road work) performs physical tasks required to construct and repair roadways. Job tasks include transporting and installing road materials (often by hand), the operation of vehicles and small machines, and directing traffic. Work takes place outside, often in remote locations and during inclement weather.

Duties and functions

1. Preparing job sites (e.g., removal of trees, rough grading, culvert installation).
2. Loading, transporting, levelling, and packing aggregates (e.g., sand, gravel, road crush) and other materials.
3. Installing and removing concrete forms for curbs and sidewalks.
4. Operating hand tools (e.g., broom, shovel, rake, wheelbarrow, sprayer, chainsaw).
5. Operating small construction machinery (e.g., ditch witch, packer, bobcat) and small vehicles (e.g., pick-up truck with trailer).
6. Directing construction machinery (e.g., pavers, rollers, and dump trucks).
7. Directing highway or street traffic on site.

Working conditions

1. Work can entail long shifts (up to 12 hours) and extended work periods (up to 14 days).
2. Work requires travel to remote locations (transport and housing provided).

3. Work performed mainly outdoors in all seasons and weather.
4. Work performed in close proximity to machinery and traffic.
5. Work entails exposure to insects, fumes, dust, and other materials related to road work.

Job specification

1. Prior experience in road construction required.
2. Ability to perform physical tasks associated with road construction, including lifting up to 100 pounds and operating hand tools and small construction machinery for prolonged periods and during inclement weather (e.g., high and low temperatures).
3. Class 5 driver's licence with no more than three demerits.
4. Training in traffic safety and traffic directing.
5. Workplace Hazard Materials Information System (WHMIS) and first-aid certified (or ability to become certified).
6. Must pass periodic worksite drug and alcohol tests.

There are three main audiences for job descriptions.

- Workers and potential workers can know that the job entails semi-skilled manual work using hand tools and small machines in the outdoors. The work also requires long shifts, unusual shift schedules, and extended time away from home. This description allows potential workers to decide if they are qualified for and interested in the job.
- Supervisors can use the job specification to make hiring decisions and the job duties to assign tasks to labourers consistent with the skills and terms of their employment contracts. Supervisors can also use the job description as the basis for assessing worker performance (see Chapter 9).
- HR practitioners can use the title and job specification to write job advertisements, classify the job, assign compensation, and perform other HR tasks. HR staff can also ensure that the requirement for workers to pass periodic worksite drug and alcohol testing

is performed within the boundaries of the law (testing is further examined in Chapters 5 and 8).

In developing a job description and a job specification, it is important to be mindful of three things. First, some aspects of jobs are more readily apparent than other aspects. For example, physical demands and activities (e.g., lifting) are often easier for job analysts to "see" than mental demands and activities (e.g., navigating office politics). Activities not readily apparent can sometimes be left out of job descriptions and specifications. This can result in workers being undercompensated and supervisors failing to hire workers with the necessary skills to do the job. Having a draft of a job description verified by workers and supervisors can identify these sorts of gaps.

Second, job descriptions and specifications are social constructions in that analysts must decide what to include and what to exclude (i.e., which KSAs, activities, and duties are important and which are not). This winnowing process can be a source of error. For example, an analyst might recognize lifting as a requirement for a building maintenance job but fail to include it as a requirement for a child-care worker. Given the gendered nature of these jobs, failing to recognize lifting as a routine aspect of child care renders such tasks and abilities organizationally invisible. Consequently, workers can be hired who are unable to do the job, supervisors might not provide workers with the equipment necessary to control the hazard posed by lifting, and organizations might be reluctant to acknowledge injuries caused by lifting. Again, knowledgeable reviewers can identify errors and omissions. Feature Box 3.5 explores the related issue of gendered emotional labour frequently overlooked in job analysis.

Third, job analysis often has difficulty grappling with activities that a worker is not formally required to perform but that are practically important to the organization's operation, such as observing social rituals (e.g., acknowledging birthdays or the births of children) or undertaking relatively thankless organizational tasks (e.g., sitting on committees or informally mentoring new hires). These tasks can enhance the functioning of a group of workers and are often performed by women. But these tasks are rarely considered "work" and tend to be ignored, trivialized, and undervalued in job analysis. This pattern suggests that organizations take advantage of women, who traditionally have been taught a moral outlook that emphasizes solidarity, community, and caring, by expecting them to do this work for free.[6]

Feature Box 3.5 Overlooking Emotional Labour

Emotional labour is the process of regulating our emotions to create a public impression in the workplace.[7] Essentially, emotional labour requires us to suppress our authentic selves and/or our reactions while on the job. For example, a worker might need to be polite to a rude customer or maintain a detached demeanour when giving a patient bad news. Although emotional labour most often occurs when workers must interact with the public, it can also be required when workers interact with co-workers or supervisors. In this way, emotional labour can be a job requirement, just like wearing a uniform or operating a piece of equipment.

Many aspects of our lives entail moderating our emotions, such as parenting and managing relationships with friends. This emotional work differs from emotional labour because of the employment context. Specifically, employers can mandate when, where, and how emotional labour occurs, leaving workers with little choice but to perform emotional labour and giving them little ability to protect themselves from the consequences of that labour. That is not to say that every worker finds emotional labour to be taxing or harmful. Indeed, some workers enjoy performing it.[8] Nevertheless, most studies find that emotional labour lowers job satisfaction and causes psychological stress for the worker.[9] By overlooking emotional labour in the job description, this form of work becomes devalued and invisible, meaning that the job becomes undervalued. Ironically, employers often cite perceived inadequacies in performing emotional labour in performance evaluations (e.g., "you need to act more professionally") even if it is not included in the formal job description.

This analysis suggests that emotional labour is an example of a psychosocial hazard. As noted in Chapter 2, employers have an obligation to identify and control workplace hazards. One barrier to controlling the hazard posed by emotional labour is its relative invisibility in job analysis. This omission might reflect that emotional labour can be difficult to "see" (unless one observes workers at work) and to quantify. It can also be highly idiosyncratic, differing among workers based on their authentic selves and reactions. Furthermore, employers have an economic incentive not to recognize emotional labour. Ignoring it allows employers to avoid compensating workers for it and to avoid the costs of protecting workers from its consequences. The requirement to perform emotional labour tends to be higher in female-dominated occupations such as retail, health care, child care, hospitality, and education. This makes emotional labour a gendered phenomenon in that its effects are disproportionately experienced by women.

Job Design

As noted above, **job design** is the process of structuring work and assigning specific tasks and duties to jobs in order to achieve an organization's objectives. In established organizations, job design is typically about redesigning jobs (or even entire workflows) to improve efficiency and/or workers' experiences of work. Both outcomes are expected to lead to increased productivity. Increased efficiency means that more products or services can be produced with the same inputs. Increasing worker satisfaction is expected to result in greater productivity.

The notion that increasing job satisfaction increases worker productivity is based on the job characteristics model. That model was originally proposed in 1976 by Richard Hackman and Greg Oldham and asserts that improving job characteristics positively alters workers' psychological states. That, in turn, results in better psychological and performance outcomes. The basic logic of the job characteristics model is intuitively attractive: better jobs make happier workers likely to work harder and more effectively. But is the underlying model correct? Feature Box 3.6 explores this model and its validity.

Feature Box 3.6 Job Characteristics Model

The **job characteristics model** asserts that job (re)design can affect worker motivation, performance, and satisfaction (see Figure 3.5).[10] This purported relationship is used to justify changing jobs in various ways. Models are simplified representations of dynamics and processes that can help us to understand the way the world works. Sometimes models are also valuable in revealing instances when the world does not quite work as one might think it does. Given this discrepancy, an interesting question is the degree to which the job characteristic model is a valid representation of what happens to workers' motivation and productivity when HR practitioners "improve" their jobs.

The job characteristics model is premised on three psychological states (meaningfulness, responsibility, and awareness) that workers can experience (see the middle column in Figure 3.5). According to the model, workers who experience these states behave differently from those who do not. These behavioural differences are said to result in improved work and personal outcomes (see the right-hand column). The degree to which these three psychological states are experienced by workers can be increased, according to the model, by altering the dimensions (or characteristics) of the job (the left-hand column) through job (re)design. In subsequent versions of this model, absenteeism and turnover have been removed as outcomes. Instead, high-quality work has been broken into high-quality and high-quantity work.

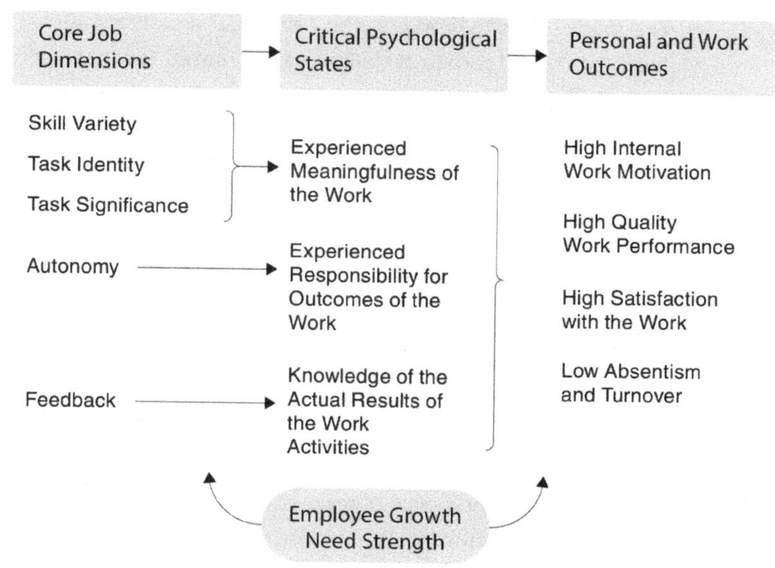

Figure 3.5 Job characteristics model
(Based on Hackman & Oldham, 1976, p. 256)

Before delving into whether this model accurately reflects reality, it is useful to unpack the job characteristics associated with improved performance.

- *Skill variety* refers to the range of skills used by a worker. It assumes that employing more skills increases the challenge of the job and thus heightens the meaningfulness of the work.
- *Task identity* refers to whether a job requires workers to complete a "whole" piece of work (e.g., assembling something completely or serving a client from start to finish) or at least to see where their work fits into the big picture. Allowing workers to complete a whole piece of work is also argued to increase meaningfulness.
- *Task significance* refers to how workers' perception of the importance of their jobs affects how meaningful they find their work. Jobs that workers view as important to others are also said to increase meaningfulness.
- *Autonomy* refers to the degree of discretion that workers have in organizing and carrying out work, and greater autonomy is said to increase workers' experiences of responsibility for the outcomes of the work.
- *Feedback* refers to workers who have clear and direct knowledge of the outcomes of their work. Increased feedback is expected to increase workers' knowledge of the outcomes.[11]

It is important to note that, with the exception of feedback, the exact mechanism by which job characteristics give rise to the desired psychological states is not particularly clear.

Since this model was initially proposed, hundreds of academic studies of it (or using it) have been performed. Research suggests that the model does a reasonable job of linking job characteristics to work outcomes, but the relationship between each core job dimension and its associated critical psychological state is much more complex and interconnected than Figure 3.5 suggests.

Research also indicates that the linkage is stronger between job characteristics and psychological outcomes (satisfaction and motivation) than between job characteristics and performance outcomes (quality and absenteeism). This difference might suggest that other contextual factors (e.g., peer norms, job security) can mediate (or influence) the relationship between job characteristics and performance outcomes.[12]

The evidence for whether the core psychological states at the centre of this model are necessary to understand the relationship between job characteristics and work performance or have any effect on that relationship is varied.[13] It is important to recognize that this nuanced analysis of the validity of the model is rarely considered in the practice of HRM. Instead, it is taken as an article of faith that job redesign will improve performance outcomes. Although this is broadly true, manipulating core job dimensions does not always result in the expected changes in worker performance or satisfaction.

The process of job (re)design typically seeks to meet four objectives:

- achieving the organization's goals to which the job contributes;
- increasing workers' satisfaction through manipulating job characteristics;
- maximizing efficiency through industrial engineering; and
- minimizing the negative impacts of work on workers through ergonomics.

In practice, job (re)design can take many forms. The steps in a workflow can be altered, and work tasks can be assigned to different jobs. Frederick Taylor's time-and-motion studies of factory work increased efficiency by making tasks simpler and more repetitive. Redesign can also include introducing new technology that can increase the productivity of workers or replace them entirely. For example, the introduction of machines and robots (e.g., the self-checkouts discussed at the beginning of this chapter) has increased the efficiency of (or replaced) human workers. Feature Box 3.7 examines an example of a job redesign involving the implementation of a call centre to manage customer requests and reduce wage costs.

Feature Box 3.7 Introducing a Call Centre

The implementation of a call centre at Athabasca University offers insights into the benefits and costs that job design can bring—some expected, some not. Athabasca University offers online university courses. Students can start any course on the first day of any month and have six months to complete the course work. They are also typically assigned a tutor available by phone or email to answer their questions and mark their assignments and exams. As registration in a course increases, the university is required to hire more tutors.

Tutors are paid in two ways. They get a monthly payment based on how many students they are assigned. This payment is unrelated to how much time they spend interacting with the students. It is essentially a form of on-call pay that compensates tutors for being available to interact with students as needed. Tutors are also paid a fixed amount for each assignment or exam that they grade. This is a form of piece-rate pay. (Compensation systems are discussed in more detail in Chapter 8.)

In 1994, the (now) Faculty of Business decided to redesign the job of tutoring to make it more efficient. Instead of being assigned to a tutor, business students emailed or phoned a call centre. The centre had scripted answers for administrative questions (e.g., "how do I book an examination?"). Approximately 80% of student queries were dealt with in this way.[14] Academic questions were referred to "academic experts" (a new title for tutors) using an electronic ticketing system. Experts were required to respond to questions within 48 hours. Students' questions would be answered by whichever expert in the course (typically there were several) was checking tickets that day.

The pay system for experts was also changed as a result of the job redesign. They were now paid by the minute for student contact. Marking remained a piece-rate system. The result was a 25% reduction in labour costs (i.e., tutor wages).[15] This significantly changed the wage-rate bargain for these workers. The online ticketing system eventually implemented also created a set of records that allowed managers to track response times and monitor responses. This significantly increased the potential for performance management, including discipline (we will examine the role of technology in performance management in Chapter 9).

Changing the wage-rate bargain subjected tutors to much greater scrutiny, and many of them initially resisted the change. Some quit. Some reduced their effort to match the new pay. Others gamed the system. For example, the greatest opportunity for these workers to recoup their lost wages was by increasing the pace of marking (because payment for marking was a fixed amount). Reducing the time spent marking to a minimum likely resulted in a lower-quality educational experience for students. For example, some tutors created a bank of assignment comments that they cut-and-pasted into essays rather than writing individualized comments.

This example suggests that job redesign can have unexpected outcomes. In this case, workers responded in unanticipated ways to changes in the wage-rate bargain. Essentially, they considered the new compensation structure unfair and modified their behaviour to respond to the (dis)incentives embedded in it. Whether the cost saving and greater administrative control were worth the resulting attrition and decline in instructional quality is open to debate.

It is interesting to note that this job redesign did not follow the prescriptions of the job characteristics model (see Feature Box 3.6). Indeed, it did the opposite of what the model suggests. By routing all contact between tutors and students through a call centre, worker autonomy and feedback were reduced. Similarly, assigning tutors only a portion of the student calls also reduced task identity and skill variety. This approach might help to explain subsequent worker attrition and gaming behaviour.

Job redesign can also entail physical alterations to the workplace. For example, an employer might replace individual offices with smaller cubicles to reduce the office space required. Or the employer might direct workers to work from home, thereby offloading office costs onto workers. Finally, job design can take the form of outsourcing some aspects of the work. For example, many employers have outsourced the HR functions of payroll and benefits administration to specialist firms.

There are several common ways that organizations attempt to redesign jobs to increase productivity and/or worker satisfaction.

- **Flexible scheduling:** Some organizations might be able to provide workers with flexibility in when they work. This can increase satisfaction by allowing the workers to manage competing demands. Organizationally speaking, though, such flexibility can complicate scheduling, supervision, and payroll.
- **Teleworking:** Allowing workers to work from home (or another location) can improve their satisfaction by reducing commuting

time and allowing them to manage competing demands better. The benefits of teleworking are gendered. Caregivers, mostly women, can experience more stress, less satisfaction, and less productivity when working from home.[16] Teleworking can also shift costs associated with providing workspaces from the organization to the worker. It can add complexity to HR tasks such as performance management, health and safety, and information privacy.

- **Job rotation**: Moving workers among jobs adds variety and can increase their skills. This can reduce, in turn, the impact of worker turnover because several workers will be able to perform a single job. Job rotation can increase costs given additional training requirements, and it does not fundamentally alter the core job dimensions identified in the job characteristics model. Workers can also resist cycling through jobs in the rotation that entail undesirable tasks or negatively affect their home lives (e.g., shift changes).
- **Job sharing**: Allowing two workers to fill a position part of the time can increase their satisfaction by allowing them to meet other demands in their lives. Job sharing can also reduce worker turnover because an employer can ask the remaining worker to cover temporarily a vacated position. Two workers, though, can complicate workflows because they must hand tasks back and forth and will slightly increase compensation costs, particularly for benefits.
- **Job enlargement**: Job enlargement entails adding tasks to a job of approximately the same complexity. This is sometimes called horizontal loading. It increases skill variety and can increase task identity. Job enlargement can also require additional training and increase compensation costs because workers must be more skilled. They might resist job enlargement if it affects the wage-effort bargain. For example, for workers who have short breaks between tasks, job enlargement can fill that time with other work. That would take away time that workers would otherwise use to recover or relax. Constantly shifting between tasks can also degrade workers' performance.
- **Job enrichment**: Increasing the autonomy of workers in how they do their work is called job enrichment (or vertical loading). It can increase skill variety, task significance, autonomy, and feedback.

Thinking back to the high-performance work system (HPWS) discussed in Chapter 1, we can see that the creation of workers' teams with expanded authority is another form of job enrichment. Again, training and compensation costs can rise, workers might resist this "opportunity" to work harder, and they might be reluctant to share their KSAs with peers because they view their knowledge as a source of power.

- *Employee empowerment*: Although job enlargement and enrichment are supervisor-controlled changes to jobs, employee empowerment allows workers to direct changes in their jobs. This approach is common in HPWS and reflects that workers can be best positioned to make changes in their jobs and workflows because of their knowledge. This approach shifts power from an organization to its workers. Although an organization can always veto changes made by employees, such an action can undercut their willingness to engage.

Many of these approaches to job design seek to increase the satisfaction (and thus performance) of workers by placing increased demands on them. The degree to which increasing demands is associated with greater productivity is questionable. Some research suggests that there is an optimal level of workload, after which workers begin to throttle back their effort per task to cope with higher volumes of work.[17] This suggests that the impact of job redesign on overall productivity might be limited.

Other limits to job redesign can include the following.

- *Worker availability*: Employers can struggle to find workers willing to accept and capable of performing a job. Employers can influence workers' willingness to work by altering wages and/or working conditions. Employers have less ability to address absolute shortages of adequately skilled workers caused, for example, by an unexpected boom in an industry absorbing existing skilled workers. The evidence for absolute labour shortages (i.e., there truly are no more workers available) is weak, and additional workers often can be enticed into the labour market by making jobs more attractive.[18]
- *Contractual or social norms*: Employers can face contractual limits on job redesign. The common law might view radical job change as

a violation of an employment contract (see Chapters 2 and 9). Provisions in a union's collective agreement can also limit an employer's ability to redesign jobs (see Chapter 10). Furthermore, workers might informally resist job redesign through individual or collective actions such as work slowdown, gaming, or turnover (see Feature Box 3.7). Customers can also resist job redesign, as shown in the opening vignette about self-checkouts.

- *Legal requirements*: Employers can also face legal limits on job redesign. Redesign that makes it impossible for a worker (or a class of workers) to perform a job based on a protected ground might run afoul of human rights legislation (see Chapter 2). For example, penalizing workers who refuse to be on call because of child-care obligations might be found to be discriminatory (depending on the circumstances).

Conclusion

Workflow analysis, job analysis, and job (re)design are foundational elements of the practice of human resource management. The information provided by job analyses in particular is required for HR practitioners to complete basic HR tasks such as undertaking recruitment and selection, determining wage rates, and organizing training. Workflow analysis also informs HR practices such as human resource planning and performance assessment.

These HR functions require practitioners to have technical skills. But they also require practitioners to exercise political acumen. The requirement for acumen reflects that information about how work is done is a source of power. Specifically, workers might object to an organization knowing exactly how fast they can work or redesigning workflow to increase productivity. This objection reflects that workers (quite reasonably) expect their employers to use that knowledge to change the wage-rate or wage-effort bargain (perhaps through job redesign). This change will almost certainly benefit employers' interests (i.e., minimizing labour costs to maximize profits), but the degree to which it benefits workers is less clear.

Ironically, exercising political acumen (and perhaps even trading off employer and worker interests) in the performance of HR tasks is often left out of the job descriptions and specifications of HR practitioners! This highlights that the contents of workflow maps, job descriptions, and job specifications are social constructions. That is, they are created by people within an organization. What is recorded in these documents is shaped, at least in part, by the interests, power, and biases of the various contributors to them. Leaving political acumen out of the job description and specification for HR practitioners allows employers to pretend that administering employment relationships is a technical task that warrants a lower level of pay. The consequences of omissions in job descriptions and specifications can affect workers unevenly, depending on their social characteristics.

EXERCISES

KEY TERMS

Define the following terms.

- Emotional labour
- Job
- Job analysis
- Job characteristics
- Job description
- Job design
- Job enlargement
- Job enrichment
- Job family
- Job rotation
- Job specification
- Observer effect
- Opportunity cost
- Position
- Reliability
- Teleworking
- Triangulation
- Validity
- Workflow
- Workflow map

ACTIVITIES

Map a workflow in an organization with which you are familiar using the following process.

- Identify the process that you will map.
- Write down the data sources, data collection methods, and verification strategy that you will use.
- Create (i.e., draw) and verify the workflow map.
- Expand the workflow map to stratify it (i.e., show which position is responsible for each step).

Perform a job analysis of a position from the job map using the following process.

- Identify the job to analyze.
- Write down the data sources, data collection methods, and verification strategy that you will use.
- Create (write out) and verify the job analysis.
- Write a job description and job specification.
- Identify instances of emotional labour.

Perform a workflow redesign using the following process.

- Identify a problem or shortcoming in the workflow that you mapped out above.
- Redesign the workflow to address the problem or shortcoming.
- Explain how the redesign will affect the job description and specification that you wrote.

DISCUSSION QUESTIONS

Discuss the following topics.

- What are the costs and benefits of workflow mapping?
- How might a job redesign both benefit and harm employers' interests?
- How might a job redesign both benefit and harm workers' interests?
- Why might workers be reluctant to participate in a job analysis?

- How can HR practitioners ensure that information gathered during a job analysis is reliable and valid?
- Why is emotional labour often invisible, and how can this problem be remedied?

SELF-REFLECTION QUESTIONS

Think about a job that you have held or that someone whom you know has held. Write self-reflections of 200 to 500 words on the following topics.

- How clearly was the workflow of this job understood by the workers doing it? How was this understanding conveyed to them? Would a better understanding of the workflow have improved their performance? Why or why not?
- What might the employer be surprised to find out if it suddenly had a perfect understanding of how the job was actually done? How might an employer respond to this new information, and how might it affect your day-to-day life as a worker?
- Which job-related factors drive your satisfaction as a worker? How do these factors align with (or diverge from) the job characteristics in the job characteristics model?
- Identify and describe two examples of when you performed emotional labour at work. Was it formally recognized in the job description and compensation structure of the job? Why or why not?
- What are three ways that this job could be enriched or enlarged? Would you want to experience these sorts of job enrichment or enlargement? Why or why not?

4 Human Resource Strategy and Planning

In September 2020, managers at Southlake Regional Health Centre in Newmarket, Ontario, announced that the hospital would be eliminating almost 100 registered nursing positions during the COVID-19 pandemic to address a long-standing budget deficit. The hospital's managers hoped to eliminate vacant positions rather than lay off staff members. The hospital was also eliminating 34 management and clerical positions and planned to cover patient care needs by hiring lower-paid staff, including 49 practical nurses and 32 other positions. The effect of this change, according to the union representing the nurses facing layoff, would be a lower quality of care and the risk of not being able to provide care during any patient surge associated with the pandemic.[1]

The decisions made by the senior managers of Southlake were the result of the hospital's **human resource planning** process. That is the process of anticipating and addressing the movement of workers into, out of, and within an organization over time. The goal of such planning is to ensure that organizations have the right number of appropriately qualified workers when and where they are needed. In Southlake's case, the hospital managers identified that the present workforce did not allow the organization to achieve its goal of providing adequate patient care within a fixed budget. Subsequently, the managers decided to alter the mix of workers to lower the hospital's labour costs. This change included deciding how to reduce a surplus of registered nurses and redistribute their work.

Human resource plans operationalize an organization's human resource strategy. As stated in Chapter 1, such a strategy is designed to assist an organization in implementing its business strategy. Consequently, we begin this chapter by examining the development of a human resource strategy before turning to explore the five-step process of human resource planning. When considering that planning, it is important to keep in mind how it can touch on issues in which the interests of labour and capital differ. In the example above, Southlake's plan to alter its workforce had significant implications for its workers. Some would see their positions disappear or be replaced by lower-paying ones. Others could see their workload intensify as they were required to cover the work of laid-off staff. Although these changes reduce upfront costs, they can have unexpected knock-on effects, including declining productivity (as workers withdraw voluntary labour), greater turnover, and higher benefit costs (e.g., more use of sick leave).

Human Resource Strategy

In Chapter 1, we explained that organizations can have three levels of strategy: corporate, business, and functional. A business strategy sets out how an organization will achieve its goals and, in the private sector, compete with rival organizations.[2] Organizations then develop functional strategies that set out how each department supports their business strategies. One of the functional strategies that organizations often have (if only implicitly) is a **human resource strategy**. It is a plan of action designed to achieve a business goal. This entails developing a set of mutually supportive HR practices that meet anticipated organizational needs based on an analysis of the business strategy and organizational context. The exact practices that an organization adopts should be selected to meet specific organizational goals rather than simply adopting "best practices."[3]

As a result, HR strategies tend to be highly idiosyncratic, so it is difficult to offer a typology of them. For example, a small organization that has adopted a cost-leader business strategy (see Chapter 1) might have a simple, reactive, human resource strategy designed to minimize labour costs and address issues (e.g., vacancies, harassment, performance) as they arise. A more sophisticated organization might have a much more proactive approach, with a unique HR strategy for each organizational unit. For example, a large non-profit with a differentiation business strategy might have different HR strategies for its small cadre of long-term and highly skilled administrators and for its front-line staff, who operate short-term projects. Its HR strategy for core administrative staff might focus on minimizing turnover through competitive wages and development opportunities and internal promotions. In contrast, its HR strategy for short-term programs might focus on minimizing costs by taking advantage of a loose labour market for front-line staff and hiring recent graduates on short-term, part-time contracts.

Organizational approaches to developing or renewing an HR strategy fall along a continuum anchored by an inside-out approach on one end and an outside-in approach on the other.[4] An inside-out approach attempts to modify existing HR practices to improve their alignment with and support of a business strategy. This approach is sometimes called an incremental strategy, in which HR changes are made (usually slowly) over time to shift organizational processes and structures toward the desired state. This approach is often adopted in mature organizations with well-established HR practices. It has a lower risk of significantly disrupting the organization, but progress can also peter out over time, especially if workers resist the approach.

In contrast, an outside-in approach selects and implements HR structures and processes best suited to supporting the business strategy and goals in anticipation of a significant improvement in organizational performance. This approach can result in dramatic shifts in HR practices (e.g., outsourcing portions of the business, changing terms and conditions of employment). Such a change can result in profound disruptions to organizational performance and entail high costs (both expected and unexpected). An outside-in approach assumes that the gains in productivity resulting from rapid change will offset the temporary costs associated with any change. In practice, most organizations will adopt a mixed approach. For example, they will try to retain (perhaps with modifications) as many existing structures and processes as possible to save money and prevent disruption when implementing new structures and processes where needed.

An organization's HR strategy can be tested for its vertical and horizontal fit.[5] **Vertical fit** refers to how well the HR strategy is aligned with the business strategy. Table 4.1 presents three HR domains (selection, compensation, training) and HR strategies consistent with each of the three business strategies from Chapter 1. These HR strategies are not recommendations. They are simply examples of typical approaches to these HR functions under each business strategy. It can sometimes be difficult to align perfectly HR and business strategies because of the circumstances within which an organization operates. For example, a garage-building company might wish to be a cost leader by developing a two-tiered labour force (with a core of highly paid workers supplemented by lower-paid temporary workers). But a tight labour market might make it impossible to attract enough qualified workers if the company offers low-wage, temporary work. This means that the organization cannot develop a two-tiered labour force.

Table 4.1 Aligning HR and business strategies[6]

	Business strategy		
HR domain	***Cost leader***	***Differentiation***	***Focus***
Selection	Hire workers who produce for high volumes of work (i.e., to maximize productivity).	Hire for KSAs related to uniqueness of product or service (e.g., customer service skills or product knowledge).	Hire for ability to innovate (i.e., to maintain market dominance).
Compensation	Minimize wage and benefit costs (e.g., developing two-tiered labour force).	Link compensation and rewards (i.e., incentives and bonuses) to outcomes related to uniqueness of product or service (e.g., customer satisfaction).	Link rewards to maintaining market dominance. Retain employees to limit loss of knowledge and impede competitors hiring away staff.

	Business strategy		
HR domain	*Cost leader*	*Differentiation*	*Focus*
Training	Hire already skilled workers. Train only for legislative compliance and to increase productivity.	Train to amplify uniqueness of product or service (e.g., increase product knowledge).	Train to support innovation (i.e., improve product or service to maintain market dominance).

Horizontal fit is the degree to which selected HR strategies complement and reinforce each other. The process of determining horizontal fit requires thinking about the interconnections of the HR domains set out in Table 4.1. The ultimate goal of assessing horizontal fit is to identify areas where different approaches do (or could) support or undermine one another. For example, an organization might decide to make a portion of its compensation package contingent on meeting output targets. This decision might incentivize staff to work quickly. But it might also (unintentionally) incentivize workers to work unsafely or prioritize quantity over quality of output.

An organization that assesses the horizontal fit of incentivizing high-volume production must consider whether the knock-on effects of this approach on quality and safety result in a net gain for the organization and are consistent with its business strategy. If either answer is no, then the organization might wish to revisit the value of linking compensation to output levels and/or consider ways to mitigate the knock-on effects. Continuing with the example above, an organization could respond to the concerns about safety and quality by creating a slightly more complex set of criteria on which to base compensation. A more complex set of criteria would require more effort for workers to understand and the organization to assess.

Human Resource Planning

Operationalizing a human resource strategy requires an organization to develop and implement HR processes and policies that result in the organization having the right number of appropriately qualified workers when and where they are needed. Organizations do this by developing a human resource plan. As noted above, HR planning is the process of anticipating and addressing the movement of workers into, out of, and within an organization over time. This plan should inform other HR functions, such as recruitment, selection, training, compensation, and performance. Figure 4.1 illustrates the five steps in human resource planning and its iterative nature.

Planning starts with an organization forecasting its labour demand (i.e., which workers will be needed) in the future. The organization then estimates the labour supply (i.e., the number and nature of workers whom it expects will be available at that time, accounting for factors such as staff turnover, vacations, and leaves). These labour demand and supply forecasts are then compared to identify where in the organization there are going to be gaps (i.e., too many or too few workers) that must be addressed to achieve the organization's objectives. A plan is then developed to ensure that the organization has the right number of workers when and where they are required. This can include planning to hire, train, promote, or lay off staff or to intensify or contract out work. The plan is then periodically evaluated to determine if it is still accurate and if it is working. This evaluation can result in more accurate forecasts and more effective plans in future planning cycles.

Organizations have different approaches to HR planning. Some do little, whereas others have much more sophisticated approaches.[7] It can be useful to think about an organization's approach to HR planning along five vectors.

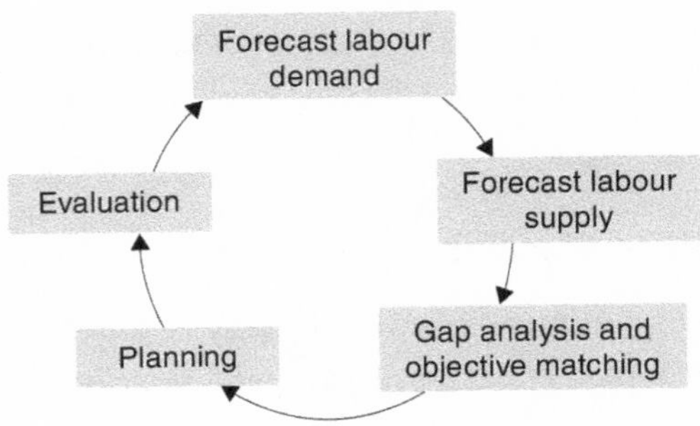

Figure 4.1 Human resource planning process

- *Informal or formal*: Organizations with formal HR planning processes typically have regular, standardized, documented, and evaluated processes with clear methodologies. Organizations with informal HR planning might engage in sporadic and ad hoc planning as needs arise (e.g., when someone quits or a new project is started).
- *Short term or long term*: Organizations can plan over different time horizons. Some might plan only in response to events (e.g., sudden growth or contraction) and look only into the near future. Others might consider multiple time frames, including a long-term plan to implement their business strategies. For example, an organization might have short-term (one year), intermediate (two to three years), and long-term (four to five years) planning horizons.[8]
- *Static or dynamic*: The adaptability of an HR plan varies among organizations. Some might be less flexible in the face of changing circumstances because of their business processes. For example, meat-packing plants struggled with the social-distancing requirements of COVID-19 because of the physical setup of their plants, which required full shifts of staff in close quarters. In contrast, restaurants could more easily adjust their staffing levels when they reduced seating and/or began offering take-out and delivery services.
- *Stand alone or strategic*: In some organizations, HR planning is focused on operationalizing business strategies. In other organizations, it informs business strategies (see Feature Box 1.6).
- *Integrated with HR processes or independent activity*: In theory, HR planning should drive other HR processes, such as recruitment and selection, compensation, and training. In some organizations, the impact of HR planning on other HR domains might be weak or inconsistent. This can reflect that the planning itself is weak or that there is a loose coupling between HR functions.

It is necessary for HR practitioners to understand an organization's approach to HR planning (and why that organization approaches planning in this way) before suggesting changes to the approach. Typically, there are reasons why an organization does things in certain ways, such as tradition, financial constraints, and internal political pressures. Understanding these constraints can help to identify where improvements in HR planning are possible and where they are not.

Forecasting Labour Demand

Estimating the number of different workers that an organization will need at some future point (e.g., in one year) is called **demand analysis**. Demand forecasting techniques can be either quantitative or qualitative. Quantitative techniques use various mathematical and statistical approaches to forecast demand and include extrapolation, trend analysis, ratio analysis, and regression analysis. Qualitative approaches rely on expert judgment and include the Delphi technique, the nominal group technique, and scenario analysis. Each of these techniques is examined below.

The planning techniques used by organizations will depend on the size and complexity of the planning tasks. For example, the owner of a concession stand at a beach might draw from past experience in deciding to hire four or five extra staff from June to September. This is an example of extrapolation, using past experience to project future demand. In contrast, a large tech company might develop short- and long-term demand forecasts using a ratio analysis to estimate how expected sales growth will drive staffing needs. The tech firm might also cope with complex drivers of labour demand (e.g., competitive pressures, regulatory changes, economic conditions) by engaging in scenario planning. In this way, the more sophisticated tech firm is tempering quantitative projections with the context provided by qualitative data (in this case, informed and reliable opinions).

Extrapolation estimates future labour demand based on past experience. Many organizations informally extrapolate labour demand. For example, a restaurant manager might know that she has hired an average of two new servers each month for the past four years to account for voluntary and involuntary turnover. This means that she will likely need to hire and train 24 new servers in the next year. She might also know that there is usually more turnover in April and August (because many of her servers are postsecondary students whose availability is driven by the school year) and will plan for similar hiring surges in the coming year.

The risk associated with extrapolation is that historical patterns are not always good guides to future patterns (see Feature Box 4.1). For example, a sudden economic boom might dramatically increase turnover at the restaurant as workers leave for more lucrative job opportunities.

Trend analysis predicts the number of employees required based on changes in another value, such as projected sales or customer numbers. Trend analysis (sometimes called indexation) is expected to generate a more accurate prediction of labour demand than straight extrapolation because there is (one hopes) a causal relationship between the index value and labour demand. For example, an HR practitioner might assume that the number of customers served (the index value) determines the number of staff needed (the labour demand).

The value selected to drive the index will vary among organizations but typically is related to the core business (i.e., good or service) provided by an organization. For example, a non-profit organization that provides home nursing care under contract to the government in three towns might expect there to be a relationship between its staffing needs and the number of older residents in the towns. Basically, it assumes that about the same proportion of residents in each town will require home care each year. The non-profit might use historical staffing and census data to create an index and thereby predict its future need for workers.

Table 4.2 is an index created for this scenario by following seven steps.

1. Populate the employee column (2019–2024) based on HR records.
2. Populate the seniors column (2019–2024) based on census records.
3. Divide the number of seniors by the number of staff each year to get an index (seniors per staff member). For example, in 2019, there were 4,532 seniors whose home-care needs were met by 50 staff. So, one staff member was required for every 90.6 seniors in the community.
4. Total the index numbers (518) and divide it by the number of years of data (six) to get the average number of seniors (86.3) whose needs were met by each staff member.
5. Populate the seniors column (2025–2026) based on the expected population of seniors (data known and accessible).

6. Forecast the number of staff needed (2025–2026) by dividing the expected number of seniors by the average index (86.3).
7. The forecast projects a need for 51.1 full-time staff in 2025 (4,412 divided by 86.3) and 50.6 full-time staff in 2026 (4,364 divided by 86.3).

This could be expressed in equation form as

$$\text{Staff required} = \frac{\text{Projected population of senior citizens}}{\text{Historical average staffing ratio}}$$

Table 4.2 Example of indexation

Year	Employees	Senior citizens	Index (seniors divided by employees)
2019	50	4,532	90.6
2020	52	4,576	88.0
2021	56	4,620	82.5
2022	49	4,588	93.6
2023	59	4,612	78.2
2024	54	4,596	85.1
Historical average staffing ratio (2019–2024)			86.3
2025	51.1 (estimate)	4,412 (census projection)	86.3 (historical average staffing ratio)
2026	50.4 (estimate)	4,364 (census projection)	86.3 (historical average staffing ratio)

Like all projections, those in Table 4.2 are only as accurate as the assumptions built into them. A key assumption in this trend analysis is that the rate at which seniors require home care is constant. If a greater (or lesser) proportion of seniors will need home care, then the historical index is not a good guide to staffing needs. That index also assumes that the number of seniors whom a worker can care for is relatively constant. A significant change in the nature of the work (e.g., providing fewer services or services by telephone) would reduce the utility of the historical index. Feature Box 4.1 explores some of the perils and pitfalls of forecasting.

Feature Box 4.1 Perils and Pitfalls of Forecasting

Human resource planning seeks to mitigate organizational risk by ensuring that the organization has adequate numbers of appropriately skilled workers. At the heart of HR planning are three beliefs.

1. It is possible to predict the future.
2. More or better data can improve our predictions.
3. Even imprecise predictions have utility.

It is useful to consider whether these beliefs are true. Individuals often use **inductive thinking** (i.e., generalizing from observations) to make predictions about the future. The peril of inductive thinking is that past patterns are not always reliable guides to what will happen in the future and, indeed, can have negative value. Consider a group of chickens. Every day they are fed by the farmer. Soon enough they come to expect food whenever they see the farmer. Until the day that she shows up and, instead of feeding them, kills them.[9]

The **narrative fallacy** can increase our vulnerability to making poor predictions through inductive reasoning. That fallacy occurs when someone takes a set of facts and (usually subconsciously) weaves an explanation from them. The chickens, for example, might have explained the regular feedings as a result of the farmer having warm feelings for them (and, to be fair, the farmer did like chicken).

Humans create these explanations because a storyline makes facts easier to retain. For example, a worker might explain a promotion to a shift supervisor as based on outstanding performance. But the promotion actually might have been given because no one else would accept it or the worker was the best candidate available to the boss (even if the worker who got the promotion is not really qualified).

Inductive thinking assumes that events are understandable. In theory, this is probably true; in reality, we all face significant limits to what we can do and know. Often important causes are hidden from us, and when creating an explanation we must choose which data to pay attention to and then interpret the data—a process shaped by our expectations, beliefs, and experiences.[10] As a result, our explanations are often overly simple or just plain wrong. Furthermore, we are often unaware of our ignorance (how can we know what we do not know?) or how our expectations, beliefs, and experiences shape our conclusions.

Additional data do not necessarily improve our predictions. We have a tendency to seek information that supports our conclusions rather than information that refutes them. This **confirmation bias** means that gathering more information might not improve the validity of our predictions. Rather, it simply makes us more confident in those predictions, regardless of their validity.

We also have a tendency to think that the world operates in a regular and thus predictable manner. As a corollary to this view, we might also expect that most change will be incremental rather than massive. This confirms our experience, say, of the seasons. Yet, like all expectations that result from inductive thinking, we cannot be sure that this incremental change is the norm in the world. Indeed, there are many examples of unexpected, epoch-changing events.

Most models of labour supply and demand assume that incremental change is the norm. These models have utility in human resource planning because that is usually true. Yet it is also useful to keep in mind that the world might not always be regular, incremental, and predictable and that irregular events can be far more important in terms of their impacts on people's lives and organizations. Canada's recent experience with COVID-19 demonstrates this point.

Overall, this examination of the pitfalls of HR planning suggests that, though it has utility, it also has limits. This analysis also suggests that it might be more valuable to spend some planning time considering how to mitigate unexpected changes (e.g., what if this organization had to shut down tomorrow? Or what if a plane crash decapitated the organization completely?) than to sweat small details (e.g., is the organization hiring enough interns this summer to meet the demand for entry-level employees in three years?).

Ratio analysis predicts labour demand using the ratio between some causal factor and the number of employees. The key difference between ratio analysis and trend analysis is that the former does not require significant historical data. Rather, it uses present-day data to estimate demand under a different scenario. For example, if the non-profit offering home care discussed in Table 4.3 considers bidding on a contract to offer home care in a fourth town, then it could use ratio analysis to determine how many additional staff in each position will be needed. We can assume that the organization knows from census data (which are readily available) that adding a fourth town will require it to serve approximately one-third more senior citizens.

Table 4.3 shows how to perform a ratio analysis in three steps.

1. Populate the current employee count column using existing HR data.
2. Multiply each current employee count by 1.33 (the estimated one-third increase) to populate the projected employee count table. (In this example, decimals have been rounded up or down to the nearest whole number).
3. For each job, subtract the current employees from the projected employees to determine the additional number required in each job category.

Table 4.3 Example of ratio analysis

Job	Current employee count	Projected employee count (33% increase)	Additional employees required by new contract
Executive director	1	1	0
Finance staff	4	5	1
HR staff	3	4	1
Care coordinators	3	4	1
Home-care staff	54	72	18

Regression analysis is a more complex technique that can be useful. Regression measures the degree that a dependent variable, in this case the number of employees needed, is linked to a set of independent variables, such as population growth, new technology, or productivity. For example, an HR practitioner might know (from observing multiple baristas over time) that a barista can consistently make six lattes in 10 minutes. The practitioner can then use this relationship to project how many baristas would be needed to make any number of lattes in a 10-minute period.

The real world is rarely as simple as the barista example above. HR practitioners, however, can use different forms of regression analysis to model the cumulative impact of multiple independent variables on labour demand using historical data. For example, our non-profit might need to model the effect on labour demand for home-care staff during a pandemic, such as (1) an increase in the number of senior citizens who will need services, (2) the delivery of some mental health services by telephone, (3) reduced worker productivity because of the implementation of time-consuming pandemic protocols for each home-care visit, and (4) increased staff sick days because of the need for staff to isolate after exposure to the virus. The estimated direction (positive or negative) and impact (large or small) on staffing can then be used to compute an overall impact. Regression analysis requires a large data set and the skill to perform and interpret the analysis. This means that regression analysis tends to be limited to large organizations with sophisticated HR departments.

One of the challenges associated with quantitative demand analyses is considering the myriad factors that can affect labour demand. Changes in demographics, technology, legal requirements, competition, internal processes, and business strategies can be difficult to accommodate in quantitative forecasts. Organizations can use qualitative forecasting techniques to predict how these factors will affect labour demand. There are three main qualitative demand forecasting techniques.

- The **Delphi method** identifies a group of experts and asks each to write a demand analysis, including the reasons and data underlying the analysis. It is generally in response to a specific question (e.g., what will be the HR demand in X department by X date?). The individual forecasts are aggregated by HR staff, and the results are shown to each expert. Based on the summaries, the experts are then allowed to adjust their individual forecasts. This process is repeated (up to five times) until a consensus on the likely future state emerges. In HR planning, experts can be line and department managers as well as other organizational actors with insight (e.g., technical staff, researchers, union representatives). The strengths of the Delphi method are its ability, derived from pooling the knowledge of multiple experts, to account for the many factors that can drive labour demand and the development of a single labour demand forecast.

- The **Nominal Group Technique** also asks a group of experts to develop individual forecasts. These experts are then brought together, each forecast is presented, and discussion on the basis of each forecast takes place. The experts then anonymously rank the forecasts, with the preferred one used to inform HR planning. This method is faster than the Delphi method but might not result in a forecast as finely nuanced as one in the Delphi method because experts select from among a small number of forecast options rather than develop a consensus forecast.
- **Scenario analysis** sees experts develop multiple forecasts in response to different scenarios. This approach helps to factor in uncertainty. For example, a firm might ask for a steady-state forecast as well as forecasts based on 10% increases and decreases in demand for the organization's product or service. Or a firm might model the effects of possible changes in operational practices. Experts might participate in the development of the scenarios (e.g., identifying the factors to consider) as well as the development of the demand analysis for each scenario. The strengths of this approach are its ability to cope with multiple factors and to draw our attention to the range of possible future states.

Qualitative demand analysis can provide a useful supplement to quantitative techniques. Qualitative techniques can also be useful when an organization considers developing a new line of business (and thus has little data from which to draw).

Forecasting Labour Supply

As set out in Figure 4.1, the second step in HR planning is understanding an organization's supply of labour at a fixed point in the future. A supply analysis includes forecasting the **internal labour supply**, which comprises the existing workforce minus turnover, as well as the **external labour supply** (i.e., the number of appropriately qualified workers available for hire). A small organization operating in a stable environment might be able to estimate its future labour supply informally by identifying who is likely to retire or otherwise move on, who could be transferred or promoted to replace them, and from where new employees might be hired. Larger organizations might use more formal supply forecasting techniques set out below.

Forecasting internal labour supply requires an organization to review information about its current workforce and then project the state of its workforce. An estimate of the future workforce requires considering the number of workers who will leave the organization. Workers can leave the workforce voluntarily (e.g., by quitting or retiring) or involuntarily (e.g., being fired or laid off or by dying). Supply analyses might also need to account for workers who are temporarily unavailable because of an event (e.g., taking parental leave or being off work because of injury or illness) or who move within the organization (e.g., promotion or transfer). The resulting forecast should have enough detail to allow an organization to identify whatever worker attributes the organization considers important at the future date. For example, an organization might track the jobs performed by workers or the skills that they possess to inform its analysis in step 3 of the HR planning process. Feature Box 4.2 discusses the role that human resource information systems can play in providing adequate data about the workforce.

Feature Box 4.2 Role of HRIS

A **human resource information system** (HRIS) is a mechanism that gathers, analyzes, summarizes, and reports important data about a workforce. An HRIS can meet multiple organizational needs. For example, it can be used to drive payroll processes (e.g., calculating wages and the amount that an employer must withhold and remit to the government for taxes), track training activity, and administer benefits. An HRIS can also be used to inform HR planning, including forecasting the internal labour supply.

The complexity of an HRIS varies among organizations. Some rely on paper files and use them manually to create necessary reports (e.g., a phone list, paycheque values). More commonly, organizations use computer systems to store data and sometimes analyze and report on it. Basic HR information collected by all organizations includes

- employee name and contact information;
- demographic data required for reporting or administrative purposes; and
- hiring date, position, compensation, and benefits.

Organizations can store such information in simple computer applications (e.g., a spreadsheet). Specific HRIS software allows organizations to store more information about employees (and applicants) and to analyze, manipulate, and interrelate information in more complex ways. More complex systems can be used to track and report on

- timesheets, attendance, and payroll;
- job descriptions and histories;
- performance assessment and management;
- training, skills inventories, and career planning;
- benefit eligibility and use;
- occupational health and safety, injury reports, and return-to-work plans; and
- other government compliance and reporting data such as employment equity and withholdings.

In terms of forecasting the labour supply, a comprehensive HRIS can identify existing and expected vacancies. If a Markov analysis (see Table 4.4) suggests that a certain number of workers are likely to move up in the organization each year, then skill inventories and performance assessment data in the HRIS can help to identify them.

An HRIS that maintains a record of unsuccessful applicants to a job can also help an organization to fill future vacancies (see Chapters 5 and 6). An HRIS can also produce useful evaluative information about the operation of each HR function and meet government or other reporting requirements. Although an HRIS can provide significant value to an organization, it can also pose risks. Digital information can be accessed by unauthorized personnel (inside or outside the organization) or used for inappropriate purposes. HR practitioners need to ensure that workers' privacy is protected (see Chapter 2). This can include limiting or tiering access or storing some HR information (e.g., medical reports) separately.

Trend analysis is a basic, but often effective, approach to forecasting supply. This approach assumes that past experience provides a good indication of future trends in turnover. For example, the owner of a small chain of bakeries might review HR records and discover that 5% of staff retire, 15% quit, and 10% are fired each year. Assuming that there are no significant changes in the environment, these percentages can be applied to the existing labour force to produce a rough estimate of the bakery's internal labour supply in future years. Trend analysis can also spark further inquiries. Annual staff turnover of 30% at the bakeries entails significant hiring and training costs. The owner might ask are there ways to retain staff who might otherwise quit? Or are there ways to adjust hiring and performance management to reduce the percentage of employees who are fired?

A more detailed approach to internal supply forecasting is a **Markov analysis**, which predicts employee movement into and out of an organization over time. Table 4.4 provides a sample Markov analysis that projects the 2025 labour supply of a chain of four clothing stores based on the 2024 workforce and historical trends in worker movement. The left-most column represents the 2024 (i.e., present-state) workforce, broken down by category of job and indicating the number of workers in each job. The columns to the right represent a forecast of where the 2024 workers will be in 2025 (e.g., same job, different job, exit). This forecast is based on historical data (expressed as percentages and then rounded up or down to whole workers) about the trajectory of workers in each job.

The Markov analysis in Table 4.4 tells us a number of useful things.

- *Turnover*: Reading rows from left to right gives HR practitioners a sense of potential turnover in each position. For example, the assistant manager row lets them see that the normal complement of assistant managers is four. Of the current four assistant managers in 2024, one is likely to get promoted to a manager, two will remain assistant managers, and one will exit the organization in 2025.
- *Internal movement*: Reading columns from top to bottom gives HR practitioners a sense of how workers move within the organization. For example, reading the assistant manager column lets them see that, by the next year, the assistant manager complement will comprise two current assistant managers and two floor supervisors who will be promoted. This pattern can suggest the kinds of training and development to offer workers in each job category.
- *Labour supply*: The projected supply row at the bottom of the table lets HR practitioners see how many workers in each job

Table 4.4 Example of Markov analysis for clothing stores

2025 2024	Manager N=4	Assistant manager N=4	HR practitioner N=1	Floor supervisor N=8	Sales clerk N=24	Shelf stocker N=4	Security N=4	Custodian N=3	Exit
Manager N=4	80% 3								20% 1
Assistant manager N=4	25% 1	50% 2							25% 1
HR practitioner N=1			90% 1						10% 0
Floor supervisor N=8		26% 2		67% 5					7% 1
Sales clerk N=24				11% 3	42% 10				47% 11
Shelf stocker N=4					86% 3				14% 1
Security N=4							84% 3		16% 1
Custodian N=3								62% 2	38% 1
Projected supply	4 (of 4)	4 (of 4)	1 (of 1)	8 (of 8)	13 (of 24)	0 (of 4)	3 of (4)	2 (of 3)	

category they are likely to have in 2025 based on existing workers plus internal promotions. This supply can be compared with the normal complement to predict how many workers will need to be hired externally in each category. For example, looking at the store clerk job category, the normal complement is 24, and the projected supply in 2025 is 13, meaning that the stores will need to hire 11 store clerks.

- *Patterns and problems*: The exit column allows HR practitioners to see patterns in worker departures. For example, 47% of sales clerks leave the organization each year. This seems like a high percentage and entails additional hiring and training costs. This might be an area that warrants further investigation. Similarly, filling supervisor and manager positions solely through promotions raises the question of whether these positions are being filled by the best candidates or simply the most convenient candidates.

Within any organization, some jobs will be more important organizationally than others, such as highly technical jobs associated with a core business function or senior management positions. Turnover in these positions can pose a significant business risk. Consequently, supply analysis can include identifying internal staff who can step into these roles. Figure 4.2 is an example of a **replacement chart**. In this example, a software development company has taken its staffing chart and identified the positions in which a sudden departure would leave the company vulnerable. The replacement chart identifies potential internal replacements, including their present performance and promotional potential. A replacement chart can also identify other characteristics of possible replacements. For example, an organization implementing an **equity, diversity, and inclusion** (EDI) program might identify candidates who meet the organization's EDI hiring goals for gender, age, ethnoracial background, or other personal characteristics where the current workforce does not match the organization's goals.

Figure 4.2 identifies that potentially there are few qualified replacements for the lead programmer and VP finance and operations positions. Since these positions have been identified as critical to organizational continuity, it might be appropriate either to develop additional internal candidates capable of taking over these roles or to identify competent external candidates.

All organizations, at some point, will fill positions with workers new to the organization. Forecasting the external labour supply available to an organization can be challenging. One issue is that, though there is a lot of data available on the labour force, the data might be poorly suited to forecasting the availability of workers at specific points in time and space. Often, for example, labour market data are backward looking. That is, they tell us how many workers were available as of the last count but not how many will be available in the future. The data can be presented at too high a level (geographically or occupationally) to tell us whether or not, say,

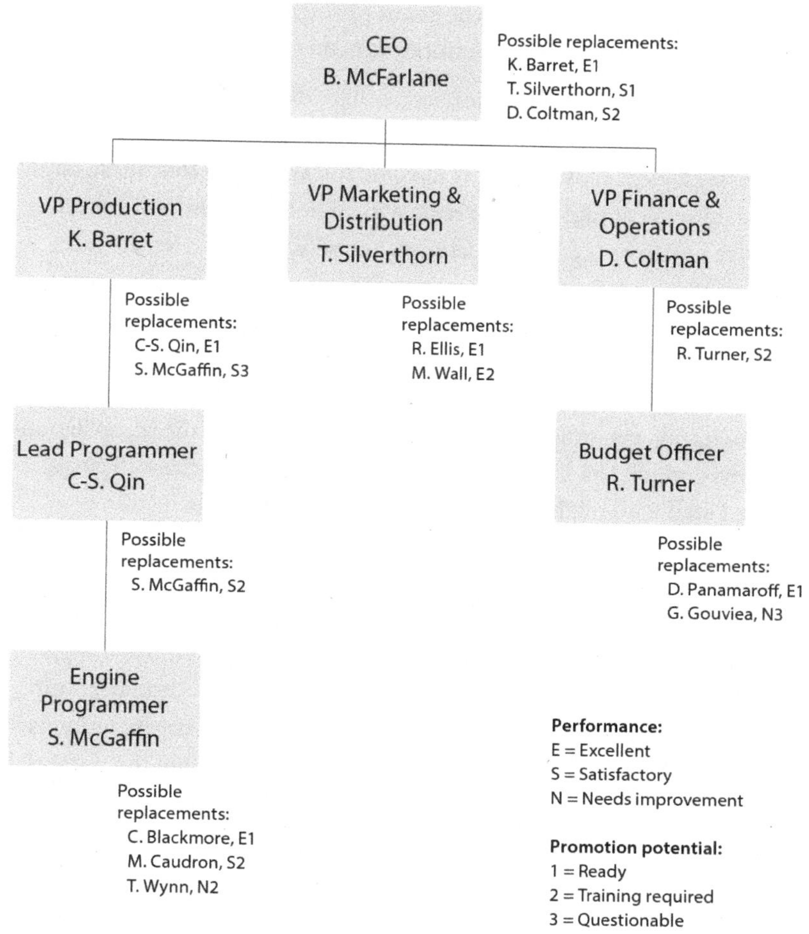

Figure 4.2 Sample replacement chart

there will be enough physical therapists available for hire in Sydney, Nova Scotia, three years in the future.

A second challenge with external labour forecasting is that many factors can affect the labour supply, and these factors can change over time. They include the unemployment rate and competition for specific skills, education and skill levels, worker mobility and attractiveness of the job location, and regulatory and technological changes. A forecast made during a period of high unemployment might not be an accurate guide to the availability of workers if the economy turns around. To forecast the external labour supply, HR practitioners need to do three things.

- *Qualifications*: HR practitioners need to identify which positions they need to fill and/or which competencies they need new hires to possess. Generally, the more specific the answer to this question, the more accurate their forecast will be because they will get fewer false positives (i.e., potential hires actually unable to do the job).
- *Time frame*: HR practitioners need to determine when the hiring will occur (e.g., within the next year? the next three to five years?). If their need is immediate, then they will look at data on the present labour force (i.e., people available for hire). If the need is further in the future, then they can look at projections about the future labour force, which can include those currently in training as well as qualified staff who might not yet be present in Canada.
- *Geography*: HR practitioners need to identify the geographic parameters of their forecasts. As noted in Chapter 1, labour markets have geographic parameters. If an organization is looking to hire a senior manager, then applicants might be willing to move a significant distance to take the job. This means that the potential labour pool might be provincial or national in scope. If an organization is looking to hire someone for a low-wage position, then the potential applicant pool might be limited to those available locally (perhaps even within walking, cycling, or transit distance).

If HR practitioners need to hire a chemist for a job with a good wage within the next year, they would likely look at data on the current supply of qualified chemists in their province or territory or even nationally. In contrast, if they need to hire 30 servers (a job that many people can perform) over the next five years at minimum wage, they will likely look at projections of unemployment in the town or city (or even neighbourhood) in which their organization operates. Feature Box 4.3 outlines key sources of data that HR practitioners can use to forecast the external labour supply.

Feature Box 4.3 External Labour Supply Forecasting Data

Forecasting the external supply of labour is a difficult task, requiring expertise and information generally beyond the scope of work for most human resource practitioners. That said, there are numerous indicators that can be helpful in gauging labour supply. In the short term, the overall **unemployment rate** is a useful place to start. The unemployment rate in Canada is usually derived from Statistics Canada data and comprises the percentage of people above age 15 without paid employment but available to work and actively seeking work.[11] The data are available by province and economic region.

There is always a certain degree of unemployment in the economy. For example, frictional unemployment comprises people who are new to job seeking or who have left their jobs to seek other ones. The labour market in Canada is considered tight when unemployment is less than 4%. If it is higher than 4%, then many organizations will be able to fill vacancies in the short term. Of course, certain occupations and skills can be in greater demand than average. Organizations that need these sorts of workers might find the external labour supply constrained.

More detailed and longer-range projections of the labour supply are also available. The government of Canada's Job Bank, though primarily a tool for workers to locate jobs, also contains labour market information by occupation and region (down to the city level).[12] Canada[13] and some jurisdictions, such as Alberta,[14] also provide public access to long-term labour market forecasts, such as Alberta's Occupational Outlook. These data sets might require specific computer skills to use. Some government departments and industry associations also provide sector-specific labour market forecasts.

The limitations on projections noted in Feature Box 4.1 also apply to internal and external labour supply forecasts. For example, an economic boom can mean that a restaurant faces higher than expected turnover (as workers seek to trade up to better jobs). This will render trend and Markov analyses based on historical data invalid. A boom can also cause the external labour supply to tighten, with fewer workers willing to make themselves available at prevailing wage rates and working conditions. Such changes can require adjustments to human resource plans.

Gap Analysis and Objective Matching

Once an organization has completed its labour demand and supply analyses, it is necessary to perform a **gap analysis**. Such an analysis determines in which jobs (or skill categories) an organization will face a shortage or surplus of workers. Although it is tempting to focus solely on the number of employees during a gap analysis, this is also an opportunity to consider other organizational goals, such an increasing equity and diversity in the workforce. The ability of an organization to "see" equity and diversity during a gap analysis turns on whether or not the organization has access to the data (perhaps from the organization's HRIS). Identifying equity-related gaps during analysis then allows organizations to develop objectives that address the gaps.

The way that an organization performs a gap analysis depends on the supply and demand forecasting methods used. This process is best illustrated with an example based on the chain of clothing stores discussed in Table 4.4. When forecasting labour demand in 2025, the chain owner primarily used extrapolation. Stable local economic forecasts and the absence of any plan to expand operations meant that she expected the chain would need the same number and type of employees in 2025 as it did in 2024. Its quantitative forecasting was modified by qualitative information generated during scenario planning. Specifically, the chain owner and HR practitioner modelled the effects of several possible operational changes in keeping with the chain's business strategy of being a cost leader. In the end, the owner decided that the chain would contract out custodial work (reducing associated labour costs by 35%). She also decided to discontinue in-store security after comparing the costs of providing security with the expected costs of theft in its absence.

The chain forecast internal labour supply for 2025 using a Markov analysis (see Table 4.4). Investigation of the high level of turnover in the sales clerk position determined that the turnover was less costly than any of the options for reducing it. The chain's forecast of the external labour supply entailed examining the local unemployment rate (currently 6.2%, forecast at 6.0% in 2025). The HR practitioner then combined the demand and supply data to identify gaps expected in the next year (see Table 4.5).

Table 4.5 Gap analysis for clothing stores

Job	2025 Demand	2025 Internal supply	Surplus (shortage)	Notes
Manager	4	4	0	
Assistant manager	4	4	0	
HR practitioner	1	1	0	
Floor supervisor	8	8	0	
Sales clerk	24	13	(11)	
Shelf stocker	4	0	(4)	
Security	0	3	3	Layoffs
Custodian	0	2	2	Contracting out
Total	45	35	n/a	

The gap analysis makes plain that, in 2025, the clothing chain will likely have both a shortage of workers in two jobs (sales clerks and shelf stockers) and a surplus of workers in two jobs (custodian and security). These projected worker surpluses and shortages can then be used to formulate strategies to ensure that the chain meets its HR planning objectives (i.e., has the right number of adequately skilled employees in 2024). Before turning to that process, it is important to note that this gap analysis identifies the likely future state for planning purposes. In reality, there can be a difference between the gap analysis and the actual state of affairs in 2025. For example, the internal supply forecast notes that, on an annualized basis, 10% of the HR practitioners turn over. Since there is only one HR practitioner position, the chain will periodically see 100% turnover in this job. Similarly, the actual shortage or surplus in any job category can vary from year to year.

Once projected surpluses and shortages have been identified, HR practitioners can develop plans to address them. Typically, an organization will develop HR objectives. Such objectives specify an outcome (or behaviour), the conditions under which it will be achieved, and the criteria by which performance will be judged. Continuing the clothing chain example, HR objectives related to the surplus of custodians might be the following.

- Contract out cleaning services to commence on July 1, 2025, at a cost savings of at least 35%.
- Terminate the employment of custodians by June 30, 2025, without triggering litigation.

When formulating an objective, it is easy to forget to include all three components (particularly criteria). To prevent this, it can be useful to break down objectives into the three components as shown in Table 4.6. Once objectives are established, an organization can begin planning how to achieve the objectives.

Table 4.6 HR objectives analysis

Outcome	Condition	Criteria
Contract out cleaning services	to commence on July 1, 2025,	at a cost savings of at least 35%.
Terminate the employment of custodians	by June 30, 2025,	without triggering litigation.

Planning

Planning entails operationalizing HR objectives, such as identifying how the organization will cope with labour shortages and surpluses. The key risk associated with a labour shortage is that an organization might not be able to implement its business strategy. The specifics of any projected labour shortage will determine the exact degree and impact of this failure. There are four main ways to address a projected labour shortage.

- *Hire new employees*: Assuming that there are unemployed workers available for work, new workers can be hired under a variety of employment conditions (e.g., full time versus part time, permanent versus temporary), depending on the organization's need and the willingness of workers to accept such terms.
- *Contract out the work*: Organizations can arrange for work to be performed by temporary staff (supplied by an employment agency), independent contractors (e.g., janitors who run their own small companies), or other companies (e.g., contracting a large firm specializing in cleaning stores).

- *Promote existing staff*: In some cases, it makes sense to promote existing staff to address specific shortages. This strategy might require making some provision for additional training or development and trigger hiring to positions rendered vacant by the promotion.
- *Intensify work*: Staffing shortages can be addressed (at least temporarily) by making staff work harder. This can entail mandatory overtime or cross-training staff, such that they can perform more tasks and potentially fill down time on the job. For example, a sales clerk could also be tasked with stocking shelves during slow periods of the day.

When deciding how to resolve a labour shortage, an organization might need to consider the relative cost of the option, the time frame (i.e., urgency) and speed at which the option can be implemented, the quality of the work that it will receive, the fit with its business and HR strategies, and the degree to which it can change approaches if problems occur. Feature Box 4.4 examines how the construction industry in Alberta dealt with long-term labour shortages during the early 2000s and the implications of this approach for different groups of workers.

Feature Box 4.4 Addressing a Shortage of Skills in Alberta's Construction Industry

Construction is a male-dominated industry, and women comprise only 5% of construction workers.[15] Indigenous workers, immigrants, and workers of colour are all under-represented. In the 2000s, an economic boom in Alberta fuelled by construction of large oilsands facilities led to a significant labour shortage among construction occupations. The provincial government developed a plan for addressing these labour shortages by attracting traditionally under-represented groups such as women, youth, Indigenous people, and workers of colour (also often called racialized workers). Employers, though, had other ideas.

A study tracking construction employment patterns found that the percentage of Canadian workers from under-represented demographics did not change despite government efforts to increase training and encourage recruitment. Employers, rather than hiring under-represented workers from Canada, turned to the use of male temporary foreign workers (TFWs) to fill labour gaps.[16] TFWs come from countries of the Global South on temporary work permits and can be deported. Because of their residency in the country being linked to their employers, TFWs were vulnerable to exploitation and mistreatment. They were also vulnerable to being laid off and sent back home when labour demand contracted. The study found that the use of TFWs created a hyper-precarious workforce.

Why did employers turn to a new source of temporary labour rather than cultivate a broader, more reliable labour pool? The answer might lie in the cost of each option. To recruit (and retain) under-represented workers from Canada, employers would have had to engage in training and education. More importantly, crucial changes would have had to be made to the sexist and racist culture found in the industry, and job redesign might have been necessary to accommodate the needs of these groups (e.g., women's child-care responsibilities make out-of-town work with long shifts more difficult). In contrast, TFWs represented a relatively inexpensive option. Aside from some administrative costs, little training was required, fewer changes to workplace culture were necessary, and the workers could quickly be removed from the labour market when the boom collapsed.

The case demonstrates how government policy can affect (and be affected by) employers' HR planning. Government policy created a cheaper alternative labour supply (TFWs) that, in turn, disincentivized employers to do the more difficult work of making more permanent changes to their workplaces. Employers' HR planning can also inform government policy. In the 1990s and 2000s, employer groups lobbied the federal government for greater access to TFWs to facilitate that option as an HR planning strategy.

Subsequently, the growing use of TFWs became politically fraught for governments, and the number of TFW permits was reduced. In their place, governments sought for a period to encourage more Canadian students to consider seeking trades qualifications. Women, immigrants, and Indigenous workers continue to be under-represented in the construction industry, suggesting that efforts have not successfully addressed barriers to their entry.

The key risk associated with a labour surplus is that the organization will have higher than necessary labour costs as workers sit idle. Idle workers represent a significant opportunity cost. There are three main ways to address a labour surplus.

- Short-term reductions in the workforce: Organizations seeking immediate reductions in their workforces can lay off their employees. **Layoffs** can be permanent or temporary and entail significant financial obligations to affected employees (see Chapter 9). Layoffs in unionized workplaces must also follow any job security provisions in the collective agreements such as the right of workers to "bump" those with less seniority to avoid being laid off (see Chapter 10). Organizations can also seek to incentivize voluntary resignations through financial packages (i.e., buyouts). And organizations can offer unpaid leaves of absence (e.g., to return to school, travel, or undertake some other non-work activity). Short-term reductions can negatively affect morale and trigger undesirable staff departures (e.g., among essential or highly skilled workers).
- Long-term reductions in the workforce: Organizations with a longer time frame for workforce reductions can realize them through attrition. For example, a **hiring freeze** takes advantage of natural worker turnover to reduce the staffing complement. A hiring freeze is a low-cost strategy but means that the organization has little control over where attrition occurs. Organizations can also offer buyout programs targeting, for example, employees close to retirement.
- Changing the terms of work: Organizations might also be able to negotiate changes in the terms of work with workers or through their unions. For example, workers might agree to job sharing (in which two workers perform a job for a portion of the week), working fewer hours, or retraining. The key risk of changing the terms of work in a non-union environment is the possibility that workers will claim they have been constructively dismissed (see Chapter 9) and seek damages.

Downsizing a workforce can often have significant effects on those workers who remain with the organization. Seeing co-workers terminated or changes to the wage-rate or wage-effort bargain can cause workers to re-evaluate the efforts that they are prepared to put into their jobs.

Workers often develop a series of expectations of how their employers will treat them (including the wage-effort bargain discussed in Chapter 1). These expectations are often called the psychological contract between workers and employers. When an employer violates the psychological contract, this can trigger anger, fear, and depression.[17] Even workers who are not laid off can experience negative feelings, sometimes called survivor syndrome, during and after downsizing. Although it can be tempting to treat these emotional effects as **externalities** (i.e., consequences that do not affect the organization), these effects can cause declining productivity, additional staff turnover, and interest in unionization.

An organization can reduce the negative psychological impacts of downsizing by how it handles departures. Downsizing in which the decision-making process is perceived by the remaining workers as fair tends to result in fewer negative organizational consequences. The perception of procedural fairness can be increased by processes that give workers voice; that are transparent, internally consistent, and based on good information; that minimize the opportunity for favouritism or bias; and that offer the opportunity for correction if there is an error.[18] Such a process can entail, however, additional costs, and organizations might need to assess the cost-benefit of procedural fairness.

Once a human resource plan has been developed, it must be communicated to those individuals whose work is central to carrying out the plan. This can include HR practitioners and line managers responsible for hiring, training, and firing staff. This step is necessary to ensure that the HR plan (designed to achieve the objectives) is actually implemented. Sharing the HR objectives and the reasoning behind them can be a useful tool for getting buy-in to the HR plan. Similarly, linking the achievement of specific aspects of the HR plan to individual performance assessments can motivate workers to take action in support of the plan (see Chapter 9).

Evaluation

The final step in HR planning is to evaluate whether the process was successful. At a high level, this means answering the question "did the organization have the right number of appropriately qualified workers when and where they were required?" There are many factors that contribute to this outcome (some of which have little to do with HR planning), so it is often more useful to assess the success of specific steps in the HR planning process.

- *Demand forecast*: Did the labour demand forecast(s) accurately predict the organization's actual labour demand? If there was a meaningful difference between forecast and actual demand, then identifying which factors explain the difference can improve future forecasts by refining the forecasting model. In contrast, if the discrepancy was related to unexpected factors (e.g., sudden economic boom or bust, major technological or market change), then it might not be possible to improve forecasting.
- *Supply forecast*: Did the labour supply forecast(s) accurately predict the organization's actual supply of labour? Again, if there was a meaningful difference between forecast and actual supply, then identifying which factors explain the difference can improve future forecasts.
- *HR objectives achieved*: Was each HR objective achieved, given the specified outcomes, conditions, and criteria? If not, then where were the points of failure, and what explains each failure? It is important to distinguish between objectives that (in retrospect) were incorrect and those that were not achieved because of the method(s) selected to achieve them during the planning stage.

Evaluating HR planning requires organizations to possess data and expend resources analyzing those data. Some organizations might choose not to undertake evaluation because they expect a limited return on investment of backward-looking evaluation. Other organizations might be reluctant to perform evaluations for fear of identifying failures. For example, forecasts can reflect a failure to predict events or patterns that, in retrospect, appear to have been obvious (even if not necessarily at the time). Or forecasts might have been inaccurate because they were adjusted at the request of institutional leaders. These failures, caused by events outside the control of the HR practitioners involved, can still result in negative reputational or employment consequences for them.

In this way, internal evaluation of HR functions has both technical and political dimensions. It is possible to mitigate the risk associated with evaluation in a number of ways. Agreeing on and keeping a record of the process and data to be used for evaluation can limit the scope of interference. Focusing on outputs (e.g., forecasts) rather than outcomes (achieving specific goals) limits the evaluation to work in the control of HR practitioners. Finally, keeping a record of interventions and other important events can provide important explanatory context for evaluations.

Conclusion

The purpose of human resource planning, ultimately, is to mitigate the risk posed to an organization by having too many, too few, or the wrong mix of workers at some point in the future. A gap between required and available workers can imperil organizational profitability and/or the achievement of its business goals. Ideally, HR planning forewarns the organization of potential gaps so that the organization can adjust its workforce. This can include adjusting recruitment and selection plans (Chapters 5 and 6) as well as approaches to training (Chapter 7) and compensation (Chapter 8). A projected surplus of workers can also result in layoffs (Chapter 9).

The opening vignette saw Southlake Regional Health Centre announce that it would lay off 97 registered nurses to address a long-standing budgetary deficit. Setting aside the question of whether these layoffs would compromise the hospital's ability to provide care during the COVID-19 pandemic, the announcement was timed to provide the five months of notice required by the nurses' collective agreement. This notice period is intended to give affected workers time to seek other work or decide to exit the workforce. By March 2021, Southlake was reporting that all of the layoffs had been achieved without involuntary dismissals (e.g., through retirements and normal turnover).[19] This timeline also allowed the health centre to hire lower-paid staff, including 49 practical nurses and 32 other positions, to maintain patient care after the layoffs.

This case is a good example of how HR planning helps organizations to identify gaps between their desired and present staffing complements with enough time to develop an effective response. It also highlights some of the limits of organizational planning. The need to reduce staffing by Southlake was driven by long-standing budgetary concerns. Yet the implementation of the layoffs took place in the context of a pandemic, the scope, staffing implications, and duration of which exceeded most of the projections available when the planning was performed. Similarly, the pandemic fundamentally altered the supply of nurses in Ontario, resulting in some hospitals, nursing homes, and laboratories offering large signing bonuses to staff units.[20] This set of unanticipated factors highlights how the limits of supply and demand forecasting can affect the utility of HR planning.

Although it is most common to associate HR planning with ensuring that organizations have the right number of appropriately skilled workers, HR planning also offers organizations an opportunity to address long-standing equity and diversity issues. Typically, organizational hiring tends to reproduce the demographics of the organization's existing workforce. The replication of existing demographic patterns through hiring practices highlights how identity factors can result in further advantage and disadvantage. Specifically, workers who possess social identities already present and accepted in an organization are more likely to be hired than workers whose social identities are not already present and accepted in the organization. Its resulting workforce might then continue not to be representative of the characteristics of the society in which it functions.

Explicitly assessing the gender, age, and ethnocultural profile of an organization's workforce is the first step in remedying under-representation of equity-deserving groups. Subsequently, an organization is able to establish equity-based targets for hiring and promotion. Achieving these targets might require an organization to identify and remedy the barriers that equity-seeking groups face.

EXERCISES

KEY TERMS

Define the following terms.

- Confirmation bias
- Delphi method
- Demand analysis
- Equity, diversity, and inclusion
- External labour supply

- Externalities
- Extrapolation
- Gap analysis
- Hiring freeze
- Horizontal fit
- Human resource information system
- Human resource objectives
- Human resource planning
- Human resource strategy
- Inductive thinking
- Internal labour supply
- Layoffs
- Markov analysis
- Narrative fallacy
- Nominal group technique
- Ratio analysis
- Regression analysis
- Replacement chart
- Scenario analysis
- Trend analysis

DISCUSSION QUESTIONS

Discuss the following questions.

- What is the purpose of human resource planning?
- Is human resource planning worthwhile for every organization? Why or why not?
- Which constraints must human resource practitioners contend with during human resource planning?
- What are some strategies that human resource practitioners can use to ensure that a human resource plan is carried out?
- How does the profit imperative shape human resource planning? What implications does this have for the inclusion of equity, diversity, and inclusion goals in human resource planning?

ACTIVITIES

Think about an organization (or a part of an organization) that you are familiar with and then complete the following activities.

- Using one of the demand analysis techniques, forecast the labour demand for the next two years. Explain to the HR director how many workers you will need to hire for each job. Identify three potential sources of error in your forecast.
- Using one of the supply analysis techniques, forecast the internal labour supply for the next two years. Explain to the HR director how many workers will be promoted and how many will exit. Identify three potential sources of error in your forecast.
- Perform a gap analysis to identify how many workers you will need to hire for each job in the next two years.
- Write one or more HR objectives ensuring that your organization will meet the overall labour demand during the next two years. Explain to the HR director the basis on which you set each of three aspects of each objective.
- Identify the implications of each objective for each functional area of human resources.

SELF-REFLECTION QUESTIONS

Write self-reflections of 200 to 500 words on the following topics.

- What was the most difficult part about forecasting labour demand in the exercise above?
- What was the most difficult part about forecasting labour supply in the exercise above?
- Think about a time when an organization that you are familiar with has been short-handed. What was the cause of this shortfall of workers? Could human resource planning have prevented this? Why or why not?
- Thinking about an organization that you are familiar with, would it be interested in incorporating equity, diversity, and inclusion factors into its HR planning? Why or why not?

5 Recruitment

Recruitment is the process of finding a sufficient number of qualified potential applicants and persuading them to apply for an existing or anticipated job opening. Organizations recruit in many different ways. Some place ads in newspapers or online. Some look at existing employees and promote them. Still others use informal networks or hire headhunting firms. One of the most interesting approaches to recruiting in the past decade was Amazon's use of artificial intelligence (AI) to power a program that crawls the web to identify and filter potential applicants for jobs.[1] The promise of Amazon's approach was automating (i.e., cheapening) the process of finding candidates as well as reducing the potential for reviewer bias when screening candidates.

Amazon soon discovered, however, that its AI had a distinct preference for male applicants. The issue was that Amazon had "trained" its AI using a data set of past "successful" applications, mostly from men. So, in essence, Amazon trained its AI to replicate the historically gendered recruiting patterns of its managers. Consequently, the AI "learned" to penalize resumés that included the term *women's* and listed women's colleges. It also learned to reward words more common on men's resumés, such as *executed* and *captured*. Amazon pulled the plug on this project in 2017.

Other organizations continue to use seemingly old-fashioned recruiting methods, such as the job fair. For example, on August 21, 2016, the Calgary Sport and Entertainment Corporation (which runs the Saddledome arena) held a job fair to find 300 workers. These part-time jobs paid at or near minimum wage. Hundreds of unemployed workers lined up hoping to capture one of those jobs. Many of them previously held permanent, full-time jobs. One worker, Kelly Murray, was quoted in a news story explaining why he was lined up. "I was working for the city—got laid off. Hard to find work after that. . . . I got work now—working for a golf course, but it will be done in two weeks. So here I am again, lining up again."[2]

Both Amazon and the Calgary Sport and Entertainment Corporation had clear recruitment strategies. Amazon was looking to recruit the best applicants in a competitive job pool by leveraging technology. The arena operator was looking to fill low-wage jobs at the lowest possible cost in a depressed economy. Each organization chose recruiting methods suitable to its goals and circumstances. In this chapter, we examine the recruitment process, including the need to develop a recruiting strategy. We also outline common methods of internal and external recruiting and consider how to evaluate the effectiveness of these methods. In Chapter 6, we will look more closely at how to select qualified candidates from the pool of applicants recruited.

Recruitment as HR Process

In medium-sized and large organizations, recruitment is usually managed by the HR department. The goal of recruitment is twofold. First, HR practitioners must ensure that enough potential applicants are aware of and apply for a position to generate an adequate number of applicants. If the applicant pool is too small, then an organization might not be able to hire a qualified person. Second, HR practitioners must ensure that the applicant pool comprises people with the required KSAs for the position. Ensuring that over- or under-qualified applicants self-select out of a job competition reduces the organizational costs of screening applicants during the selection process. It is important to remember that potential applicants also use the recruiting process to learn about the organization and, based on what they learn, decide whether or not they would like to work there.

Figure 5.1 offers a visual representation of the recruitment process and demonstrates its connections to other HR processes. A recruitment strategy must be aligned with an organization's broader business strategy (see Chapter 1). For example, an organization that pursues a differentiation strategy based on offering high-quality customer service will almost certainly have a different recruitment strategy compared with an organization that has adopted a cost-leader strategy.

Importantly, Figure 5.1 illustrates that recruitment does not begin when the HR department is asked to post a job advertisement. Rather, recruitment begins when HR practitioners develop a recruiting strategy informed by other HR functions. The specific tools, methods, and actions adopted to recruit applicants should flow from this strategy.

The process of job analysis (see Chapter 3) will determine the nature of the job as well as the required KSAs of applicants. Job design can shape the potential pool of applicants. For example, high-paying jobs that can be performed remotely might attract a large pool of applicants. Low-paying jobs that must be performed in a specific region might draw applicants only from the locally available pool of workers.

Finally, an organization's human resources plan (see Chapter 4) and staffing needs identified by managers will inform the number of positions that must be filled and identify external factors that will affect recruitment. For example, organizations that seek to increase the proportion of their workforces drawn from traditionally under-represented groups (e.g., Indigenous people, women, or workers of colour) might need to take specific steps to recruit applicants from these groups. Similarly, it is important to know whether the recruitment will take place in a context of labour shortage or oversupply.

Figure 5.1 Recruitment process

Recruiting Strategy

The purpose of a recruiting strategy is to ensure that an adequate applicant pool is available for the selection process. When deciding how to go about recruiting staff, HR practitioners must consider several factors. First, they need to know which positions need to be filled. This includes understanding the requirements of the positions and the number of hires required. Then they need to consider the availability of candidates with the required KSAs for the position and where to find them. These factors can guide the recruiting methods that they adopt. Not surprisingly, organizations often employ different recruiting strategies for different jobs.

For example, if an organization wants to hire a small number of candidates who have KSAs not widely available, then an HR practitioner might consider looking inside the organization (i.e., internal recruiting) or adopting a more focused external recruiting strategy (e.g., hiring a search firm, buying targeted advertising, or using existing workers' professional networks). In contrast, if an organization wants to hire a large number of candidates, and there are many potential applicants with the required KSAs, then an HR practitioner might rely on unsolicited applications, untargeted advertising, and online postings.

These examples illustrate the need to identify the recruiting methods most likely to secure an adequate number of qualified applicants at the lowest possible cost. Although cost is an important constraint in developing a recruiting strategy, there are additional factors to consider. Other HR goals (e.g., increasing the demographic diversity of the workforce) can affect the recruiting strategy and suggest that alternative or additional methods are required. Feature Box 5.1 discusses diversity in the workplace. Organizational policies can also constrain the methods available. For example, an organization that prioritizes recruiting from within will start with that strategy.

Feature Box 5.1 The Diversity Dilemma

Many employers have begun to incorporate "diversity" as a strategic goal in recruitment and selection. Diversity is generally understood to mean making an organization's workforce more representative of society by increasing the presence of traditionally under-represented groups in the workplace, such as women, workers of colour, youth, Indigenous people, persons with disabilities, and 2SLGBTQ+ people. Greater diversity can reflect a commitment to social justice or an effort to comply with employment equity requirements. Organizations can also expect that increased diversity will boost productivity, improve their reputations, or create healthier workplace cultures.[3]

Common approaches to increasing diversity include training managers and HR practitioners to identify and correct organizational practices that discourage diversity, altering job descriptions and workplace arrangements to accommodate under-represented candidates, implementing "blind" recruitment techniques that remove markers of gender or ethnoracial backgrounds from applications, and establishing quotas for hiring under-represented groups. Some argue that these efforts undermine merit-based hiring (i.e., hiring the most qualified candidates possible). There is little evidence to support this claim.[4] This is partly because practices that result in the over-representation of straight, white, able-bodied men in a workforce are likely not merit-based because they exclude highly qualified applicants who possess different identity factors.

Despite these approaches, the data suggest that workplaces are not becoming all that more diverse.[5] One reason is that the approaches, by themselves, are inadequate to remove the substantial barriers facing traditionally under-represented groups in society and the labour market. The causes of under-representation are deeply structural and embedded in society's racist, sexist, ableist, and ageist roots. A further challenge is that workers from equity-deserving groups are often expected to assist an organization with identifying and remediating inequitable practices (in addition to performing their regular work). This places significant additional workloads and psychological burdens on these workers. It can also make them the targets of pushback against diversity initiatives by other organizational actors, who might feel threatened. This can lead, in turn, to burnout, discrimination, harassment, and attrition of workers from equity-deserving groups.[6]

Furthermore, many efforts to increase diversity rely on stereotypes that further dehumanize certain workers. For example, advice on attracting young workers often focuses on what "they" are looking for in work (e.g., work-life balance or opportunities for additional training).

This stereotyping erases the differences that exist among young workers. For example, many prioritize income over other aspects of a job because of their financial obligations.

Replacing one set of stereotypes (e.g., young workers are lazy, have no commitment) with another (e.g., they want flexibility in and meaning from work) simply shifts the narrative that marginalizes groups of workers. It is unlikely to increase meaningfully their rate of participation. And prescribing job flexibility and meaning as a solution to youth uninterest in a company also ignores cross-cutting class interests (see Feature Box 1.2), such as a need for decent wages and working conditions.

A key barrier to increased diversity can be the immediate financial and social costs that organizations might seek to avoid by maintaining their existing workforces. Changing existing work processes and cultures can be disruptive. As the revelations of the #MeToo and Black Lives Matter movements show, workplaces have a long way to go to eradicate the sources of inequity. Nevertheless, ignoring calls to address inequities increasingly creates reputational and legal risks. Conversely, addressing these issues is the right thing to do and might be a source of long-term competitive advantage.[7]

Incorporating non-traditional HR goals, such as increasing diversity, can be challenging in developing a recruitment strategy. If the organization has no experience or no internal resources for how to meet those goals, then it might not know how to start. One method to achieve such goals is to reconsider whom the organization has traditionally targeted for recruitment and consciously make efforts to reach out to new networks and groups. Organizations can also turn to external consultants for assistance in incorporating diversity into recruitment and selection.

Recruiting strategies must also grapple with an organization's reputation in the broader community. Organizations might have a macrolevel reputation (sometimes referred to as their brand). Many large corporations work hard to establish brands. A brand includes how the organization is perceived as an employer. When you think of Google, what do you think of? Likely you think of a "fun" and empowered workplace, with nap pods, video games, ping pong tables, and flexible work hours. That is part of Google's brand, and it feeds into its recruitment strategy. Even though recent reports highlight that Google's working conditions include sexual harassment and employee protests, the images that the name evokes continue to be powerful.[8] That is the power of a brand. Google has to process hundreds of unsolicited job applications a day, attributable to its strong brand.

Organizations also have reputations at the microlevel. Workers, customers, and neighbours have direct experiences with an organization—about how well workers are treated, customer service, or product quality. Collectively, these perceptions make up an organization's reputation in a community, and that, too, can affect recruitment. If the local community widely believes that the organization is a "bad employer," then it will be harder to attract candidates. In a way, the microlevel reputation can be more difficult for an organization to correct as it operates through informal channels and networks. Conversely, a positive reputation in a community can make recruitment easier. A recruitment strategy needs to take into account whether the employer is perceived positively or negatively by the pool of potential workers from which it is recruiting.

Practically speaking, a recruitment strategy might need to respond to an organization's reputation by reinforcing a positive belief about the organization, highlighting a little-known aspect, or countering a negative perception. For example, if the organization has had a high-profile, bitter strike with its workers, then the recruitment strategy immediately after it might need to incorporate the union's assistance or demonstrate a degree of goodwill for working collaboratively with the union going forward. Similarly, if the organization has made a major contribution to its community, then a recruitment strategy might be able to leverage the resulting goodwill.

Once a recruiting strategy has been developed, often it can be reused to fill subsequent vacancies, assuming that the considerations driving the strategy remain valid. A challenge for HR practitioners is that organizational recruiting strategies can fossilize yet be used even when they are no longer appropriate. For example, the declining importance of daily newspapers in the lives of Canadians might suggest that relying on newspaper advertisements is no longer an effective use of advertising dollars.

The techniques discussed at the end of this chapter can provide data to assess the effectiveness of existing techniques and the internal political capital necessary for HR practitioners to drive changes in recruiting behaviour.

Internal Recruitment

Internal recruitment is the process of drawing from existing employees to fill positions. Many organizations, in particular larger enterprises with sophisticated HR departments, utilize promotions and lateral transfers as preferred methods for filling vacancies. Internal recruiting has four advantages for organizations.

- *Cost*: The organization does not have to advertise the position, and internal hires require much less training and orientation.
- *Risk*: Past performance is often a reliable predictor of future job success. Internal hires are known quantities, and organizations can make more accurate evaluations of their potential compared with external candidates.
- *Incentive*: The potential for promotion can incentivize behaviour desired by the organization among other employees, such as exerting extra effort or complying with directions that a worker might otherwise find objectionable.
- *Loyalty*: Opportunities for growth and advancement in an organization can make workers more loyal to the organization and, consequently, work harder, thereby reducing turnover.

Internal recruitment is most effective when the organization has valid and reliable measures of workers' past performance and an inventory of their KSAs. For these reasons, internal recruitment can be linked closely with training (see Chapter 7) and performance management (see Chapter 9). Internal recruitment is also more effective when workers believe that the process of selection is fair. For example, many unionized workplaces have seniority provisions embedded in a collective agreement negotiated by the employer and the union. These provisions make the duration of a worker's service a factor (to varying degrees) in determining eligibility for promotion or transfer. Provisions that make clear factors to be considered in promotion decisions and the process by which decisions are made increase the transparency and fairness of decisions. Although seniority provisions are often criticized as undermining merit-based staffing practices, in practice they have complex effects, associated with lower turnover and higher overall wages, as well as mixed effects on productivity.[9]

There are four main methods of internal recruitment.

1. *Internal job posting*: Distributing a job posting to existing employees is a transparent way to generate a list of interested candidates. Internal job postings rely on applicants to self-select. Self-selection can mean that some qualified candidates will not apply and that some unqualified candidates will apply. Even a rudimentary career development process (see Chapter 7) can improve understanding among workers of the jobs for which they are qualified.
2. *Succession planning*: A succession plan identifies and tracks potential successors for important positions, including an evaluation of their suitability. The replacement charts discussed in Chapter 4 are an example of succession planning. When a vacancy occurs, qualified candidates can be approached directly.
3. *HR systems*: Organizations possess large amounts of information about their workers (e.g., addresses, social insurance numbers, wages, and benefits). Some organizations also compile data on performance, KSAs, and interests to identify and evaluate candidates for promotions or transfers. This approach makes internal recruitment more efficient but less transparent. The measures recorded in a database are likely limited and can result in overlooking suitable candidates whose strengths might not be recorded.
4. *Nominations*: Asking someone (e.g., a supervisor) with knowledge of both the position and the workers to recommend someone can be an efficient way to identify potential candidates. Because of a lack of clear criteria, nominations can be unreliable and invalid and appear to be unfair. Furthermore, they can replicate existing inequities in the workplace since powerful actors are likely to put forward the names of their protégés and allies. Despite these

shortcomings, nominations are one of the most common methods of internal recruitment because this approach is quick and allows powerful organizational actors to extend their influence in the workplace.

Selecting an internal recruiting method often requires trading efficiency with transparency. Internal recruiting can also be politically complex, with internal stakeholders sometimes exerting pressure to have their preferred candidates selected. Furthermore, unsuccessful internal candidates might remain in the workplace and bear some animus toward the successful candidate or decide to seek employment elsewhere.

Internal recruitment might not be appropriate if the position requires highly specialized skills that no one else in the organization is likely to have. For example, it might not be possible to find an internal replacement for the sole IT technician at a toy manufacturing company because none of the other employees was hired for their IT skills. Internal recruitment also tends to reproduce existing skills, attitudes, and perspectives because candidates are already immersed in the organization's culture. External recruitment might be more desirable for an organization that experiences rapid industry change, begins a new line of business, or seeks to diversify its workforce or change its culture.[10] External recruiting can also be required if internal recruiting does not (or is unlikely to) yield a satisfactory candidate.

External Recruitment

External recruitment refers to the process of communicating with people outside the organization to attract candidates to fill a vacant position. External recruitment is inevitable for any organization. Even if internal recruiting fills a vacancy, it creates a new vacancy to fill. And, sometimes, there are simply too many vacancies (or too few qualified internal candidates) for an organization to rely on internal hiring. External recruitment is more expensive and time-consuming than internal recruitment. It also entails a higher risk of making a bad hiring decision because the employer has much less and lower-quality information—much of it gleaned second hand from resumés, interviews, and references—on which to base a selection. Nevertheless, by broadening the potential labour pool outside the organization, external recruitment can bring new perspectives, experiences, and skills into the organization.

There are eight main methods of external recruiting.

1. *Unsolicited applications*: Employers regularly receive resumés from individuals seeking work, by mail or email or when applicants visit a worksite in person. Some organizations might triage such applications and retain those resumés that fit expected vacancies.

2. *Advertising*: Advertising job vacancies in newspapers and magazines or on the radio, billboards, buses, and the internet can be an effective way to reach a large audience. The rate at which views are converted to applications, however, can be low unless ads target likely candidates.

3. *Online postings*: More than half of Canadian job seekers report looking for work online.[11] This includes searching organizations' websites, looking at job-posting aggregator websites (e.g., Monster.com), and using social media. Paid online advertising can be both more tightly targeted and less costly than traditional print advertising.[12] The reach of online advertising creates the risk that an organization will be flooded with applications from unqualified candidates. To reduce the resulting costs of selection, organizations might need to develop a system for quickly filtering out frivolous applications.

4. *Job fairs*: Job fairs bring together employers (often by industry or geography) and potential workers (e.g., the one at the Saddledome in the opening vignette). Although job fairs can be time consuming, they allow organizations to interact directly with applicants. This lets an organization put its best foot forward and make preliminary assessments of candidates.

5. *Educational institutions*: Postsecondary institutions offer career services for students. Accessing job posting boards and campus career fairs can be an effective way to recruit educated but inexperienced employees.

6. *Employment agencies*: Some employers contract with employment agencies to find applicants. **Executive search firms** (sometimes called headhunters) can help employers to find new senior executives. Although convenient, executive search firms are expensive and tend to focus on moving existing executives around rather than seeking new talent. At the other end of the spectrum are **temporary employment agencies** that have a roster of workers available for short-term assignments (alleviating the need for recruitment and selection). The fee for "temps" dispatched to an organization is often 20% to 30% of the salary paid to the worker. The worker often remains an employee of the temp agency and can face contractual barriers to accepting permanent work with the contracting organization.
7. *Employee referrals*: Existing employees can be effective recruiters, especially if an organization provides a financial incentive when a referral is hired. Employees are more likely to recommend someone to work for an organization that they themselves consider to be a good employer. But referrals also tend to perpetuate the existing demographic make-up of the organization.
8. *Professional associations/unions*: Many professional associations provide job postings to their members. This can be an effective way to recruit applicants with specific credentials. Similarly, many unions have hiring halls that coordinate the provision of workers for jobs. Hiring halls are most common in construction, in which building trades workers tend to work on time-limited projects and the union provides a useful service in connecting them to the next project. Some maritime, printing, and professional unions also have hiring halls.

Table 5.1 shows the external recruiting methods used by Canadian employers and how they have changed in the past few years. Of particular note is that, though online methods are growing in popularity, informal methods continue to be an important source of applicants for employers. The decline of newspaper advertising is also notable.

Table 5.1 Recruitment methods[13]

Method	2015 (%)	2023 (%)
Online job boards	65.9	79.5
Personal contacts, referrals, informal networks	65.6	74.4
Company website	51.9	63.7
Social media	32.4	61.7
Employment agency/headhunter	15.3	25.3
Newspaper ads	20.4	10.2

On the worker side, although 45% of workers report applying for work online, between 70% and 85% of jobs are still filled through informal networks (mostly since most job openings are never publicly posted).[14] So, though the internet has become a key tool in recruitment, employers are wise to keep in mind that informal avenues of finding and attracting candidates continue to be a crucial part of a recruitment strategy.

Feature Box 5.2 Recruiting International Workers[15]

Canadian employers have long recruited workers, especially skilled workers, from other countries. More recently, they have begun recruiting lower-skilled workers to fill labour shortages and to reduce labour costs. The federal government restricts the ability of non-citizens to reside and work in Canada. Employers that wish to access foreign workers have three options.

1. The federal government operates a variety of temporary foreign worker (TFW) programs. These programs typically provide foreign nationals with a work permit valid for a fixed period of time (e.g., two years) that might or might not be renewable. These programs often restrict the occupations for which a work permit will be issued, such as agricultural work or live-in caregiving, and/or stipulate the geographic region in which TFWs must reside. Permits are often "closed," meaning that the worker is legally permitted to work only for the employer named on the permit. These programs can also require a foreign worker to have an employer sponsor the worker and can limit the ability of

the worker to change employers while in Canada. Lower-skilled workers usually come via TFW programs.

2. The federal government has also entered into a series of international mobility programs (IMPs) with other countries. IMPs usually target higher-skilled occupations. Foreign nationals are still required to apply for a work permit, but it has fewer restrictions than those granted through the TFW programs, including being "open," meaning that they are not restricted to working only for one employer (i.e., they can quit and find new jobs).
3. Employers unable to find a Canadian citizen or permanent resident to perform skilled work can make a job offer to a foreign national. The candidate must then apply for entry into Canada under one of several federal streams leading to permanent residency. Applications are screened against criteria (e.g., education, skill, experience, language ability, age, adaptability) and offers of residency extended on a competitive basis. This process can be lengthy, and this stream is significantly smaller than the TFW and IMP streams.

Workers from another country often face difficulty attaching to the Canadian labour market. Several factors contribute to this difficulty. Workers might have trouble getting their credentials recognized in Canada. This can result in their inability to find employment in fields for which they are qualified. They might also have difficulty convincing employers that their employment experience is comparable to work in Canada. Workers might be unable to provide employment references acceptable to Canadian employers. HR practitioners who wish to tap into the skills of internationally trained workers might need to consider varying job requirements to account for these factors.

Foreign workers, especially those coming through the TFW programs, tend to be more vulnerable to exploitation and mistreatment. In part, this vulnerability results from restrictions placed on their permits, reducing their labour mobility and making them more dependent on their employers. Many foreign workers are also workers of colour from poorer nations, making them more likely to experience racism and other discrimination.

Job Postings

A **job posting** is a descriptive summary of a position, its requirements, and the conditions of work. It is required regardless of which recruiting method is used. The content of a job posting is normally derived from a job description and specification (see Chapter 3) and then modified to account for the requirements of the specific position for which the organization is recruiting. For example, if the Ministry of Labour is hiring a policy analyst, much of the job posting will be derived from the generic policy analyst job description and specification. But the job posting might also include position-specific requirements, such as knowledge of federal-provincial labour market training agreements and the location of the position. Job postings can sometimes be developed in other ways given time pressure or the inability to perform a sophisticated job analysis. For example, a supervisor might be tasked with quickly outlining the main duties and qualifications of a position.

Feature Box 5.3 contains the typical elements of a job posting along with an example of each element. The level of detail contained in a job posting will vary depending on where the posting is publicized (e.g., newspaper ads tend to be shorter than postings hosted on the company website). Although all postings need to provide basic information, a well-designed posting will provide the potential applicant with a clear picture of what the job will be like and the kind of candidate whom the organization is seeking. The more descriptive and precise the posting, the more effective it will be in attracting desired candidates and dissuading those not appropriate for the position. It is important to remember that the posting is the one opportunity that the organization has to persuade someone to apply. A well-constructed posting should give applicants a sense of the workplace and how they can expect to be treated by the employer. In other words, a job posting should be more than a listing of job attributes. It should be a promotional advertisement for the organization as a whole.

Feature Box 5.3 Sample Job Posting

This job posting for a construction labourer is based on the job description and specification presented in Chapter 3 (Feature Box 3.4). The left-hand column identifies the element of the job posting, and the right-hand column provides an example of each element.

Element	Example
Name of company and job title	ABC Road Construction Ltd. keeps motorists safe by ensuring that roads remain in good repair. ABC is seeking up to 10 construction labourers to perform road work.
Nature of job	Labourers assist in the construction and repair of roadways, including transporting and installing road materials (often by hand), operating vehicles and small machines, and directing traffic.
Starting date and duration	These positions are available for immediate start dates and will continue for the duration of the road work season (ending approximately October 31).
Location and hours of work	These full-time positions will require travel throughout the province (travel and housing provided) for periods of up to two weeks. Applicants are expected to be available to work overtime while on site.
Job duties	Duties include • preparing job site (e.g., removal of trees, rough grading, culvert installation); • loading, transporting, levelling, and packing aggregates (e.g., sand, gravel, road crush) and other materials; • installing and removing concrete forms for curbs and sidewalks; • operating hand tools (e.g., broom, shovel, rake, wheelbarrow, sprayer, chainsaw); • operating small construction machines (e.g., ditch witch, packer, bobcat) and small vehicles (e.g., pick-up truck with trailer); • directing construction machines (e.g., pavers, rollers, and dump trucks); and • directing highway or street traffic on site.
Conditions of work	In addition to shifts of up to 12 hours and extended work periods (of up to 14 days), the job requires travelling to remote locations in the province (transport and housing provided), working outside in inclement weather, and working near traffic and other road construction–related hazards.
Qualifications	Applicants must be able to perform physical tasks associated with road construction, including lifting loads of up to 100 pounds and operating hand tools and small construction machines for prolonged periods and during inclement weather. Applicants must have prior experience in road construction, possess a Class 5 driver's licence (no more than three demerits), be WHMIS and first-aid eligible (certification preferred), and pass periodic worksite drug and alcohol testing.
Salary and benefits	Wages are $30 per hour plus a comprehensive benefits package with RRSP matching.
Contact information	Submit resumés in confidence to Zoe Murthy, Lead Hand <address and email>.

Note that this posting conveys enticing aspects of the job (e.g., wages, benefits, housing) as well as unattractive aspects (e.g., long days, travel, drug testing). This **realistic job preview** allows applicants for whom these conditions would be unacceptable to opt out of the competition before applying. This approach is designed to increase the likelihood of converting applicants into hires and ensuring that they stay on the job.

Applications

The purpose of recruitment is to generate a pool of qualified candidates for a job. Typically, organizations collect written information from each candidate. This information is then analyzed during the process of selection to identify potential hires for further consideration. As a result, any recruiting strategy must include a method of collecting applicant information. The most common approach is to request an application package that includes a cover letter, resumé, and, often, a list of references. Cover letters and resumés provide applicants with significant latitude to share relevant information but entail higher costs for an organization given the time required to analyze applications. Asking for cover letters and resumés might be appropriate when the number of applicants is expected to be smaller and when there is a need for a deeper understanding of their experience and aptitudes.

An alternative is to require candidates to complete a standardized **application form** (either paper or electronic). Application forms collect specific information that the employer is seeking in a standardized format. In addition to basic personal information, the form might ask for previous work experience, education and other certification, and whether the candidate meets job-specific criteria (e.g., a valid driver's licence). It might also ask for references. Application forms are useful when there are many positions to be filled or the job is relatively straightforward and less information is needed to make a decision. The forms can be processed quickly given the standardized format.

In designing an application form, it is important that the form collects only information relevant to making a selection. This means that the form should be structured such that any information on personal characteristics listed as **protected grounds** in human rights legislation (e.g., age, ethnoracial background, gender) is defensible as necessary for the process of selection. Table 5.2 presents some sample application form questions with commentary on potential pitfalls and proposes alternative questions. In developing an application form, it is important to be mindful that questions can also indirectly reveal inappropriate information. For example, asking for the date that someone graduated from high school could reveal their age.

Table 5.2 Questions to avoid on application forms

Question	Comment	Recommended alternative
How old are you? Date of birth	Age is relevant only if the job or its duties are prohibited for minors.	Are you over the age of 18?
Are you a Canadian citizen?	Citizenship is relevant only when determining if someone is legally eligible to work in Canada.	Are you legally allowed to work in Canada?
Gender	Gender is almost always irrelevant to a hiring decision.	Do not collect.
Family status	Family status is relevant only if it affects workers' availability to work.	Are you able to work irregular hours (or night shifts or in other locations)?
Health	Health is relevant only if it affects the ability to perform tasks that are bona fide occupational requirements.	Can you lift 100 pounds?

Electronic applications are a convenient and effective mechanism. Web-based applications can force applicants to complete them fully before submission as well as allow them to upload documents. Electronic applications also allow organizations to store, process, and share applications internally. (We will discuss in the next chapter the effects of online applications on selection procedures.) Care must be taken to protect the uploaded data to prevent breaches of the applicants' privacy. Feature Box 5.4 examines the broader issue of privacy in the recruitment process.

Feature Box 5.4 Recruitment and Privacy

Applicants provide employers with a significant amount of personal information. As noted in Chapter 2, Canada's privacy laws, particularly as they apply to private sector employers, are exceptionally varied. Generally speaking, employers have an obligation to protect the personal information provided to them by job applicants. There are three main ways in which organizations can ensure the privacy of applicants' information during recruiting.

- *Collect only necessary information*: Collect only the information required for recruitment and selection. It would include basic contact information as well as information required to assess a candidate's suitability for a position. Examples of information unnecessary during recruitment and selection include a social insurance or driver's licence number, birthdate, marital status, and dependants. The information can be collected after hiring if it is necessary to administer the employment relationship.
- *Control access to information*: Access to applications should be restricted to those directly involved in the hiring process. This means that long-established norms, such as accepting application forms dropped off at the front counter of a business, might not be appropriate (unless the recipient is part of the hiring process). Similarly, applications should be stored in a secure location.
- *Destroy information*: Organizations should have a clear process of document retention and destruction once hiring has been completed. This can be as simple as shredding all documents other than the successful candidate's application (which would become part of that worker's personnel file). Or an organization can retain all applications and related documents for a fixed period of time (e.g., three months) in case any issues arise. If an organization expects to hire again for the position, then it might wish to retain applications for a longer period to draw from them in the future without reposting the job.

Developing clear processes for recurring organizational tasks, such as handling applications, helps to ensure that organizations do not inadvertently expose themselves to risk. Clearly documented processes also ensure that organizations can manage transitions more easily when HR practitioners and managers join and/or leave the organizations.

Evaluating Recruitment Efforts

Evaluating recruitment efforts allows an organization to understand and improve its performance. An important question, though, is how to define the word *effective*. Simply asking "did the position get filled?" does not generate information that can be used to guide future recruitment efforts. And it is important to distinguish between recruitment and selection functions. A wildly successful recruitment effort that generates lots of qualified candidates might not result in a hire because of something that happened during selection.

To determine how to evaluate a recruiting process, HR practitioners should start by identifying the goals and context of the recruitment. For example, they might ask how many applications from qualified candidates the organization was trying to generate. Was finding candidates from a particular demographic group a priority? Were there any special events or issues (e.g., skills shortage, undesirable job characteristics, organizational scandals) that might have affected recruitment? The goals and context help to determine which evaluation technique should be used and how its results should be interpreted.

There are a number of common measures used to evaluate recruitment efforts. **Yield ratios** measure the percentage of candidates who move through each stage of the recruitment and selection processes for each recruitment method utilized. This allows us to compare the effectiveness of different methods of advertising. For example, if a recruiter has to fill 10 vacancies, then the recruiter might use both newspaper ads and website postings to draw attention to the vacancies. For each approach, the recruiter might measure the total number of applications generated, the number of applications by candidates who meet the qualifications for the job, and the number of successful applicants. The results of such an analysis are set out in Table 5.3.

Table 5.3 Example of yield ratios

	Website	Newspaper ad
Applications received	100	50
Minimally qualified applicants	30 (30%)	10 (20%)
Applicants hired	5 (5%)	5 (10%)

In this example, the website generated twice as many applications as the newspaper ad. The website also generated a greater proportion of minimally qualified applicants (30%) than the newspaper ad (20%). But applicants who responded to the newspaper ad were more likely to be hired (10%) than applicants who responded to the website (5%). If the recruitment goal was to maximize the number of acceptable candidates to review, then the website performed better. If the goal was to maximize the proportion of applicants who are hired, then the newspaper ad was a more effective recruitment method.

A second way to assess recruitment is to determine the cost per applicant or hire of different recruiting methods. Table 5.4 continues the website and newspaper example and suggests that the website posting had a much lower cost per applicant, per qualified applicant, and per hire than the newspaper ad. In determining the cost of each method, it is worthwhile to consider both direct costs (e.g., charge for an advertisement) and indirect costs (e.g., staff time used).

Table 5.4 Example of recruitment cost

	Website	**Newspaper ad**
Cost	$300	$10,000
Cost per application	$3 ($300/100)	$200 ($10,000/50)
Cost per qualified applicant	$10 ($300/30)	$1,000 ($10,000/100)
Cost per hire	$60 (300/5)	$2,000 ($10,000/5)

The yield ratio and cost-per-hire data allow HR practitioners to consider whether newspaper advertising is worthwhile in the future. In determining this, it is useful to know whether it would have been possible to fill all 10 positions from the 30 applicants generated by the website posting. And, if it was possible, then it would be useful to know whether doing so would (or did) result in a significantly less qualified applicant pool. Answering these questions might require discussions with the selection committee and/or an analysis of the hired and rejected applicants.

In theory, an organization that seeks to increase the diversity of the candidate pool might evaluate the degree to which its recruiting efforts generated applicants from each targeted group. The data might then be compared with the demographic make-up of the organization or labour market. In practice, collecting demographic data with which to categorize applicants can be problematic. Although candidates can be asked to self-declare whether they fit into a specific equity category, some candidates will be reluctant to do so because of fear of discrimination. Some employers encourage self-disclosure by making statements in the job ad that encourage candidates of diverse backgrounds to apply for jobs. Ascribing certain characteristics to applicants through observation (e.g., based on a name, photo, or personal presentation during an interview) is a fraught process and best avoided.

Organizations interested in improving their recruitment and selection processes might also query candidates about their experiences with different aspects of the process (e.g., ease of application, clarity of communication, timeliness of response). However, it is important to keep in mind that such inquiries gather information only from candidates who have applied, thereby excluding potential candidates who self-selected out of the competition. This exclusion suggests that the utility of information collected from such inquiries might be limited.

Conclusion

Successful recruitment takes planning, understanding of the economic and organizational context, and careful implementation. Although recruitment might seem to be a straightforward HR function, and in many ways it is, organizations can make mistakes, usually because of inadequate planning. It is easy to get swamped with too many applications or not to get the attention of the best candidates.

Amazon's recruiting woes in the opening vignette suggest a number of things about both recruitment and selection (the subject of Chapter 6). First, a key risk of recruiting is unintentionally replicating the existing staffing complement. Amazon did that by training its AI using historical data. But HR practitioners are also vulnerable to unconscious bias, which can influence how they structure job postings and where they look for applicants.[16] Various forms of bias, and the errors that they can cause, are discussed in Chapter 6.

Second, though organizations face significant pressure to minimize costs, not every cost savings is a good idea. Although the example in Tables 5.3 and 5.4 suggests that it is a good idea to stop advertising in newspapers because of the high cost per hire, newspaper ads can provide access to an important pool of applicants. In the Amazon case, automating recruitment and selection looked like a great way to reduce HR costs. In practice, however, the system ended up working no better than the traditional approaches to recruiting that it was developed to replace.

Third, it is important to recall that workers are forming impressions of an organization while they are being recruited. A poor impression—whether caused by bad press, inadequate compensation, or a poorly presented or managed recruitment process—can cause workers to decide not to apply for a position. Potential applicants with lots of other options (i.e., generally the most desirable candidates) are likely to be the first to walk away from a job posting.

EXERCISES

KEY TERMS

Define the following terms.

- Application form
- Executive search firm
- External recruitment
- Internal recruitment
- Job posting
- Protected grounds
- Realistic job preview
- Recruitment
- Temporary employment agencies
- Yield ratio

DISCUSSION QUESTIONS

Discuss the following topics.

- What is the value in developing a detailed recruitment strategy?
- Which factors go into deciding on a recruitment strategy?

- What are the pros and cons of internal recruitment?
- What are the pros and cons of external recruitment?
- How are yield rates calculated?
- Which criteria should be used to evaluate the recruitment process?

ACTIVITIES

Complete the following activities.

- Find an application form online. Review the information gathered in the form. Is the form gathering any information that it should not be? Why? Is there another way to word any problematic question to make it more appropriate?
- Consider a job that you recently held. Write a job posting of up to 600 words for placement on a website that accurately describes the job and might entice a potential applicant to apply for it. Then rewrite the posting in 200 words for placement in a newspaper ad.

SELF-REFLECTION QUESTIONS

Write self-reflections of 200 to 500 words on the following topics.

- What were the challenges in writing the job postings for the exercise above? How did the two postings differ? How did you decide which information to exclude for the shorter posting?
- In the last job or volunteer opportunity that you applied for, how/where did you hear about it?
- Think about the last job or volunteer opportunity that you applied for. Which features of the job or volunteer opportunity or the posting persuaded you to apply? What lessons can you draw from this about recruiting strategies?
- If you were to design a recruitment process with the goal of attracting under-represented groups to your organization, what steps would you take to achieve that goal?

6 Selection

Recruitment is only the first step in a hiring process. Once a roster of candidates has been found, there needs to be a method for determining which candidate(s) to hire. Selection processes need to be carefully designed. A poorly designed process can lead to a cascading sequence of consequences for an organization. For example, the Canadian Museum for Human Rights in Winnipeg was recently embroiled in controversy about its hiring practices.

A racialized worker complained of being repeatedly overlooked for promotions despite being more qualified than the white co-workers who got the promotions. Another racialized worker complained that new openings at the museum routinely went to a manager's white friends, whereas black acquaintances of racialized workers were not even contacted for interviews. A third worker reported being told by their manager that they would get into "trouble" if they provided a positive reference for a racialized co-worker whom the manager did not like. A black volunteer who routinely worked 40 hours a week without pay was repeatedly overlooked for a paid position doing similar work.

These events were documented by an external investigator hired to examine workers' complaints about discrimination at the institution.[1]

The investigator found significant shortcomings in hiring practices at the museum, including

- a lack of representation by members of non-white groups on hiring committees;
- a lack of "blind" screening procedures;
- job criteria that were not bona fide job requirements (but could create barriers for racialized workers, including overly stringent bilingualism requirements);
- a lack of a formal policy addressing equity in hiring; and
- no consideration of equity-based hiring objectives in the selection process.

The investigator also found a sexist, racist, and homophobic workplace culture perpetuated, in part, by the museum's hiring practices.

The irony of a human rights museum being found guilty of discrimination is jaw dropping. Nevertheless, the story is a stark reminder that issues of racism, sexism, and other forms of systemic discrimination can occur in any workplace. The investigator's report highlights that both lax hiring practices and the absence of formal policies addressing equity can perpetuate and intensify systemic biases in the workplace.

The case of the museum also demonstrates the important role that selection plays in creating a workplace culture. Who gets hired and how to shape the characteristics of the workforce and workplace norms. Designing a strong process of selection helps an organization to find workers who meet its needs (however they are defined). It also helps an organization to change its workforce and culture. In this way, selection, just like recruitment, is an important tool that organizations can use to implement their human resource strategies successfully.

The Selection Process

Selection is the process of analyzing applicants to identify the candidates who best meet the requirements of an open position. "Best" often refers to how closely a candidate's knowledge, skills, abilities, and other characteristics align with the job specification for the position. A good selection process should result in workers who are successful in their jobs and stay with the organization over time. Figure 6.1 outlines the main steps

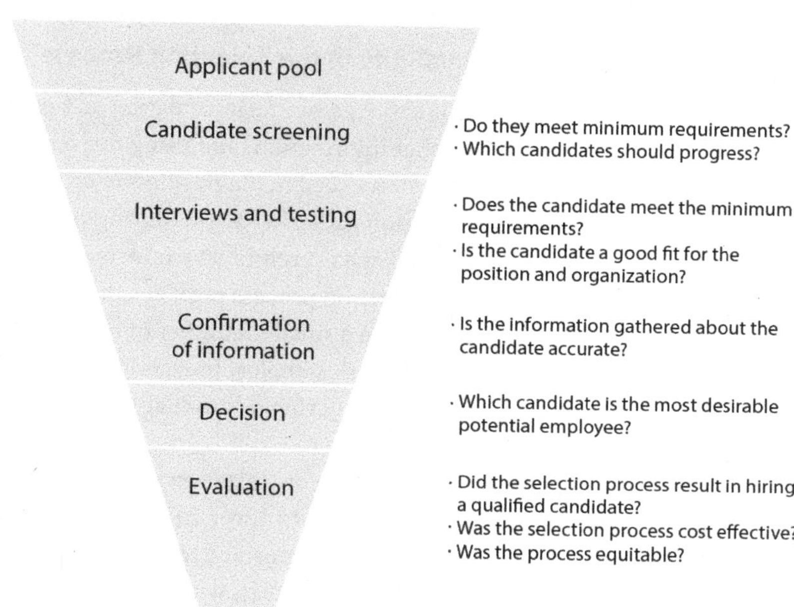

Figure 6.1 The selection process

in the selection process and the key questions to be answered at each step. Sometimes these steps will be taken consecutively and sometimes concurrently, depending on the nature of the job, timelines, and chosen selection strategy. The order of the steps can also vary.

Whether they know it or not, organizations have a hiring strategy for each position. Making that strategy explicit allows HR practitioners to ensure that it makes sense and is compliant with the law. An explicit strategy also allows HR practitioners to evaluate the effectiveness of the selection techniques used and to make improvements. In this chapter, we outline each step in the selection process, including the key considerations, the tools available, and when to use them. We conclude the chapter by offering some ways to evaluate the effectiveness of the selection process.

Relevance, Reliability, and Validity in the Selection Process

At its core, the selection process is about gathering information on a candidate, evaluating and analyzing that information, and using the results to predict whether the candidate will succeed in the position in order to inform the hiring decision. Information gathering begins during recruitment, when an organization decides what preliminary information to require candidates to submit. The selection process provides the opportunity to collect more information from a smaller number of candidates as the pool is narrowed. Interviews, work samples, tests, and reference checks are all common methods for gathering additional information during the selection process.

A key question is which tools provide an organization with the information that it needs to select a candidate to hire? In deciding what information to collect and consider, it is important to know whether or not it is relevant to the hiring decision. That is, will the information help you to predict whether a candidate will be successful if hired? It is also important to know whether or not the information is accurate. The concepts of validity and reliability can be helpful when considering what information to collect on candidates and use during selection.

As discussed in Chapter 3, reliability is the degree to which the information that HR practitioners collect is consistent over time. For example, if they administer a test, then it should produce a consistent result each time it is administered. If they test the same person twice and get different results, then the test might not be a good measure to use. The desire for reliable information can affect how they collect information on candidates. For example, if they are interested in knowing about someone's educational attainment, they might get a more reliable answer by asking for transcripts than they would by relying on a candidate's resumé or statements in an interview. A transcript will provide the same answer each time they look at it.

Measures must also be valid (i.e., measure what they claim to measure). For example, if HR practitioners are interested in knowing how fast a potential cashier can work, they might time how quickly the candidate can scan and bag groceries during a simulation. This test is only valid, however, if the candidate's actual performance matches the test result.

If candidates consistently perform better on the test than they do on the job (perhaps because there are no customer distractions during the test), then the simulation might not be a valid test.

Validity takes three forms relevant to selection.

- **Criterion validity** is the degree to which a measure's results are correlated to actual performance of some aspect of the job. A skill test, for example, has criterion validity if candidates who score higher on the test also perform better on the job.
- **Content validity** is the degree to which the content of a measure matches the content of the real-life situation. In other words, does the tool evaluate relevant aspects of the job in question? Is it missing pieces (in the scanning and bagging example above, the impact of customers was missing), or does it include content not present in real life?
- **Construct validity** is the degree to which the tool measures something real and relevant. What is being measured must be real. Sometimes this is self-evident, such as measuring typing speed. Other times it is not. For example, an HR practitioner might want to measure a candidate's honesty. But how does one measure a concept as complex as honesty? What is being measured must also be relevant to the job. Examining the job specification can be helpful in determining the relevance of the information that an HR practitioner is considering gathering.

To be useful, the information collected and used in the selection process must be valid, reliable, and relevant. If the information is not valid and reliable, then it is unlikely to be useful in predicting a candidate's performance and thus of little use in making a hiring decision. Complicating matters, some jobs lend themselves to more valid, reliable, and relevant measurement than others. It can be easier to ascertain which selection criteria are relevant in routine jobs (e.g., working on an assembly line) than it is for jobs in which the duties are highly variable and/or rely on workers who exercise significant discretion in completing tasks (e.g., residential plumbing repairs or customer service). For this reason, it is important to develop selection processes appropriate for each job or position.

Candidate Screening

The first step in the selection process is **candidate screening**. During this process, each application is analyzed with the goal of removing from consideration candidates who do not meet the minimum requirements and are unlikely to be good fits. The end result should be a manageable number of high-quality candidates who can be more thoroughly vetted. Screening can require reviewing the applications several times. If there are many applicants, then an HR practitioner might first review each application to determine whether the applicant meets the minimum requirements for the job set out in the job specification. Often the minimum requirements are objective and quantifiable and related to education, years of experience, professional certification, and so on. The need for clear criteria should shape the job posting (see Chapter 5). For example, if education is an important factor, then stating a minimum requirement of "a university undergraduate degree in X field" is preferable to a more general statement such as "possessing postsecondary education." The former creates quick and clear demarcation during selection, whereas the latter leaves too much room for judgment. If the candidate screening criteria are vague, then that might suggest the job specification (Chapter 3) requires additional work.

Once candidates who do not meet the minimum job specifications are removed from the applicant pool, it might be necessary to conduct a second round of evaluation to identify which of the minimally acceptable candidates will proceed to the interview stage and/or the testing stage. Having a clear numerical target during this stage is helpful (e.g., we want to interview a maximum of four candidates and hire one). This target can be informed by past experience with hiring as well as the costs and benefits of expanding this **short list** of candidates to evaluate further.

This second phase of screening can be more difficult because all candidates are minimally qualified. During a second round of screening, the criteria used should be closely linked to the job specification so that the decisions are anchored in the actual needs of the job. It is important not to evaluate the applicants in an informal, "gut feel" way. Doing so can introduce an array of issues regarding bias and undermine validity and reliability. A better approach is to establish a matrix to allow for a multivariable evaluation. An evaluation matrix could involve a grid in which each criterion that a candidate meets is checked.

Table 6.1 shows an example of an evaluation matrix based on the job posting for a labourer presented in Feature Box 5.2. Since this is a second-level screening, the organization knows that all applicants have met the basic qualifications. This screening assesses whether or not each applicant has experience with each of the six main job duties. A matrix is useful because a visual representation of each candidate's match with the screening criteria can create a shared understanding of the candidate's qualifications and facilitate decision making. In this case, Table 6.1 suggests that Candidates C (four of six) and D (five of six) seem to have the widest range of experience with the job duties.

A matrix can be made more complex when warranted. For example, Table 6.2 adapts the matrix presented in Table 6.1 to allow each reviewer to assign applicants points for each duty based on the applicant's level of experience. This approach creates a slightly more nuanced assessment of each applicant. When comparing Tables 6.1 and 6.2, for example, note that Candidate D is the highest rated in both grids. But the second highest rated in Table 6.1 is Candidate C (who has the broadest level of experience), whereas in Table 6.2 Candidate A is rated higher (because of much more experience).

Neither matrix is better than the other; each just measures different aspects (breadth versus depth) of the candidates' experience. Which one you choose will be determined by which aspect is most important. It is also possible to add complexity by weighting each column in Table 6.2

Table 6.1 Sample evaluation matrix

Candidate has experience/displays aptitude in the following tasks.

	Job Site prep	Handling aggregates	Using hand tools	Using small machinery	Directing machinery	Directing traffic	Score
Candidate A	X		X		X		3
Candidate B	X	X	X				3
Candidate C	X		X	X	X		4
Candidate D	X	X	X		X	X	5

Table 6.2 Extended evaluation matrix

Candidate has experience/displays aptitude in the following tasks.

	Job site prep	Handling aggregates	Using hand tools	Using small machinery	Directing machinery	Directing traffic	Overall score
Candidate A	3	0	3	0	2	0	8
Candidate B	3	1	1	0	0	0	5
Candidate C	2	0	1	2	1	0	6
Candidate D	2	1	2	0	3	2	10

Scoring: 0 = no experience; 1 = <1 year of experience; 2 = 1–3 years of experience; 3 = >3 or more years of experience.

differently. For example, if having long experience using small machinery is highly desirable, then you might multiply whatever score candidates get on this column by two. This would shift the scores in Table 6.2 such that Candidates A and C tie with eight points each.

Ideally, the screener should have no awareness of the sex, ethnoracial background, age, or other characteristics of the candidate. This is because research has consistently shown that unconscious bias among screeners affects their choices. For example, resumés with "white"-sounding names are more likely to get candidates interviews than identical resumés with "non-white"-sounding names.[2] A similar effect is found regarding sex,[3] and, as an intersectional analysis would predict, women whose names suggest that they are persons of colour experience a compounding bias.[4] **Blind screening** controls for bias and ensures that screening decisions better reflect candidates' abilities.[5] A different approach to reduce bias in screening is to adopt **identity conscious screening**, in which the screener actively searches for candidates from marginalized groups to select for interviews. This practice is controversial but can be effective in increasing diversity in the workplace.

Some organizations use technology to automate all or part of the screening process. The software, often called applicant tracking systems (ATS), searches for key words, phrases, or characteristics identified by the organization to filter the candidate pool. This technology improves the efficiency of screening by evaluating hundreds of resumés in seconds but also comes with trade-offs. Clever applicants can fool the ATS by tailoring their resumés to "match" the key aspects for which the organization might be searching. The internet is full of websites offering tips on how to "beat" ATS. Also, ATS can entrench existing hiring biases. The person programming the system establishes the criteria and keywords that it will search for and therefore can embed biases into the program against certain social characteristics. For example, in Chapter 5, we discussed Amazon's artificial intelligence recruiting system and how its algorithm taught itself to discriminate against women.

A final, but less common, tool that can be used for screening, especially at the second step, is a **screening interview**. It allows the screener to gather information on the candidate that might not be available on the resumé or application form. Screening interviews are typically short, often take place by telephone or video conference, and focus on specific qualifications or qualities needed for the job. The advantage of screening interviews is the richness of information that they can provide in making a difficult screening decision. They are a resource-intensive way, however, to gather information, requiring logistical arrangements and personal engagement. Also, they risk introducing bias into the screening process. They might be most appropriate when the candidate pool is relatively small, the job requires KSAs that can be assessed easily through a conversation, or the job is at a high level in the organization (thus warranting the extra cost).

Interviews

Once the applicant pool has been winnowed to the desired size through screening, organizations can begin to collect more detailed data on short-listed candidates to make a hiring decision. By far, **interviews** are the most common technique as well as one of the most maligned. An interview consists of a series of questions posed to a candidate to draw out information on the suitability of the candidate for the job. Candidates feel a great deal of pressure in interviews since they know that their answers are being closely evaluated. They also complain about strange questions, such as "if you were an animal, what kind of animal would you be?" On the employer side, interviewers can struggle to discern an authentic answer from someone prepared to tell the interviewer what the candidate believes the interviewer wants to hear. Some people perform better in an interview situation than others. Research shows that poorly designed interviews end up being both invalid and unreliable in predicting employment outcomes.[6] Subjectivity and personal bias easily creep into decisions based on interviews, including biases related to ethnoracial background, sex, disability, and other characteristics. There is no way to "blind" interviews.

So why bother with them? Because, when well designed, interviews can provide a richness of information that no other selection tool can. Interviews provide insights into the candidate as a person and allow for an evaluation of skills and abilities that goes beyond keywords and formal qualifications. As a result, interviews are an excellent tool for evaluating how well a candidate will fit into the existing organizational culture. Interviews are also the only moment when a candidate can ask questions of the employer, which can also enhance the likelihood of finding a good fit (see Feature Box 6.1). Plus, people have a legitimate need to "see" the person who might be joining their organization. As imperfect as they might be, interviews satisfy many selection needs. But interviews need to be designed and executed carefully to address their inherent weaknesses.

Feature Box 6.1 Interviews as a Two-Way Street

Organizations use interviews to collect data on candidates. Less recognized is that candidates also use interviews (and the broader selection process) to collect information on and evaluate a potential employer. One outcome of this dynamic is that candidates can opt out of the selection process. Sometimes candidate attrition is good for an organization since a candidate might self-identify as a bad fit. Other times candidate attrition can deprive organizations of the most qualified candidates.

Undesirable candidate attrition can be the result of an onerous selection process or suggest that the employer is undesirable. Extensive psychological testing, for example, might be time consuming and feel intrusive to candidates. In response, those with other options might choose to drop out of the selection process.

Similarly, a badly managed selection process can result in candidate attrition and poor hires. A selection process by the government of Alberta saw all candidates who had applied to positions in a similar pay grade placed in a pool. Each was interviewed by a random set of managers using generic questions. Then all were called together, broken into groups, and told to build a LEGO kit jointly while being evaluated by managers. It was not stated what this approach was intended to assess (perhaps teamwork, leadership, and followership) or how assessment would take place.

Many candidates dropped out of the selection process after what they termed the "Hunger Games" Lego event. This attrition resulted in "gold rush" hiring in which managers sought to hire any candidate who met the minimum qualifications (in order to fill empty staffing lines) before the pool of potential candidates was exhausted. Managers often made offers of jobs for which candidates had not applied (but were in the same pay band). Hiring decisions made during this process created performance problems for years afterward.

In structuring a selection process, HR practitioners need to consider carefully how it will affect candidate retention and attrition. A demanding process might well be warranted sometimes. But a process out of step with what candidates experience elsewhere requires clear justification. And gimmicky selection processes, such as the government of Alberta's "Hunger Games" approach, are generally best avoided.

Interviews can take many forms, from an impromptu session with a manager when a candidate drops off a resumé to formal, structured proceedings with set questions and a panel of interviewers. The nature of the job, the organization, and the resources available for the selection process help to shape the type of interview that is appropriate. There are four decisions to make when setting up an interview process.

1. Medium: Most interviews are conducted *in-person*. If resources are scarce and/or candidates are out of town, then a **telephone interview** might be conducted. It deprives the interviewer(s) of visual cues, such as body language, but it can blind the candidate's ethnoracial background, disability, and potentially

gender. Another alternative is an *online interview* through video-conferencing software.

2. Formality: **Unstructured interviews** do not have an established set of questions. The interviewer(s) can craft questions in response to the flow of the interview. Usually, evaluation criteria are similarly informal, with interviewers going with their overall impressions. On the other end of the spectrum are **structured interviews**, which have pre-established and standardized questions and evaluation standards. In between are **semi-structured interviews**, which have standardized questions but allow room for interviewers to respond to information that comes out in the interview.
3. Format: Who participates in an interview and when can vary. *One-on-one interviews* consist of one interviewer and one candidate. *Panel interviews* consist of multiple interviewers who interview one candidate. A **sequential interview** *process* has the interviewee move from one interviewer to another in sequence, usually answering different questions at each stage.
4. Content: Three types of questions can be asked. **Knowledge and background questions** probe factual information about candidates and their skills and knowledge. These questions can supplement information provided in the application, or they can be designed to confirm certain information. **Situational questions** pose scenarios that candidates might be confronted with in the position and ask for their responses to the situation. **Behavioural questions** look backward, asking candidates to reflect on an experience in the past, talk about their actions, and possibly indicate how they might act differently today. Interviews often have a mixture of each type of question, depending on the nature of the information sought.

Decisions on the characteristics of an interview depend on the nature of the position being filled and the organizational resources available. In general, the research has found that unstructured interviews are more likely to have issues with subjectivity and bias.[7] During such interviews, the interviewer is more likely to evaluate candidates based on overall impressions. Research has shown that interviewers are more likely to develop positive impressions about candidates similar to them,[8] which can perpetuate existing inequalities in a workplace as well as increase the risk of a human rights complaint.

Nevertheless, unstructured and one-on-one interviews have their place. If there is a need for a quick decision and the job permits a straightforward evaluation of fit (e.g., hiring for a temporary labourer job), then an unstructured, one-on-one interview can be worthwhile. Bias in such an interview can be reduced through a consistent set of questions and the use of rigorous scoring criteria. Having more than one interviewer, preferably with different perspectives, to provide a range of viewpoints can also reduce selection bias. As for the types of questions to use, behavioural and situational questions have similar levels of validity and reliability.[9]

HR researchers often point to an overall lack of predictability for interviews, citing people's flawed ability to evaluate other people.[10] These researchers prefer selection methods that remove human subjectivity and fallibility from the calculation. Yet interviews remain the most popular form of selection process. Research often overlooks the human aspect of selection. People have a need to know and understand the people with whom they will be working. Individuals tend to trust their own judgment, even if it is flawed, over that of computers or test results. One strength of interviews is that they are opportunities to see the whole person and not just test scores. Because of human bias, seeing the whole person can create as many problems as it solves, but there are ways to structure interviews to minimize the impact of that bias. Interviews will likely continue to be the most popular form of selection tool for a long time to come.

Interview Mistakes and Training

Mistakes are easy to make during an interview. Asking the wrong question or incorrectly evaluating an answer can have consequences for the success of the selection process. Table 6.3 examines some of the most common interview mistakes, regardless of which type of interview is selected.

Table 6.3 Interview errors and remedies

Type	Issue	Remedy
Inadequate planning	Not knowing what information to elicit or how	Clear questions grounded in the job specification
Halo and horns effect	A single positive or negative characteristic that colours the overall evaluation of a candidate	Clear evaluation criteria and multiple interviewers
Snap judgment	Premature decision on a candidate based on the first impression	Interviewer training
Candidate order	Relative strength of preceding or subsequent candidates that can skew evaluation results	Clear evaluation criteria and evaluation completed immediately following an interview
Serial-order effect	Interviewers who might have a better ability to remember the first and last items in a series (e.g., interview candidates, candidates' answers in interviews)	Clear evaluation criteria and evaluation completed immediately following an interview
Leading questions	An interviewer who telegraphs a desired answer in how the question is asked or how feedback is given	Neutrally phrased questions and interviewer training
Talking too much	Long-winded answers or discussions that can prevent completion of the question set	Interviewer training
Non-verbal cues	An interviewer who subconsciously judges a candidate on irrelevant criteria (e.g., appearance, mannerisms) or discriminatory criteria (e.g., gender, ethnoracial background, age)	Clear evaluation criteria and interviewer training
Similar-to-me bias (sometimes called likeness or affinity bias)	An interviewer who rates candidates based on similarity of characteristics (e.g., demographic, personality) to self	Clear evaluation criteria and interviewer training

Although there is no way to eliminate fully biases, mistakes, and subconscious tendencies in interviews, their impacts can be reduced with appropriate training. Training interviewers should be a part of the selection planning process. Interviewing is a skill and, as such, can be taught. Training can include three aspects of interviewing.

- Interviewers need to know how to ask questions in a neutral manner as well as how to evaluate the answers and apply a scoring guide (see "Making the Decision" below). Some tips in effective note taking can also be of assistance.
- Training should address interview management, including making the applicant feel at ease, remaining in control of the interview, and engaging in good listening practices.
- Most importantly, training should address issues of bias and non-verbal cues. Training people to spot their biases is a difficult task and can require repeated efforts. That said, the only way to prevent bias from interfering with the selection process is to make interviewers conscious of their biases and how to overcome them.

Selection training can include opportunities for simulation, role playing, or job shadowing to make the interviewer comfortable with the process. Training should also include basic knowledge of the position to be filled and its job specification so that the interviewer can identify candidate responses relevant to the position. Interviewers should also be trained on the evaluation scheme.

When they have discretion in the questions that they ask, it is imperative that interviewer training includes discussion of interview questions to avoid, for practical and human rights reasons. Vague questions provide little useful information on which to base a selection decision. An example of a vague question is "what is your biggest weakness?" It is not connected to the job specification, does not speak to identifiable qualities of the candidate, and creates too much room for providing an inaccurate answer. Of course, most candidates will say that their major flaw is that they are perfectionists or work too hard. Metaphorical or trick questions are more popular recently but no less problematic. Asking a candidate what kind of animal they would be might seem to be creative but does not elicit a response that can be meaningfully evaluated (e.g., how do we know whether a "lion" or a "bear" is better suited for a position?).

Preventing litigation on human rights issues is another reason to teach interviewees about which questions to avoid. Certain questions, even innocently framed ones, can lead to accusations of discrimination and concerns about breaches of privacy (see Chapter 2). All interview questions should be related directly to the position, specifically the job specification. Even when a question is related directly to a job requirement, it is important to be careful how it is framed. Table 6.4 offers some examples of questions about legitimate job requirements that can still run afoul of human rights and some alternatives. It is useful to note that the "bad questions" outlined in Table 6.4 also fail to extract the information needed to evaluate a candidate properly. In contrast, the "good questions" avoid possible litigation and extract the information required for the selection process.

Table 6.4 Questions to avoid in an interview

Job requirement	Bad question	Protected grounds	Recommended/ better (?) alternative
Cash handling or working with vulnerable clients	Do you have a criminal record?	Record of offence (some jurisdictions)	Are you eligible to be bonded? Can you pass a child welfare check?
Working shift work or on call	Do you have children?	Family status	Can you work the night shift? Are you available to work on call?
Able to work legally in Canada	Where were you born?	Citizenship/ nationality	Are you able to work legally in Canada?
High school diploma	When did you graduate from high school?	Age	Do you hold a high school diploma?

Training should also address the potential for human rights issues to emerge from candidate disclosures. For example, a candidate might ask about on-site child care or flexible hours and, in doing so, disclose that they have four young children. The candidate's family status is of no relevance to the selection process. Having this information poses a small organizational risk: if the candidate is not hired, then they might attribute the decision to their family status. The best option here is for an interviewer to answer the specific question and move on. No record of the question should be made so that it does not influence subsequent decision making.

A final component of training is to teach and remind interviewers that, during the interview (including the informal "chit-chat" as it gets under way), the interviewer is in a position of power over the candidate. The candidate needs the job and is competing against others for it. The interviewer will decide who gets the job. It is more imperative for the candidate to react and respond to the perceived needs of the interviewer than vice versa. This creates a power dynamic that must be openly recognized and managed by interviewers. Off-hand comments, even a compliment about a tie or shoes, can be interpreted by the candidate as subtle messages about how they are perceived. The power dynamic can turn an innocent remark (e.g., "nice blouse you have on") into a subtle power move, reminding the candidate that the interviewer is the one doing the evaluating. It can also make the candidate feel uncomfortable or unsafe.

Applicant Testing

Some employers use tests to measure aspects of a candidate's skills, aptitudes, and personality. Like interviews, the purpose of testing is to elicit information to inform the selection decision. Tests are often asserted to provide more objective measures of candidates than interviews because they remove human bias. Tests are often (but not always) quantitative, making it easier to calculate their validity and reliability. Testing can be expensive and resource intensive.

In broad terms, there are two kinds of tests used during the selection process: demonstration and predictive. **Demonstration tests** measure a candidate's knowledge, skills, or ability to do tasks by putting the candidate through a series of tasks, scenarios, or questions that can reflect the knowledge or skills required to perform a job. They are demonstrative because they ask the candidate either to demonstrate what they know about the job currently or to perform some aspect of what the job will entail. There are a few kinds of demonstration tests.

- *Work knowledge tests* pose questions or scenarios to the candidate that relate to the job. These questions or scenarios might focus on technical aspects of the work or facts that someone in the job would need to know. The key is to ensure that the questions are linked directly to the job specification and the work that needs to be performed. The candidate can be evaluated based on how well they answer the questions.
- *Work sample/simulation tests* ask the candidate to engage in a part of the work. The candidate might be asked to perform a series of duties related to the work or given a simulated situation in which they need to take action. For example, a candidate for a communications job might be asked to write a media release and a newsletter article within a certain time frame. A bus or truck driver might be asked to navigate a route and successfully park the vehicle. Simulation tests can involve live simulations involving other workers, such as a mock OHS accident investigation.
- *Physical ability tests* require the candidate to perform a series of physical tasks or undergo physical tests to determine their physical capacity to perform the duties of the position. They might also involve sensory or perception tests. As shown in Chapter 2, though, employers need to be careful to design physical ability tests to test capabilities that are real proxies for the position or BFORs.

The value of demonstration tests is that they provide useful information about a candidate's ability to perform the duties of a position and allow an organization to compare the performances of several candidates. The position-specific nature of demonstration tests means that they must be designed for the job. This can make such tests resource intensive to conduct. Simulations require coordinating many people, which is logistically challenging and requires much advance planning. The creation of demonstration tests also requires expertise by the tester in both the job and the test design.

Predictive tests measure aspects of the candidate's personality or preferences. These tests are not directly related to the duties of the position. Rather, they attempt to measure qualities of the candidate that an organization believes predict their success in the position. Predictive tests can take several forms.

- **Cognitive ability tests** measure candidates' mental capabilities. General cognitive tests, commonly referred to as IQ tests, measure verbal or written comprehension, quantitative ability, and reasoning or logical ability. There are also specific cognitive ability tests that measure only those aspects of cognitive ability relevant to the job. Many cognitive ability tests are available, and they can vary significantly in content. They share the goal of creating a quantified measure of a person's cognitive capacity.
- **Personality tests** examine elements of a person's basic traits, such as introversion or extroversion, agreeableness, conscientiousness, openness to new experiences, and emotional stability. A key assumption of such tests is that certain personality traits are more likely to lead to success in certain positions. Similarly, interest inventories seek to measure how well the candidate's personal interests align with the job requirements. Like cognitive tests, myriad personality tests are available commercially.
- **Integrity tests**, sometimes called honesty tests, assess a candidate's predilection toward honesty. Questions focus on scenarios related to breaking rules, stealing, or lying. Integrity tests can be stand alone and overt, or they can be embedded in personality test questions.
- **Medical exams** involve a physical examination and possibly other health tests (e.g., conducted on blood or urine samples) to establish a candidate's ability to meet the physical requirements of the job and to identify any problematic health-related issues (e.g., drug use, uncontrolled diabetes). The invasive nature of medical exams suggests that they should be conducted only near the end of the selection process and only on the leading candidate. Drug tests, a popular but controversial form of medical exams, are discussed in Feature Box 6.2.

Feature Box 6.2 Drug and Alcohol Testing during Selection

Some employers require prospective employees to submit to a drug and alcohol test prior to commencing employment. The assumptions underlying such testing are that impairment increases the risk of a workplace incident and that testing can reduce the frequency of impairment on the job. Although this logic makes intuitive sense, research suggests that it is not necessarily accurate.

There is mixed evidence about the effect of drug and alcohol testing on workplace injury rates. Some studies show small improvements in injury rates, whereas others do not. The absence of compelling evidence of the efficacy of testing should give us pause. Testing companies would benefit significantly from evidence that drug testing increases safety. That these companies have not managed to find such evidence suggests that testing does not increase safety.

One potential explanation of the lack of evidence about the efficacy of testing is that the underlying assumption (substance use is an important cause of injuries) is incorrect. There is compelling research to suggest that drug use is not an important cause of injuries. That is not to say that being impaired never contributes to a workplace incident (or that being impaired on the job is a good idea). Rather, it simply suggests that, if drug use does not meaningfully contribute to the occurrence of workplace injuries, then testing will not reduce injury rates.[11]

Despite this research, many employers continue to require pre-employment testing. It is most often required for **safety-sensitive positions**. They are positions in which impairment can cause a catastrophic incident that would injure the worker or others. The law on pre-employment testing is complicated. In Canada, alcohol and drug addiction are considered a disability and therefore protected under human rights legislation. Employers are not allowed to discriminate against workers on the basis of their addictions. This protection means that drug tests should not be used in the selection process.

After an offer of employment (conditional on passing a drug or alcohol test) has been made and accepted, employers can require workers in safety-sensitive positions to take and pass a test before commencing work. If a worker fails the test and claims that they have an addiction, then the employer must accommodate them. In practice, this means establishing a clear policy that provides access to treatment and counselling. Firing or otherwise penalizing the worker for their disability would contravene human rights legislation.[12]

Despite the legal complications, pre-employment drug and alcohol testing remains common in some industries (e.g., transportation, construction). For these employers, the risks associated with a human rights complaint are outweighed by the expected benefits of identifying and removing workers who might be impaired on the job. In practical terms, few workers are willing to challenge employers, in particular prospective employers, on testing because they fear not being hired or let go at the end of their probationary periods.

Workers can be resistant to testing for several reasons. Some view it as a violation of privacy and an intrusion into their private lives. Workers might also legitimately question whether testing measures impairment. Whereas blood-alcohol testing does measure impairment from alcohol, drug testing does not measure impairment. Rather, it measures the presence of residue related to past drug use in the worker's body. For this reason, workers often argue that it is not the employer's business to know what they did on their time off if that activity does not affect workplace safety. Pre-employment testing is even more controversial since it makes assumptions about future behaviour based on a test that measures past behaviour.

Furthermore, workers might argue that testing does not make workplaces safer. Instead, they might suggest, employers can use testing illegitimately to exert control over workers. For example, employers might discourage workers from reporting injuries (which can attract government inspectors and increase workers' compensation premiums) by requiring injured workers to take a drug or alcohol test. This policy causes workers to consider whether it is worth their while to report an injury.

None of these predictive tests measures anything directly connected to a position, so it is reasonable to ask how they help an organization to make a better selection decision. The utility of these tests flows from their track records (as measured by researchers) in predicting future job success (usually defined as a worker who remains with a new employer for a period of time or how well the worker performs the job). If studies find a statistically significant correlation between these tests and increased success, then the tests are deemed useful. It is worth noting that, at times, the effects found can be fairly small.[13]

One of the challenges of evaluating the predictive power of these tests is that they can only show statistical correlation (i.e., A and B occur together) and not causation (i.e., A causes B). When studying human behaviour in a real environment, it is not possible to control all of the variables, so HR practitioners can never be certain what caused the success. Furthermore, studies of predictive tests need to create a simple and measurable definition of success. What a successful selection looks like will differ from organization to organization and from occupation to occupation. This caveat is not meant to dismiss the validity of research on these tests but to remind us that HR practitioners need to look at a range of tools and evaluate, based on the evidence of their efficacy, which ones work best for their organization and its goals.

Some also argue that these tests are problematic for a different set of reasons. They are invasive since they ask personal questions and make judgments about a worker's intelligence, personality, and tendencies. Workers might argue that employers should not be entitled to know this kind of information about them because it is beyond the scope of the employment relationship. This argument suggests that the instrumental value of the tests in marginally improving selection success is not worth the violation of workers' privacy and dignity.

These types of tests also need to be understood in the context of power dynamics in the employment relationship. Employers are not just looking for workers who can competently perform the job. They are also looking for workers easy to manage. Personality and integrity tests can also be used to select workers who will be more compliant and cooperative with management and to weed out workers who might resist authority, agitate for a union, or stand up for their rights. For example, an employer might test for agreeableness (i.e., trusting, cooperative, collaborative). Employers desire this trait in workers because such workers will likely integrate more easily into a team. They are also less likely to challenge authority or criticize an employer's decisions.[14]

Predictive tests are usually utilized as a supplement to other selection tools, including interviews. They can provide useful additional information not accessible through other tools. This explains their growing popularity. Nevertheless, the shortcomings and problematic use of these tests should be considered when deciding whether they are a practical addition to the selection process.

Reference and Qualification Checks

One of the last steps in the selection process is to confirm the qualifications of the candidate and to check with people who have experience with the candidate. For some jobs, a criminal record check might also be needed. This step is usually performed only once the preferred candidate is identified or when only a couple of candidates remain in contention because it is resource intensive. Each check serves a different purpose.

- **Qualification checks** involve confirming that candidates possess the necessary registrations, certifications, credentials, or qualifications that they claim to have. It can involve contacting schools, professional regulatory bodies, or other relevant bodies that can confirm the information provided by the candidates. Qualification checks are part of an organization's due diligence to ensure that its workers are indeed qualified to perform their jobs. Qualification checks are also an honesty test.
- **Reference checks** involve contacting individuals to solicit their opinions of candidates and their suitability for a job. Since references are selected by a candidate, checks need to be conducted carefully. The goal is to move beyond general platitudes and solicit information related to the demands of the position and the workplace context that the candidate will be entering. Questions should address situations that the candidates might experience in the new workplace (e.g., how do you think the candidate will respond to an open space workplace?) or specific elements of the job (e.g., this is a fast-paced job; how well can the candidate think on their feet?). It can be useful to ask references to provide examples of how the candidate handled specific situations or performed specific tasks in the past. Candidates can also provide letters of reference. They are typically less useful than a telephone call because they do not provide any opportunity to ask job-related questions. The research indicates that reference checks should be used to verify findings from other parts of the process and not to predict how well a candidate will perform in the job.[15] Some groups of workers, such as those new to Canada, might

have difficulty providing references. This requirement can then discriminate against them.

- **Criminal record checks** will reveal whether a candidate has been charged with or convicted of a criminal offence. Successfully passing a criminal record check (or a child welfare check) might be a bona fide occupational requirement for certain positions (e.g., working with a vulnerable population). Usually, the candidate needs to apply for the criminal record check after being hired and then provides the result to the employer before beginning work.

Before conducting a reference or qualification check, it is important to seek consent from the candidate to make the necessary contacts. The checks should also be conducted in accordance with relevant privacy legislation to ensure that private information is handled appropriately (see Chapter 2). Despite the growing practice of checks, organizations should refrain from checking applicants' social media accounts, as explained in Feature Box 6.3.

Feature Box 6.3 The Perils of Checking Social Media

Approximately 70% of employers report checking candidates' social media accounts before making a hiring decision, and over half indicate rejecting applicants based on what they find.[16] Social media—such as Facebook, Twitter, and Instagram—are easy to access, and most people's accounts are publicly accessible. Employers can find information that they cannot easily glean through interviews or application forms, and many believe that the posts and photos can reveal a candidate's character and "personality."

However, this practice can lead employers down a dangerous path. First, social media accounts reveal information about applicants that employers should not be considering in their decision making, including a person's gender, ethnoracial background, sexual orientation, disability, political views, and religious affiliation. If an organization makes a hiring decision based on what it finds in a social media feed, then it might be violating a candidate's human rights. In addition, even information that does not reveal prohibited grounds, such as photos of the candidate socializing, can lead an employer to make false inferences about the candidate.

Research shows that access to social media information leads employers to make decisions based on informal impressions not related to the job rather than on valid criteria.[17] In other words, employers derive incorrect conclusions from what they find on social media. Studies have also shown that decisions made using social media information are not correlated to job performance or retention, meaning that the information gathered does not lead to better hiring decisions.[18]

Checking social media has little upside for the selection process and can have significant downside in terms of legal liability. Given the popularity of this approach to selection, however, candidates should consider cleaning up their social media feeds or strengthening their privacy settings to protect themselves.

Making the Decision

After gathering a range of information on candidates, an organization must decide whom to hire. A few candidates might be eliminated during the selection process as unsuitable. Usually, though, an organization will have two or more candidates among whom to choose. A decision strategy can help those charged with selection to weigh the information and determine the best candidate(s). Two broad decision-making strategies are commonly used.

Many organizations adopt an intuitive strategy. Those making the selection will look at each of the minimally qualified candidates and balance several factors.

1. *Organizational needs*: There might be pressing organizational needs that the hiring must meet. For example, production pressure might require a candidate who can get up to speed quickly. Or the organization might need to prioritize hiring underrepresented groups.

2. *Key qualifications*: The job specification outlines the minimum qualifications necessary for the job. Some candidate qualities will be more important than others in the performance of the job, and candidates with greater strengths in these areas might be preferable.

3. *Suitability*: Candidates need to fit into the organization's culture and environment. For example, some will function better than others in a loud, crowded workspace with a collaborative atmosphere. Similarly, some will have a working style more consistent than others with an organization's norms. That said, too much emphasis on "fit" can reinforce existing biases within the organization and cause appropriate candidates to be overlooked because they do not fit the "image" of the organization. Emphasizing fit can also result in candidates who will not challenge the dominant culture of an organization, which might not be desirable.

On this basis, an organization will make a hiring decision. The key drawback of this approach is the potential for inserting bias into the decision process. Bias can take one of two forms. First, human decision making is a complex matrix of reason and emotion. Individuals are often persuaded by factors not relevant to the decision, many of which are subconscious. These unrecognized factors can lead to incorrect weighting of qualities or to blind spots. The result can be a suboptimal decision. Second, intuitive approaches are more likely to replicate existing employment patterns in the organization. For example, similar-to-me bias and a focus on fit (see Table 6.3) can result in candidates from under-represented groups being overlooked.

To address such concerns, many organizations turn to more quantitative approaches, which can involve constructing a scoring system to apply to each candidate. The criteria for the position are listed and weighted, reflecting their importance based on the established goals. Candidates are scored based on those criteria, and those with the highest scores are selected. Some types of information are easier to score than others. Test scores are easily applied. Interview results require a bit more discretion in assigning scores. One advantage of this approach is that it forces decision makers to focus on each criterion, and a candidate's fit based on that criterion, rather than a general, overall assessment.

Table 6.5 provides a simple example of a selection score card based on the job specification for a construction labourer (road work) set out in Chapter 3 (Feature Box 3.3) and extended through Chapter 5. Those charged with selecting a candidate assign a point for each required quality for each candidate.

- The number of points available for each quality reflects its importance. For example, experience can provide a candidate with up to three points (out of a total of 10).
- The number of points scored increases with the candidate's qualifications. For example, candidates with more experience receive more points in the experience category.
- Some qualities or levels of performance are listed as automatic failures (AFs). Candidates who do not possess these qualities are automatically deemed unsuitable for the job and discarded.

Table 6.5 Sample score card

Quality	0 Points	1 Point	2 Points	3 Points
Years of experience	<1	≥1–<3	≥3–<5	≥5
Machines successfully operated	0 AF	1–2	3–4	≥5
Hand tools successfully operated	0 AF	1–2	3+	
Traffic training	No	Yes		
WHMIS training	No	Yes		
First-aid training	No	Yes		
Lift 100 pounds	No AF			
Driver's licence ≤ 3 demerits	No AF			
Suitability	No AF			
Total points				

When making multiple hires, these scores can be used in different ways. Top-down selection sees an offer made to the candidate with the highest score. Additional offers are made by working down the list until all of the positions are filled. As an alternative, an employer can adopt a banding approach, by which candidates are clustered into groups (e.g., by quartiles).

Within each quartile, the sequence of offers is made based on other, non-scored considerations. For example, if an organization wants to hire more women, offers might be made first to women in the top quartile of candidates and then to men in that quartile. A bottom-up selection can also be used, in which a minimum score is set, and candidates who fall below that score are eliminated, whereas those above that score are either selected or move on to a second step in the decision process (e.g., a second interview, consideration of other criteria, etc.).

The development of scoring criteria entails trade-offs that HR practitioners should consider. For example, in Table 6.5, having job experience is not a requirement, but it is awarded a significant number of points. Using a top-down selection approach (i.e., hiring the candidate with the most points) means that the selection system might work against younger workers or newcomers to the occupation. This kind of built-in bias might be justifiable because (at least theoretically) it reduces training costs. It is worth considering, however, whether hiring younger workers might be desirable for other reasons. An organization with an older workforce, for example, might wish to hire younger workers in order to attenuate the risk caused by many workers retiring at the same time. The extra costs associated with hiring less experienced workers might be justified in this case and warrant a reweighting of the selection scorecard in Table 6.5.

The Job Offer

It is important to move through the entire selection process quickly because candidates are likely to apply for multiple jobs, and good candidates can be snapped up quickly. For this reason, once a selection is made, usually an initial offer is made via a phone call. The call should be to the point, offering key information such as wage rate, starting date, and so forth. The candidate might request some time to consider the offer or discuss elements of it further (e.g., make a counteroffer on the wage rate). It is important for the person making the offer to know which elements are negotiable and be prepared to negotiate them, including knowing the permissible range of acceptable terms.

The phone call is usually followed with a written offer, which becomes the official offer of employment. This is not the employment contract, signed once the offer is accepted, but for both clarity and convenience the written offer should include the following elements.

- Job title
- Compensation, including bonuses
- Benefits, including items such as a moving or car allowance
- Starting date
- Probationary period
- Union membership (if applicable)
- Conditions to which the offer is subject (e.g., successful drug test, criminal record check)

It is possible that the candidate will turn down the offer. In such a case, an offer is then extended to the next most qualified candidate. For this reason, it is usually advisable to identify more than one potential hire and to hold off on notifying unsuccessful candidates until a hire is confirmed. When a candidate accepts the job offer, an organization moves to settle any outstanding conditions and prepares to finalize the employment contract and orient the new hire to the organization (see Chapter 7).

The final step of selection is to notify unsuccessful candidates. The time to do that is when the hire is finalized (i.e., the candidate has accepted and met any outstanding conditions). Typically, only those candidates interviewed or asked to take tests are contacted. The notification should be brief and polite. Unsuccessful candidates might ask why they were not chosen. The response should be honest and measured. A good strategy is to focus on the strength that distinguished the successful candidate. This approach allows for a clear indication of why the choice was made while not pointing out shortcomings of unsuccessful candidates. It is important to remember that second and third choices might be appropriate, and you might want to consider them for future openings, so maintaining a positive relationship can be advantageous.

Failed Searches

Although most selection processes result in hiring the required number of workers, sometimes a selection process does not result in a hire. A failed search happens most often when no qualified applicants applied for the job, an organization cannot make an offer that a qualified candidate will accept, or delays in or changes to a selection process render the competition moot. In some cases, especially when hiring to a position of key importance, a failed search is a better outcome than hiring someone simply to fill the position.

It is useful to identify why a search failed. This understanding can suggest ways to prevent a repeat in the future. There are several potential explanations for a lack of qualified candidates.

- There might be few potential candidates who meet the qualifications. This might require altering the job design so that more candidates are qualified or expanding the geographic scope of the recruitment effort.
- Word of the job opportunity did not reach potential applicants in time for them to apply. This might require a more extensive and/or longer recruitment effort.
- The job opportunity was not sufficiently enticing to potential applicants. This might require revisiting the compensation, duties, or working conditions of the job. It might also suggest that a review of the employer's reputation is warranted.

An organization unable to negotiate an acceptable offer might suggest that the compensation or working conditions associated with a position are not competitive. In contrast, unexpected internal changes and delays are simply a fact of life and not usually within the control of an HR practitioner.

Evaluating Selection Efforts

Evaluating the effectiveness of the selection efforts allows an organization to understand and improve its performance. An important question, though, is how to define what is effective. Simply asking "did the position get filled?" does not generate information that can be used to guide future selection efforts. It is also important to look at both the recruitment efforts (see Chapter 5) and the selection efforts. Although there is clearly overlap, they have distinct goals that should be considered separately.

To determine how to evaluate a selection process, HR practitioners should start by identifying the goals and context. Was it important to hire candidates at a low cost? Or alter the composition of the workforce in some way? Or is success about finding candidates who meet certain performance criteria? Once they know what the goals were, they can select an evaluation method that will give them the answers that they seek. Two common approaches to assessing selection are looking at the time that it took to fill a vacancy and a new hire's quality of fit.

Time lapse measures the time that it takes to fill the vacancy, including selection time. The number of days from when the postings/ads first went out to when the successful candidate accepts the job offer assesses the efficiency of the process. This measure more often examines the selection process since it is easier to control timelines on the recruitment side by establishing closing dates et cetera. Time is not always the most important factor, and for some positions slower might be better if it allows an HR practitioner to find the right person (e.g., hiring a new chief executive officer who will chart the direction of the organization). Nevertheless, this measure is useful if the concern is filling vacancies quickly to prevent downtime, reducing the need for overtime, or overworking existing employees.

Quality of fit considers post-selection outcomes of the process. Looking at turnover rates among new hires after a certain period of time, productivity of new hires, new hire job satisfaction, or other performance ratings can provide useful information about how effective the process was in finding the appropriate candidates for the vacancies. These measures require a period of time to elapse before they can be used.

In theory, an organization that seeks to increase the diversity of the candidate pool might evaluate the degree to which its selection process altered the percentage of employees from each targeted group. The data might then be compared with the demographic make-up of the organization or the labour market. In practice, collecting demographic data with which to categorize applicants can be problematic. Although candidates can be asked to self-declare whether they fit into a specific equity category, some will be reluctant to self-disclose because of fear of discrimination. Ascribing certain characteristics to candidates through observation is a fraught process and best avoided.

Organizations interested in improving their selection processes might also query candidates about their experiences with different aspects of the process (e.g., clarity of communication, timeliness of a response, perceptions of an interview). Such inquiries gather information only from candidates who moved through the selection process.

This exclusion suggests that the utility of information collected from such inquiries is limited.

Overall, evaluation of a selection process is difficult. Some metrics, such as cost and time, are easy to measure and can increase efficiency but do not speak to the effectiveness of the process. Most of the evaluation measures only indirectly address process effectiveness. Turnover and job performance speak to the success of finding employees who can do their jobs. But none of them can reveal whether the "best" candidate was hired since there is no way to measure that. In the end, selection evaluation needs to be iterative, a process of looking back and forth between the process and the outcomes and reflecting on how selection methods can be improved.

Conclusion

The controversies at the Canadian Human Rights Museum point to how inadequate hiring practices can lead to more complex problems at an organization. The poor hiring practices led to the creation of a workplace culture steeped in discrimination and unfairness. New hires perpetuated that unfairness since they were selected through a flawed process. The situation spiralled out of control, and eventually the organization was thrown into crisis. Along the way, dozens of workers were mistreated. Not all of the problems at the museum can be blamed on the hiring process, but it played a significant role.

One of the lessons from the museum vignette is that selection processes need to be carefully designed and implemented. The process of selection needs to be effective at its core function: that is, identifying candidates who are appropriate fits for the positions and organization. But it must also be fair, transparent, and accountable. Ultimately, selection is not just about finding the right candidate but also a key process in producing and reproducing a workplace environment that operates by determining who is hired and how they are hired. This means that HR practitioners responsible for selection need to be mindful of the broader context in which their decision is made.

Most of the research on selection focuses on finding workers who are the best fits for the jobs. Much less of it addresses how selection feeds into broader workplace dynamics. The good news is that it is possible to do both things. Designing a rigorous selection process that aligns with broader organizational goals will help to create a healthier workplace environment. A well-designed process of selection reduces the impact of individual bias and thus reduces the risk of replicating unhealthy workplace dynamics. And though no process can guarantee that the "best" candidate is selected, it can minimize the mistakes that lead to a "bad" candidate being selected.

EXERCISES

KEY TERMS

Define the following terms.

- Behavioural question
- Blind screening
- Candidate screening
- Cognitive ability test
- Construct validity
- Content validity
- Criminal record check
- Criterion validity
- Demonstration test
- Identity conscious screening
- In-person interview
- Interests test
- Knowledge and background question
- Medical exam
- Online interview
- Panel interview
- Personality test
- Physical ability test
- Predictive test
- Qualification check
- Quality of fit
- Reference check
- Safety-sensitive positions

- Screening interview
- Selection
- Semi-structured interview
- Sequential interview
- Short list
- Situational question
- Structured interview
- Telephone interview
- Time lapse
- Unstructured interview
- Work knowledge test
- Work sample/simulation test
- Yield rates

DISCUSSION QUESTIONS

Discuss the following questions.

- What are the goals of candidate screening?
- Why are validity, reliability, and relevance important for the selection process?
- What are the shortcomings of interviews as a selection method? How can they be overcome?
- What are the strengths and weaknesses of the different types of tests used in selection?
- Which steps can HR practitioners take to minimize the impact of unconscious bias in selection?
- Which criteria should be used to evaluate the effectiveness of a selection process?

ACTIVITY

Complete the following activity.

- Review the job requirements for the construction job profiled in Chapter 5 and in Figure 6.1. Write interview questions for a structured, one-on-one, in-person interview that will solicit pertinent information about the candidates.

SELF-REFLECTION QUESTION

Write self-reflections of 200 to 500 words on the following topics.

- Why do you think employers prefer interviews, even knowing about their shortcomings, over other selection techniques?
- In your opinion, how relevant is the information gleaned from personality, interests, and honesty tests for the selection process?
- Think about the last job interview that you participated in as a candidate. How would you describe your mental and emotional states? Were you aware of the power imbalance between you and the interviewer(s)? How did that imbalance manifest itself during the interview?

7 Orientation and Training

Organizations offer training to improve individual, group, and organizational performance. Training can improve the productivity of the workforce by introducing new methods of working or integrating new equipment. Organizations might also be legally required to perform some forms of training. As stated in Chapter 2, for example, organizations are required to provide training to workers on the safe handling of any hazardous chemical that they are required to use on the job. Finally, training can also be used to reward good workers, improve unsatisfactory performance, and build skills as part of organizational succession planning.

In practice, training is often one part of a response to an organizational problem or issue. For example, the Calgary Fire Department has been accused of long-standing and systemic racism by current and former firefighters.[1] Chris Coy, Calgary's first black firefighter, rose to the rank of captain before retiring in December 2020. He recounts hazing, social exclusion, and a culture of fear. Another firefighter described an episode 10 years earlier in which a stuffed pink panther toy was placed in a uniform belonging to a black firefighter, had shoe polish smeared on its face and hands, and was hung from a rafter in Fire Station 5. "It was a mock lynching," said Coy. "I was outraged, but the victim didn't want to do anything because he feared a backlash."

After multiple investigations, Calgary's current fire chief, Steve Dongworth, admitted that his department has a problem with racism. A part of the department's response included providing staff with inclusivity and active bystander training—in which firefighters are taught to take action in the face of behaviour that jeopardizes the health and safety of their colleagues.[2] Offering training is often an attractive solution to organizational problems because it frames the issue as a result of ignorance (rather than malice), usually among workers, and assumes that the issue can be remedied via education. It is important for HR practitioners to be mindful that focusing on the proximate (or most immediate) cause of a problem can obscure other actors and factors that contribute to the performance problem (i.e., the root cause). Failing to address root causes can mean that the performance problem persists even after the training has been completed.

There are two main approaches to training. **Off-the-job training** sees workers receive training at a place and/or time separate from their normal work, such as in a classroom during the work day or online after work has ended. Off-the-job training often entails formal instruction in a classroom setting and remains the most commonly offered type of training in Canada.[3] Self-paced online training is a close second. Workers can also receive **on-the-job training**, often provided at their workstations by their supervisors or co-workers. For example, new workers often learn how to do tasks through on-the-job training. Job rotations and apprenticeships are other forms of on-the-job training (the latter being supplemented by formal classroom instruction). Workers can also engage in self-directed, on-the-job training as they identify gaps in their knowledge, skills, and abilities while doing work and then take action to address these gaps.

In this chapter, we introduce the key steps in developing training for workers. This approach is based on the **instructional systems design model** *(ISD)* of training and development. This model is outlined in Figure 7.1 and begins with conducting a needs assessment to find out who needs what training. Subsequently, during the design phase, the training objectives, content, and methods are determined. Then it is necessary to determine how an organization will assess whether or not the training was

Figure 7.1 Instructional systems design model

effective. In this chapter, we will also consider the application of training by workers to their jobs (called the transfer of training) and how to assess an organization's return on investment from training. Finally, we discuss new worker orientation and career development.

Feature Box 7.1 The Role of the State in Training

Workers do not arrive in the workplace as blank slates. Rather, they bring with them KSAs that they have accumulated during their lives. Their prior experiences include education and training provided by the state. State-based training serves two important roles. First, it provides basic skills. Consider your own experience in the K–12 system. A key outcome for most students is the development of basic literacy and numeracy skills. These skills often form the basic building blocks for subsequent job-related KSAs. The K–12 system is almost exclusively funded by the state in Canada, and each province and territory will have developed a comprehensive curriculum that students are expected to master.

Workers might also have completed some postsecondary training, usually funded partially by the state. Postsecondary training often develops or expands occupationally useful skills. The public postsecondary system includes colleges, universities, and technical schools that deliver programs leading to certificates, diplomas, degrees, and trade qualifications. Workers can also pursue formal education at private career colleges.[4]

Although the development of employment-related KSAs is an important function of state-funded training, this training also entails the inculcation of certain values and beliefs in students that are useful to employers. This is the second role of state-based training. These KSAs are often called the **hidden curriculum** of education. The term *hidden* can be a bit misleading. This process is not hidden in the sense that it is a secret conspiracy. Rather, this curriculum is hidden in plain sight because it is the accepted norm.[5]

Think back to your own K–12 experience. It likely entailed attending a school five days a week for seven hours a day. In the classroom, the teacher determined what happened, for how long, and what behaviour was acceptable. Students were rewarded for carefully following directions and punished for disrupting the work of others. Punishment was applied via social pressure, loss of privileges, suspension, and expulsion. Your performance was periodically assessed using assignments and tests, although you might have noticed that some students—perhaps those deemed "good" (by virtue of their behaviour or because they belonged to a particular identity group)—often received better grades than students deemed "bad," regardless of their respective performances.

These structures and processes closely mirror those of a traditional workplace. In this way, the school system teaches future workers that they must be punctual, obedient, and diligent—characteristics that most employers desire in workers. The K–12 system also teaches students to expect limited discretion in what they do during the day and when and how they do it. Students learn that deviations from the "rules" will result in punishment. They also learn that who they are can affect how they are treated and that their gender, heritage, and class can affect what they can expect in life.[6] The lengthy process of **acculturation** that students face normalizes employers' authority in the workplace, including their "right" to determine what training is required, who should receive it, and how it should be delivered.

Needs Assessment

A **needs assessment** (sometimes called a needs analysis) is the process of identifying gaps between desired and actual worker or organizational performance. During this process, HR practitioners also decide which gaps can be addressed by training and how to prioritize them. The needs assessment process is fairly straightforward and set out in Figure 7.2. HR practitioners first identify a concern, usually a gap between the desired performance and the actual performance.

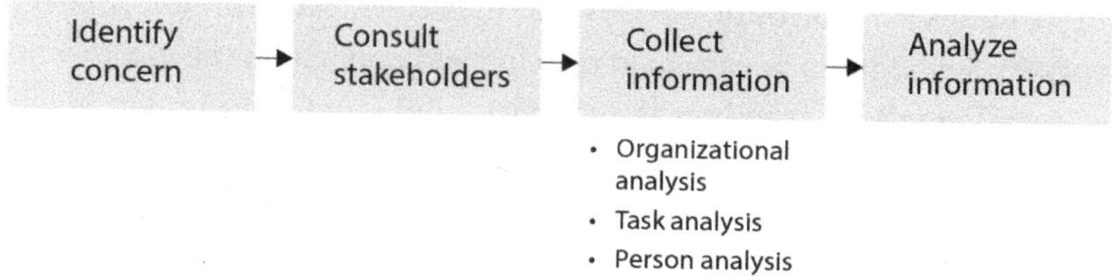

Figure 7.2 Needs assessment process

Concerns are often identified through routine monitoring of worker or organizational performance (e.g., increasing defect rate, loss of revenue, growing worker discord). At other times, concerns surface as a result of specific events, such as the allegations of racism in the opening vignette or a regulatory change.

Once a concern is identified, it is often useful to discuss it with those affected by or knowledgeable about it. Internal stakeholders can include workers, supervisors, and managers, and external stakeholders can include customers, clients, or regulators. This discussion can help to flesh out the nature of the performance gap as well as its potential organizational consequences. Discussing a concern with stakeholders can also be an important way to generate support within the organization for the eventual training intervention. At this point, an organization can sometimes conclude either that the concern is not worth addressing (e.g., the cost of training would exceed the value realized by improved performance) or that training would not be an appropriate intervention.

If an organization decides to proceed with the needs assessment, then it collects three different kinds of information to understand or flesh out the problem further. An **organizational analysis** examines an organization's strategy, environment, resources, and context to determine whether or not training is needed to help the organization achieve its goals. Training should be aligned with and help to advance an organization's business strategy and goals. Environmental factors (e.g., competitors, market or technological changes, economic factors, regulatory changes) can affect the need for and utility of training. Organizational resources (i.e., time, money, internal expertise, political will) shape an organization's ability to design and deliver training. Finally, the organizational context, such as the attitudes and norms of workers and managers, can profoundly affect workers' willingness to engage in training and apply it on the job.

A **task analysis** examines the job tasks and conditions under which they are performed to determine which knowledge, skills, or abilities are required to perform a job effectively. Ideally, an organization will have up-to-date job descriptions and specifications that can be used to consider the importance, frequency, and difficulty of each task that a worker must do. This analysis of tasks can identify and prioritize topics to address in training and can be supplemented through discussion with knowledgeable informants or other members. Table 7.1 provides a list of needs assessment techniques. Obtaining feedback on a task analysis can also be a way to generate support for the eventual training intervention.

Table 7.1 Needs assessment techniques

Technique	Process	Considerations
Observation	Observation can be structured (e.g., time-motion or behavioural frequency studies) or unstructured (e.g., informal walk-throughs).	Observation can be low cost and offer highly relevant information about performance in the workplace. Observers often must be knowledgeable about the work that they are observing to make accurate judgments. Workers can alter their behaviour while being observed (observer effect).
Surveys	Written questionnaires can ask respondents to report behaviours, beliefs, concerns, and suggestions. Different questionnaires can be used for different groups.	Questionnaires are inexpensive and quick to administer and, if anonymous, can offer candid information. Depending on the nature of the questions, the results can also be easily tabulated. Formulating valid questions can be a difficult process. Response rates are often low, so the results might not be reliable. Questionnaires might not be the best way to get at causes or solutions. Respondents might experience recall error, which can compromise validity.

Technique	Process	Considerations
Interviews	We can speak individually and directly with those who have knowledge of an issue. This can be an open-ended conversation or entail a set of scripted questions. It is also possible to facilitate group discussions about issues (e.g., a focus group).	Interviews can provide opportunities to probe for causes and solutions. Often they will generate a more nuanced understanding of an issue. Interviews can also help to build support for the eventual solution. They are time consuming to perform and analyze. Strong personalities or organizationally powerful individuals can skew the results, particularly in a group setting.
Tests and work samples	Tests can be administered to generate quantitative data on proficiency and the presence of knowledge, skills, and abilities. Work samples can also be assessed to provide insight into the same factors.	Tests and work samples are good at identifying gaps in performance but less useful in identifying solutions. They are most effective when the desired performance is easy to identify or quantify. Testing can be expensive and does not necessarily reflect real-world behaviour. Where available, work samples can reduce these challenges.
Documentary review	Organizational documents can be easily accessible sources of information about performance. They include plans, manuals, reports, job descriptions and specifications, employee records, memos, and minutes. Other documents that can have value include research reports, industry journals, regulations, and best practices documents.	Documents can be easy to access, identify expected outcomes, and offer useful examples of what other organizations have done in response to similar performance gaps. Documents might not be helpful in identifying the causes of performance issues in a specific workplace.

A **person analysis** identifies who needs to be trained. It requires studying who performs tasks related to the performance issue and how well their actual performance matches the desired performance. This entails identifying desired performance, assessing the gap between it and actual performance, and identifying barriers that the worker encounters in trying to meet desired performance. Considering the barriers to performance can help HR practitioners to understand whether training is an appropriate response (e.g., when there is a knowledge or skill gap) or whether some other intervention might be more effective, such as redesigning the job or the reward structure, supplying needed tools or equipment, or discipline or dismissal.

The outcome of a needs assessment is information that lets an organization plan an effective training program. For example, such an assessment identifies which performance gaps exist and how they might be resolved through training. It identifies where in an organization training is required, what kind of training is needed, and who requires the training. Finally, it provides the information required for an HR practitioner to write training objectives and to develop techniques to assess whether the training was effective. Typically, training is the best solution when the following conditions are met.

- The task is difficult and performed frequently.
- Correct performance is critical to meeting organizational goals.
- Performance expectations are clear, with an appropriate reward structure.
- The employee does not know how to do the work.
- Other solutions (e.g., coaching, discipline) are not effective and/or are not cost effective.[7]

Organizations can be reluctant to conduct a needs assessment given the cost, both in time and in money. Sometimes problems can be (or appear to be) so pressing that immediate action might be required. For example, organizational leaders might respond to bad publicity about a sexual harassment complaint by mandating organization-wide training, even though the problem might be resolved more effectively through the discipline process (see Chapter 9). If organizational leaders have already diagnosed the problem(s) and prescribed solution(s), then they might be reluctant to have their decisions questioned and possibly overturned. When circumstances prevent a full needs assessment, an expedited assessment focused on identifying training objectives can still be better than nothing.

Designing Training Programs

Designing a training program generally begins with the development of one or more training objectives. The objectives shape the training content and methods likely to be the most appropriate. A **training objective** specifies what workers are expected to be able to do after the training is over. Training objectives are typically derived from the needs analysis and have three components.

- *Performance*: What behaviour will the worker display after training?
- *Circumstances*: Which tools will workers use, and under what time constraints and conditions will they be expected to display the behaviour?
- *Criterion*: What is the acceptable level of performance?

Table 7.2 contains some examples of training objectives. They are broken down into three parts to illustrate each component.

Table 7.2 Sample training objectives

Performance	Circumstances	Criterion
Clerks will keyboard	at a rate of 65 words per minute	with 99% accuracy.
First responders will control active bleeding of patients	in the field using a pressure bandage	within two minutes.
Staff assessing mortgage applications	shall calculate monthly payments	with 100% accuracy.
Policy analysts will assess incoming correspondence to	identify key issues requiring a response	within one hour of receipt of the correspondence with 95% accuracy.

The workers displaying the behaviour can be a category of workers (e.g., all front-line staff) or persons performing a specific job task (e.g., anyone operating a vehicle). It is often worthwhile considering how and when an organization will evaluate whether or not a worker is meeting the criterion. Sometimes testing is effective (e.g., keyboarding), whereas other times observation on the job is more practical (e.g., speed of controlling bleeding). If mastering the behaviour can take some practice, then it might make sense to delay evaluation to allow for practice. If there is concern that the worker might stop demonstrating the behaviour over time, then periodic testing or observation might be appropriate. Training booster sessions can also be used.

Once training objectives have been established, HR practitioners must identify the specific training content that workers must learn in order to meet the objectives. This is often expressed as an answer to the question "what is to be learned?" The needs assessment can offer useful guidance in identifying specific KSAs that must be taught. Other sources of information, such as job descriptions or specifications or equipment manuals, can identify a particular performance and level of skill required. These sources, in turn, help HR practitioners to determine the training content required.

Determining that content can help HR practitioners to grapple with the question of whether to develop training in-house or purchase training from external providers. Purchasing training can include acquiring access to existing classroom or online training (e.g., courses provided by a local college) or contracting with a provider to develop and/or deliver on-site training. Organizations might choose to outsource training to reduce the cost and time required to develop training as well as to access expertise and resources not available in-house. The advantages of in-house training include greater control of the content (e.g., using organizational terminology and values), a lower long-term cost (because the organization owns the training materials), and trainers who have a better understanding of the audience and the organizational context.

Once the training content has been identified, HR practitioners must select the method(s) by which they will deliver it. Table 7.3 summarizes common training delivery methods. Some methods can be delivered on- or off-site, whereas others might require access to specific equipment. It is common to use more than one training method to deliver material to maximize learning and retention.

Table 7.3 Training delivery methods

Method	Summary
Lecture	• A lecture is primarily a one-way method of conveying information. Lectures can take place face-to-face, such as in a classroom. They can also take place online, whether live or prerecorded. Written training material (whether on paper or online) that students work through on their own is another form of one-way communication. • Lectures are effective in conveying large amounts of information at low costs. They are not generally effective in developing skills or changing attitudes. Lack of retention and "information overload" can be issues. Short lectures can be effective when combined with other, more active, delivery techniques.
Interactive	• Interactive training—whether in-person or online—allows back-and-forth communication between trainer and trainees and possibly among trainees. This approach can engage trainees, provide opportunities for questions, and build group consensus. • Interactive training tends to be more expensive than lectures because fewer people can be accommodated effectively in a single class or session, and it can take more time to move through content. Trainers must also be prepared to manage participants.
Behaviour modelling	• **Behaviour-modelling training** (BMT) sees a trainer demonstrate how to perform a task. Trainees are then given an opportunity to imitate the trainer and provided with feedback to improve their performance. BMT can be effective in teaching interpersonal and motor skills. This can occur in a classroom or on the job. A variant of BMT is coaching (or mentoring), in which a more experienced person provides advice and assistance on a one-on-one basis. Coaching can take place in a formal framework with a clear plan. Alternatively, it can occur casually in the workplace. Sometimes coaching occurs in the context of performance management (see Chapter 9). • When BMT occurs on the job, it is sometimes called job-instructed training. Many of us have likely experienced a supervisor or knowledgeable co-worker who has shown us how to do different parts of a job when we first start. Employers can also use job-instructed training when workers are cross-trained through a job-rotation system. Feature Box 7.2 discusses job rotation in greater detail.

(*continued*)

Table 7.3 Training delivery methods (*continued*)

Method	Summary
Case study	• Case studies ask trainees to discuss, analyze, and solve problems based on realistic examples. Case studies are typically more engaging than lectures. Their primary use is helping trainees to develop and integrate analytical and problem-solving skills in a real-world context. • Case studies can be time consuming to prepare, and trainees need adequate time to process the information and then work through the cases. Shorter cases (sometimes called *case incidents*) can be used to illustrate a specific problem or apply specific knowledge or skills.
Role playing and simulation	• Role playing sees trainees practice new behaviours in safe environments. After role playing, they have an opportunity to debrief their experience and consider how they might improve their performance in the future. Role playing can be an effective way to develop interpersonal skills and change attitudes. • A simulation is a more complex and lengthier form of role playing. Simulations can be conducted with a group of people (e.g., a collective bargaining simulation) or be computer-mediated training (e.g., a flight simulator). Simulations are typically expensive to develop and operate but provide trainees with realistic opportunities to practice skills.
Performance aids	• A performance aid assists workers to do a job correctly. Worksite signage is a common example, such as a set of procedures posted on the wall by a machine or reminders to wash one's hands before handling food. Performance aids can reinforce training and help training transfer (see below). • A performance aid is typically designed to reduce the cognitive load on a worker (i.e., having to remember the steps and sequence). This approach to training is particularly effective when a performance is infrequent, important, and complex and can be done slowly enough that the worker can refer to the aid. Over time, aids can lose their effectiveness if they are static, for they become too familiar, and workers stop "seeing" them.

The most important consideration in selecting a training method is its alignment with the training objective and content. For example, if an organization wants workers to apply specific manual skills to their jobs, then the method of delivery likely needs to include an opportunity for workers physically to practice and master those skills. In this case, hands-on training or a simulation might be more effective than watching a video of someone else perform the skill. That said, a video might be an effective way to impart basic information at the start of training on what workers will be able to do by the end of training. Other factors that can help us to decide which method of delivery is most appropriate or practical include the following.

- *Cost*: The organizational resources (time and money) available and the expected return on investment (see below) place limits on the methods that can be selected.
- *Trainer preference*: Trainers might have clear preferences for and/or limited repertoires of training techniques, which can shape the methods that they can use.
- *Trainee preference*: Workers might also have clear preferences for how training is conducted. Workers' skills and abilities can also shape which methods are viable.

Trainee characteristics might also be important to consider when selecting who should participate in training. Sometimes trainees might already possess some of the KSAs that the training seeks to impart. In these cases, it is possible to truncate (or enrich) the training. Other times adults might not have the foundational skills (e.g., literacy or numeracy) required to be successful in the training and can benefit from preparatory work first. Assessing trainee readiness is one way to enhance the success of training. Organizations can also provide slightly different training to different categories of workers. For example, in a large organization, workers might receive training different from that of supervisors.

Feature Box 7.2 The Politics of Job Rotation and Cross-Training

One way that employers can expand workers' skills is through **job rotation**. It entails shifting a worker between two (or more) different positions or jobs such that the worker is eventually able to perform both. In addition to building workers' skills, job rotation can be used to improve morale and engagement by offering workers variety in the tasks that they do. As noted in Table 7.3, job rotation can be one form of job-instructed training.

Job rotation is sometimes associated with **cross-training**. It entails a worker acquiring KSAs associated with a different job. Cross-trained workers can undertake job rotation (i.e., performing the other job), or they can use acquired KSAs to perform their base positions better. For example, construction workers might acquire some of the KSAs associated with a site foreperson so that they can serve as lead hands (i.e., a carpenter who also organizes work on the job site). Understanding the lead hand job, in turn, might cause them to think and act differently (e.g., how they sequence tasks and use materials) when doing carpentry tasks.

Job rotation is most effective when there is a clear plan in place to which both the workers and the supervisor agree. Organizations can see job rotation as a way to reduce the risk of being caught short-handed because of illness, resignation, or sudden growth. The potential downsides of job rotation include workers who develop broad, but shallow, skill sets (i.e., a jack-of-all-trades is a master of none) and workers who feel a reduced sense of ownership of a specific job or task (thus becoming more likely to let problems slide).

Workers can have mixed views about job rotation. Some will be interested in expanding their KSAs to increase their job security or marketability. Others might appreciate some variety in their day-to-day work. That said, workers who have highly specialized knowledge or skills might be uninterested in job rotation because other workers with this knowledge or these skills can reduce their job security and power.

Workers can also worry that cross-training will allow their employers to increase the intensity of their work. For example, an employer might add tasks to a worker's duties when the worker develops new skills, causing the worker to work harder. If there is no change in the absolute level of work that needs to be done, then this sort of redistribution can also result in the employer needing fewer workers.

This analysis again draws our attention to the differing interests of employers and workers as well as differences in interest among workers. Accounting for workers' interests and getting their "buy-in" when considering the implementation of training programs (e.g., job rotation) will increase the likelihood that workers will engage fully in the training, and the organization can realize the full value of that training.

An important consideration in selecting a training method is that workers tend to learn more quickly and retain training longer if they have an opportunity to use the training content as part of the training.[8] This approach is called **active practice** and makes a certain amount of sense if we think back, for example, to our own experiences learning to drive a car. It is certainly possible to explain how to drive in a classroom lecture (a good way to start). But the opportunity to practice driving is essential to understanding how to apply that knowledge and for application of that knowledge to become habitual and automatic. Feature Box 7.3 outlines 10 ways that training can be organized to improve its effectiveness.

Feature Box 7.3 Conditions of Practice

The effectiveness of active training suggests that HR practitioners can organize training in ways that enhance workers' learning. These **conditions of practice** are steps that can be taken before training begins as well as techniques that can be used during training to maximize learning and retention.

Pre-training interventions include the following.

- Preparatory information provides trainees with base knowledge and an overview of the training to reduce stress and in order to prepare themselves.
- Goal setting by trainees ahead of training can increase both their investment in the training and their focus during it.
- Advance organizers provide trainees with a structure into which they can organize the information that they learn in training.
- Attentional advice identifies for learners ahead of training which aspects of the training are the most important to pay attention to and incorporate into their existing knowledge and skill sets. This activity can also happen during training.
- Metacognitive strategies (thinking about how one learns) introduced before the training begins can help trainees to evaluate their progress and improve their performance during training.

Interventions during training include the following.

- Part learning breaks down a complex performance so that trainees can master each component before integrating it into a whole performance.
- Task sequencing refers to teaching the parts of a performance in the sequence in which they will occur in the workplace to help learners relate the steps to one another.

- Practice with training content tends to be most effective when spread over time, such that workers have time to absorb and integrate the content.
- Feedback during training provides trainees with opportunities to correct errors, builds confidence, and maintains engagement.
- Overlearning content enables a performance to become automatic. Overlearning requires practice during and after training. It might be appropriate for tasks that workers must perform often and in which automatic performance yields significant gains in productivity. Overlearning is also appropriate when workers are learning content that they will not use very often but must execute perfectly when used (e.g., emergency procedures).

The conditions of practice implemented before and during training interact with the degree of active practice and the desired training outcomes. For example, if an organization wants trainees to be able to perform what they have learned in settings similar to the training setting (called possessing **routine expertise**), then it might use fewer conditions of practice and fewer active learning methods. This is because the expected performance does not require learners to be able to adapt their performance much. If, conversely, an organization wants trainees to be able to apply their training in diverse settings and circumstances (called possessing **adaptative expertise**), then it might wish to incorporate more conditions of learning as well as active practice. This can include allowing trainees to make mistakes so that they can understand why it is important to perform tasks in certain ways.

Delivering Training

Once training objectives and methods have been determined, the next step is to develop a lesson plan. A **lesson** is a cohesive unit of instruction with specific training objectives. A **lesson plan** outlines the sequence of events that will take place during the lesson. Developing a lesson plan is an opportunity both to nail down all of the details of the training and to work through how each event in the training contributes to achieving the training objective and is related to the other events. Typically, a lesson plan will include

- the training objective(s);
- when and where the training will take place;
- any materials, equipment, or supplies required; and
- an outline of events with an approximate time allocation for each event.

Achieving a training objective often requires several events to occur. For example, it might be necessary to introduce some concepts (short lecture), consider how they might be relevant to the training objective (group discussion), show trainees how to apply the concepts (demonstration), and then allow the trainees to practice applying the concepts (role playing and feedback). When reviewing the lesson plan, it can be useful to apply Robert Gagne's checklist of nine events of instruction that help learning to take place.

1. Gain trainees' attention by telling them why the training matters.
2. Describe the objectives of the training so they can relate it to their jobs.
3. Stimulate recall of prior knowledge to help trainees integrate training.
4. Present the material to be learned.
5. Provide trainees with guidance about how best to learn the material.
6. Give trainees the opportunity to practice with the training content.
7. Provide informative feedback to improve trainees' performance.
8. Assess trainees' performance to see if training objectives have been met.
9. Assist in transferring training to the workplace.[9]

The last two instructional events (assessing performance and training transfer) are discussed below.

Feature Box 7.4 Diversity, Equity, and Inclusion Training

Historically, organizations have responded to societal changes through training. For example, growing awareness of gender inequity in the 1980s and 1990s led organizations to offer training designed to reduce sexual harassment and gender discrimination more broadly. Recent attention to the inequitable treatment of people on the basis of their gender, ethnoracial background, sexual orientation, or disability have resulted predictably in an increase in training that deal with issues of equity, diversity, and inclusion (EDI) to address the systemic roots of inequities in organizations.

EDI training is most effective in altering participants' thinking, beliefs, behaviour, and skills when it targets both awareness and skill development, is substantial and conducted over a period of time, is mandatory, and is linked to other diversity initiatives, such as a cohesive strategy leading to broader organizational change.[10] The presence (or absence) of these characteristics is thought to reflect the underlying degree of management's commitment to EDI. These factors are also often absent in EDI training initiatives.

One of the issues facing HR practitioners tasked with implementing EDI training is that EDI challenge powerful social narratives. For example, embedded in most people's beliefs about education and employment is the view that hard work and ability are rewarded (see Feature Box 7.1). The idea that society is a meritocracy—that our success in life is based on our efforts and skills—is deeply embedded in the psyches of many people. Yet the analysis of intersecting identity factors in Feature Box 1.1 highlights that such factors (which have nothing to do with ability or work ethic) play profound roles in the level of success that individuals achieve.

Grappling with the idea that career success is driven, at least in part, by factors beyond anyone's control can be very threatening to people's conceptions of themselves and their understandings of the world. Suggesting alterations to long-standing organizational practices (e.g., the criteria for hiring, promotion, and compensation) in the name of increased equity can turn this relatively abstract threat to people's self-conceptions and worldviews into an immediate and concrete threat to the financial and career interests of those who have benefited from the existing system. The resulting anxiety and anger are often difficult for workers to get past.

So why do organizations use training to address complex issues such as this? One explanation is that potentially profound organizational change requires workers to change their attitudes, beliefs, and behaviours. Earnest and thoughtful training is an effective way that organizations can prompt and guide that process of change. A less charitable explanation is that training can sometimes be a performative response to pressure. That is, organizations might wish to be seen as responsive to EDI issues but not incur the organizational costs of serious reforms. Short-lived, one-off training can create the appearance of action and shift responsibility for change onto individuals, yet it is ineffective in generating lasting changes in organizational cultures.

Evaluating Training

Organizations spend a significant amount of money providing training. Not surprisingly, an organization might want to know the outcome of the training. Some organizations also might want to know whether the benefits of the training outweigh the costs of providing it. In this section, we discuss **training evaluation**—the process of assessing the outcome of training for workers and organizations.

There are different approaches to evaluating training. An organization can collect data to improve training or to assess the value or outcome of training. Evaluations can also be descriptive (i.e., have trainees learned the material?) or causal (i.e., did the training cause a change in behaviour?). Organizations can also collect data on trainees' perceptions, changes in their KSAs, the rate at which training is applied on the job, or the effect of the training on organizational outcomes.

The decision-based evaluation model asserts that evaluators should select which aspects of training to measure and how to measure outcomes based on the purpose for which they will use the results.[11] This requires training evaluators to know why they are conducting an evaluation. For example, if the purpose of training is to justify the expenditure on training in terms of organizational outcomes, then there is little sense in measuring trainees' reactions. Conversely, measuring the application of training on the job might be of little interest if we're focused on determining whether specific instructional methods result in an improvement in trainees' KSAs. This knowledge helps evaluators to select what to measure and how to measure it. Decision-based evaluation also suggests that evaluators understand the barriers to evaluation (see Feature Box 7.5), which can pose practical constraints on what is possible.

Feature Box 7.5 Barriers to Evaluation

Many organizations evaluate workers' reactions to training and the learning that has taken place. Relatively few organizations assess whether workers apply training on the job or whether the training results in improved organizational performance.[12] There are numerous barriers to such evaluation.

Evaluating the impact of training on organizational performance is a complex undertaking. It requires us to understand both how an individual's work relates to organizational goals and how training shapes the individual's performance. For example, an organization might be concerned about the rate of manufacturing defects in a product. If the organization can identify the frequency with which a worker (or group of workers) makes an error and can monitor this frequency after a training intervention, then it might be possible to assess broadly whether the training was an effective intervention. If it is possible to ascribe a cost to each error, then it might also be possible to calculate the value of the training and compare it with the costs of the training (see below).

It is uncommon for organizations to have such a clear indication of how training can affect organizational outcomes. Furthermore, such evaluation entails additional organizational costs (time and money). Workers can also be reluctant to have their performance evaluated because they fear consequences. Finally, it can be difficult to isolate a performance from other contextual factors such that an organization can be confident that the assessment has measured the training effect. Other changes in the environment (e.g., new supervisors, changes in seasons) can affect performance in ways that can be hard to control for.

There can also be resistance to evaluation by trainers. They might worry that the barriers above will make it difficult methodologically to establish whether their training has had an effect. And, if the evaluation shows few, no, or negative impacts, then trainers (also workers themselves) might worry about their future employment.

A number of different variables can be measured when evaluating a training program.

- *Reactions*: Trainees' opinions on facilitation, training techniques, materials, course structure, assessment process, and utility of training can be measured to guide changes to future training sessions. Reactions are often measured with questionnaires.
- *Learning*: What trainees learned in training can be measured using a pre-test and a post-test, with the difference in KSAs being attributed to the training.
- *Behaviour*: Changes in an individual's behaviour can be measured through self-reports, observing trainees on the job, or monitoring work behaviour (e.g., absenteeism or defect rates).
- *Results*: These are measures of the impact of training on organizational performance. They can include tracking changes in cost, production, quality, and speed. As noted in Feature Box 7.5, given the many factors that can affect these indicators, it is important to be cautious about inferring causality (i.e., that training caused the changes). It might be necessary to adopt more complex data collection designs to control for other factors. It might also be worthwhile to measure changes over time to see whether the effect of training persists.

If an organization wants to calculate the **return on investment** (ROI) in training, then it needs to determine the monetary cost of the training as well as the value of its results. Training costs can include

- direct costs, such as the trainer's salary, equipment rentals, material costs, catering and travel costs;
- indirect costs, such as a portion of the administrative costs of running a training function;
- developmental costs associated with creating or purchasing the training content; and
- trainee-related costs, such as the costs of wages that must be paid when staff are training.

Calculating the financial benefits of training can be trickier. It can be hard to quantify reductions in costs or increases in revenues directly caused by the training. And sometimes the value of a benefit is in dispute, so someone has to decide what number to use. This can reduce the validity of the estimate of benefits. Assuming that an organization has satisfactory estimates of training costs and benefits, it can calculate the ROI using this formula:

$$\text{Return on investment} = \frac{\text{Benefits} - \text{Costs}}{\text{Costs}}$$

If the ROI is greater than 1, then there was a net benefit from the training. That is because, for every dollar spent, the organization yielded some amount greater than one dollar in return. If the ROI is less than 1, then there was no net benefit from the training. Some benefit might have been provided, but it was outweighed by the costs. In calculating an ROI, it is important to remember that there can also be non-monetary benefits to training, such as improved morale or greater staff retention, which are difficult to quantify and that ROI is only one metric for evaluating the effectiveness of training.

Training Transfer

Training transfer is the application of KSAs acquired during training on the job over time. It is important to pay attention to training transfer because not every trainee will necessarily apply the training when they return to their normal duties. There are numerous barriers to training transfer, including lack of opportunity to use new skills and limited support for doing so. Training transfer can be maximized by ensuring that workers have immediate and frequent opportunities to apply their training and support from their supervisors to do so. If workers are reluctant to apply their training, then an organization might develop a performance-management plan (see Chapter 9) that identifies expected behaviours or outcomes and periodically assesses them.

Training transfer can also diminish over time. This can reflect workers who forget training or fall back into old routines. It can also be a function of organizational factors (e.g., workload or lack of support) pressuring workers to adopt different behaviour (e.g., taking shortcuts). Where a relapse reflects workers who forget what they learned, booster training or the addition of performance aids can address the problem. If there are structural pressures that cause workers not to use their training, then identifying and remedying them are likely to be more effective in ensuring training transfer than is attempting to alter the workers' behaviour and requiring retraining.

Orientation

A common form of training that most workers experience is **orientation**. It familiarizes new workers with their duties, organizational expectations and processes, and co-workers. The organizational purpose of an orientation is to minimize the time that it takes for a worker to begin making a contribution, to inculcate organization-specific knowledge and values, to comply with regulatory requirements (e.g., telling workers about workplace hazards and controls), and to ensure that the organizational investment made to hire the employee is not lost because of attrition.[13]

Orientations can take different forms. They can be formal and standardized. They often include

- an introduction to co-workers;
- an outline of expectations regarding attendance, comportment, and dress;
- an explanation of job duties, standards, and how the worker will be evaluated;
- a discussion of compensation, benefits, and other HR-related matters;
- a health-and-safety orientation; and
- an overview of the organization, its purposes, and its key activities.

Orientations can also be protracted. For example, they can involve a series of events over the first few days, weeks, and months of employment, timed to provide new workers with information as it becomes important and needed. Orientations can also be very informal, with a supervisor or co-worker making introductions, showing a new employee the ropes, and answering questions.

When an organization does not provide new workers with an orientation, they will still learn about their jobs and the organization. The risk here is that what workers might learn can be undesirable from the perspective of the organization. There is no way, of course, for an organization to prevent workers from learning whatever they wish. After all, they have both agency and an interest in getting the lay of the land (e.g., How long is a coffee break? Whom should I never be alone with in a room? Is anyone actually checking when I come and go?). But providing an orientation is an important way for an organization to shape how new employees see their work and their roles.

Recently, some organizations have developed **onboarding** processes. Onboarding is a systematic effort to socialize employees so that they integrate more fully into and identify with the organization to reduce attrition. Onboarding can include pre-arrival information to help new workers understand their work and workplace and to answer basic questions. This can include brief introductions to co-workers, tours of the workplace, or a pre-arrival mentoring program. Upon an employee's arrival, onboarding can include a personalized welcome, with a workspace ready for the employee, a planned orientation, and someone designated to address questions.[14] The research on onboarding suggests that the most significant increases in organizational commitment and job satisfaction are associated with onboarding activities that allow new workers to develop formal and informal relationships within the organization.[15] Sometimes, though, what organizations call onboarding is simply a trendy renaming of traditional orientation activities.

Career Development

Some organizations use systematic training to develop the skills of existing workers in order to shape their development in a specific way. This approach to employee development can be part of an organization's HR strategy (see Chapter 4) and be designed to meet expected labour demand through internal recruiting and succession planning (see Chapter 5). **Career development** efforts can be formal or informal arrangements. For example, in a smaller organization, a manager might identify a high-performing worker for additional training and mentoring to ready that worker for an expected vacancy. A larger organization might have clearly developed hierarchies of jobs that workers can expect to progress through as their KSAs become broader and/or deeper. This progression of jobs can create a **career path** within an organization. A career path can include lateral moves within an organization designed to broaden a worker's experience by exposing that worker to different organizational areas or functions as well as to assist them in developing a network of relationships throughout the organization. It can also include vertical moves upward as a worker earns promotions.

As noted in Chapter 1, there has been an increase in precarious employment in Canada over time. In thinking about the impact of growing employment precarity on organizations' willingness to invest in career development, it is useful to remember that not every worker experiences increasing precarity. Rather, growing precarity often masks the development of a **dual labour market**, in which some workers continue to have well-paying, secure work with benefits. The wages and working conditions of those workers with "good jobs" might be subsidized by workers with "bad jobs" (i.e., low wages, no benefits, high insecurity). Organizations can still see value in providing career development for workers in the primary labour market, on whom organizations might rely for leadership and stability. Organizations, however, might be less inclined to invest in workers in the secondary labour market because they do not expect to recoup the costs of training workers whom they expect to be in the organization for a short time.

Conclusion

The purpose of training is to improve organizational performance. Training does this by enabling workers to behave differently. This includes developing their KSAs and assisting them to change their behaviours. Training is most effective when some sort of knowledge or skills gap is an important factor in whatever is degrading organizational performance. If other factors are (also) at work, then training might not be the best or sole way to address the performance issue. Solving complex problems can require an organization to re-examine how work is designed (Chapter 3), how staff are hired (Chapters 5 and 6), and how performance is managed (Chapter 9).

Think again of the opening vignette and the racism identified in the Calgary Fire Department, which has provided staff with inclusivity and active bystander training, in which firefighters are taught to take action in the face of behaviour that jeopardizes the health and safety of their colleagues. This approach frames racism as a result of ignorance (rather than malice), usually among workers, and assumes that the issue can be remedied via education. A group of active and retired firefighters publicly called for the department to offer a more comprehensive response that includes

- public acknowledgement of the existence and severity of the toxic workplace culture;
- a public inquiry into job-related suicides;
- recognition of PTSD caused by workplace abuse;
- an independent investigation of workplace abuses;
- a revised process of promotion;
- representative hiring and promotion committees;
- anti-racism training delivered by experts with lived experiences;
- a zero-tolerance standard for racism, bullying, harassment, assault, or toxic behaviour in the workplace; and
- official recognition of BIPOC and female trailblazers.

This list of actions reflects the belief that training can be a part of an organizational response to a problem but, on its own, might be insufficient. The reaction from the Calgary Fire Department to the group's recommendations reflects that organizations often make trade-offs when considering how to respond. "In fairness, some of those are things we're already doing," Fire Chief Steve Dongworth said. "But we will take a close look at those nine recommendations. Where they're practical and aligned with our approach, we'll move those forward."[16]

Although it is not clear what the Calgary Fire Department considers when it assesses whether a recommendation is practical and aligned with its approach, it is possible to make some guesses. The costs of adopting recommendations are likely a factor. There can be direct costs associated with providing independent investigations or recognizing trailblazing firefighters. But likely there are also indirect costs. They can include reputational costs if investigations of racism and work-related suicide reveal further racism that, in turn, can cause increased turnover among existing staff and difficulty recruiting new staff. Altering processes of hiring and promoting can also require ceding power to traditionally marginalized groups, which can be organizationally complicated and fraught.

The point of this analysis is that training, though often presented as a technical process (see Figures 7.1 and 7.2), is also a deeply political one. Someone (usually the employer) selects who gets what training. When the training is done, that person can compel the trainees to exhibit the desired behaviours and, if desired, attach rewards or penalties to those behaviours. And, as demonstrated by the opening vignette, training can be used to defuse demands for deeper structural change by framing outcomes as the products of workers.

EXERCISES

KEY TERMS

Define the following terms.

- Acculturation
- Active practice
- Adaptative expertise
- Behaviour-modelling training
- Career development
- Career path
- Conditions of practice
- Cross-training
- Dual labour market
- Hidden curriculum
- Instructional systems design model
- Job rotation
- Lesson
- Lesson plan
- Needs assessment
- Onboarding
- Off-the-job training
- On-the-job training
- Organizational analysis
- Orientation
- Person analysis

- Return on investment
- Routine expertise
- Task analysis
- Training evaluation
- Training objective
- Training transfer

DISCUSSION QUESTIONS

Discuss the following questions.

- Why do organizations engage in training?
- Why is a needs assessment important? And why is it often neglected?
- How does a training objective improve training?
- Which factors influence the selection of a training method?
- Which conditions of learning do you think are the most useful?
- Which of Gagne's nine events of instruction do you think get the least amount of attention and why?
- What are important barriers to effective training evaluation?
- What might the consequences be when organizations do not provide new employees with orientations?

ACTIVITIES

Complete the following activities.

- Select a training experience that you have had and perform a needs assessment, emphasizing the task analysis.
- Develop a training objective based on the task analysis that you performed.
- Select a training method to achieve the training objective that you developed.
- Write out how you would teach someone to drive a car using Gagne's nine events of instruction.

SELF-REFLECTION QUESTIONS

Write self-reflections of 200 to 500 words on the following topics.

- What was the best training experience that you have had, and why was it good?
- What was the worst training experience that you have had, and why was it bad?
- How could the worst training experience have been improved?
- Why do you think that the organization might continue to offer the bad training?
- Think back to starting a new job. What information would you have wanted to know that you did not receive?

8 Wages and Benefits

In 2000, Edmonton entrepreneurs John and Laurel Rudolph purchased a struggling dry-cleaning chain called Page the Cleaner. At the time of purchase, the company had been losing money. The previous owner paid most of the staff the provincial minimum wage and provided no benefits. Staff turnover was high and morale low. Upon taking over the company, the Rudolphs introduced a health benefit plan and linked wages to a local **living-wage market-basket indicator** (a calculation that determines what income a worker needs to pay for the necessities of life), a change that nearly doubled the hourly wage. Soon turnover declined, productivity increased, and morale improved. The company began turning a profit.

The Rudolphs found that higher wages led to a higher quality of candidates for jobs, lower training and orientation costs, and greater employee investment in the success of the company. The combination increased the profitability of the company. "People who are paid better respond with greater loyalty to their employer," said John a few years later. "It was a double win—our staff was happier and our profits went up."[1] Today Page the Cleaner is a prominent, successful, northern Alberta business. It has continued with the practice of linking wages to living-wage indexes.

At first glance, what happened at Page the Cleaner seems to be counter-intuitive. The new owners increased their labour costs by increasing wages and benefits without raising prices, yet the company increased its profits. Conventional wisdom would have predicted the opposite outcome of these changes. Instead, increasing wages lowered other labour-related costs and increased employee productivity, leading to increased profitability. The case demonstrates that wages and benefits are more than a line in an organization's operating budget. They need to be seen as part of an organization's overall HR strategy since they can affect other aspects of operations. Also, the case is a reminder that paying wages as low as the labour market will bear might not be the best strategy for an employer. Rather, a range of factors needs to be considered in determining compensation.

In this chapter, we look at the process of establishing and monitoring wages and benefits. We examine the different forms of compensation, discuss how to determine the right compensation package, and consider the effectiveness of different types of compensation. As you read through this chapter, it is important to note that wages and benefits take many forms, some more obvious than others. Many call the package of wages, incentives, benefits, and rewards that organizations provide to workers **total compensation** (or total rewards) to reflect the range of forms that it can take. Total compensation includes the base wage (or salary) and any additional monetary payment such as overtime pay or incentive pay. It also includes benefits such as health or dental plans and pensions. Less obvious forms of compensation include vacation entitlement, share-purchase agreements, fitness or health packages, travel allowances, payment of professional association fees, flexible scheduling, and professional development opportunities. Even workplace amenities such as snacks, resting spaces, or on-site child care are part of the total compensation package. Thinking of compensation as only the salary and health-care plan risks missing things that workers value and consider when deciding whether to take or remain in a job.

Pay Structures

How does an HR practitioner go about determining the appropriate wage and benefit package for an organization or specific jobs within it?

Basing compensation on only one or two factors, such as each worker's bargaining power (i.e., their ability to demand a higher wage based on their skills and availability) or the average of wages in the industry, can quickly lead to inconsistent compensation. That, in turn, often leads to dissatisfaction among lower-paid workers and possibly internal strife, turnover, and poaching from other organizations. The overall approach to wages and benefits should reflect an organization's overall strategy, financial capacity, and position in the market. Internal factors also matter.

The first step in developing a compensation strategy is to establish the **organization's pay structure**. It is the level or range of pay for each job in the organization relative to the pay for other positions within the structure. A number of factors must be considered when creating the pay structure, including legal requirements, external forces, organizational priorities, and issues of equity and equality.

As discussed in Chapter 2, each jurisdiction in Canada establishes a set of minimum employment standards with which organizations must comply. These standards include minimum wage levels (which differ among jurisdictions), paid vacation and other leave entitlements, overtime premiums, and possibly maximum working hours. These requirements form the floor (or minimum) compensation that must be paid. The common law can also affect pay decisions. For example, substantially altering compensation packages is a form of wrongful dismissal (called constructive dismissal) and can trigger a claim of wrongful dismissal (see Chapter 9). This highlights the importance of correctly establishing the initial pay rate for a worker. All jurisdictions also have human rights provisions that prohibit **wage discrimination** on the basis of immutable personal characteristics. Some jurisdictions also require a form of pay equity among workers (see Feature Box 8.1).

Feature Box 8.1 Pay Equity Legislation

In Canada, certain groups of workers are paid, on average, less than other groups. For example, in 2022, women earned 86.7 cents for every dollar earned by men.[2] Men of colour earned 78% of what white men earned, and women of colour earned only 59% of what white men earned.[3] Workers with disabilities do not fare much better, earning only 73% of what non-disabled workers earn.[4]

Although it can be tempting to explain away these patterns as a function of age, education, job choice, experience, and performance differences, these factors do not appear to explain the majority of the observed differences. For the most part, researchers accept that the unexplained gap is a function of structural and systemic discrimination in the labour market. For this reason, it is important to consider the effect of intersecting identity factors (see Chapter 1) on the practice of human resource management.

Increasingly, organizations must grapple with pay (in)equity, both to comply with the law (see Chapter 2) and to prevent reputational harm. In general terms, ensuring **pay equity** entails analyzing and accounting for differences in compensation that do not reflect legitimate considerations (e.g., job tenure, performance). Pay equity takes a number of common forms.

- *Equal pay laws*: Human rights legislation in every jurisdiction prohibits paying workers differently on the basis of immutable personal characteristics (e.g., gender, disability, age) when performing the same job. For example, an employer cannot pay women mechanics less than men mechanics who perform the same functions simply on the basis of their gender (e.g., men need to earn a family wage).
- *Equal pay for equal work*: Some jurisdictions require an employer to pay the same wages to workers who perform "substantially similar work." This requirement typically applies only on the basis of gender. For example, a man doing inventory maintenance in a warehouse and a woman in the same warehouse doing shipping and receiving do similar work (in different parts of the warehouse) and, all other factors being equal, should be paid the same.
- *Equal pay for work of equal value*: A few jurisdictions go a step further (again just for gender) and require some (usually large) employers to conduct an analysis of each job classification. The goal of this analysis is to ensure that jobs predominantly filled by women are paid the same as jobs of equal value predominantly filled by men. Equal value is determined by evaluating the skill, effort, responsibility, and working conditions of a job. An example

is administrative assistants at a construction company (mostly women) being paid less than construction labourers (mostly men).

These different approaches reflect that the premise of pay equity (i.e., all workers should be fairly compensated for the work that they perform) is contested. Specifically, the premise challenges deeply held notions that many employers (and governments and workers) hold regarding the value of specific jobs or types of work. The idea that the work performed by a personal care aid is worth "less" than the work performed by a mechanic reflects deeply rooted sexist and racist stereotypes.

This contestation over the relative value of different types of work (and workers) is often obscured by technical discussions about how to conduct such analyses (i.e., how to determine "value"). Indeed, implementing pay equity can be technically daunting. Comparing two occupations that, on the surface, are unlike one another is tricky. Few HR practitioners have ready access to the tools necessary to conduct such an analysis.

Even when the parties agree to an approach to determine equity, the calculations to determine whether pay equity has been achieved can be complex and convoluted. In 2019, the union representing University of Alberta academic staff signed a "landmark" agreement with the employer to increase the wages of women who were full professors by almost 6% (while freezing the salaries of men at this rank) and to provide a one-time payment to other women academics.[5] Although some lauded the agreement for addressing a long-standing pay inequity, others disagreed with the formula used to determine the inequity and lambasted the exclusion of other women university workers from the wage increase.

The external environment also shapes the possible pay structures that an organization can develop. The external environment includes economic conditions, competitors' decisions, inflation, and workers' options for employment. Setting pay structures too low compared with competitors' wages can make it harder to attract qualified workers. It is important to understand the economic and competitive environment. There are four external factors to consider.

- *State of the economy*: Short-term and long-term trends in the economy shape the wage levels and other forms of compensation required to attract and retain workers. For example, an economic boom can increase the number of workers required by an organization as well as competition among organizations for those workers. Data on economic trends are often available from governments (particularly Statistics Canada), local economic development agencies, or chambers of commerce.

- *State of the labour market*: The labour market is both shaped by the economy and has its own specific dynamics. Organizations should pay particular attention to the balance between labour supply (the number of qualified workers available) and labour demand (the number of jobs available). Usually, the labour market will have a surplus of workers (i.e., more workers than jobs, often called a loose labour market), which gives employers an advantage and allows them to set lower wage levels. At other times, demand for labour is high relative to the supply (called a tight labour market), and labour shortages can occur. In those circumstances, it might be necessary to increase wage rates or otherwise improve the terms and conditions of work to be able to attract qualified workers. Assessing the balance between demand and supply requires more than looking at the unemployment rate, for different occupations, industries, and regions can experience dynamics distinct from the overall trend. There is a range of statistics, some highly localized, measuring the labour market that can be accessed to conduct an analysis. We should also remember that labour markets are shaped by the actors within them. Of particular note is that the state, by changing policy, can affect the demand-supply balance in favour of one party or another (usually employers). For example, expanding employer access to temporary foreign workers can help employers to avoid the consequences of a tight labour market by expanding the pool of available workers.
- *Other organizations' behaviour*: The pay structure and compensation offered by other organizations that need similarly qualified workers affect the ability to attract and retain workers. Documenting and analyzing other organizations' pay structures comprise a *wage survey*. It can be conducted informally by reviewing job postings and making inquiries or formally by accessing local wage statistics from government or economic development agencies.

- *Cost of living and inflation*: The **cost of living** (e.g., the cost of essentials such as food, shelter, and transportation) varies from region to region. It affects both the prevailing wage rate in the area and how likely workers are to move into or out of an area. The cost of living is affected over time by **inflation** (the rate of increase in the cost of living). Consumer Price Index (CPI) rates are available at the municipal and regional levels. These issues are taken up in more detail in Feature Box 8.2.

Feature Box 8.2 Inflation and the Cost of Living

Inflation is the increase in the prices of goods over time. What this means for workers is that the amount of goods and services that they can buy with their wages (i.e., the purchasing power of a wage) decreases over time. In Canada, inflation is often measured using Statistics Canada's Consumer Price Index. The CPI periodically measures the cost of a basket of goods and services. Changes in this cost are used to calculate the rate of inflation. This information then allows us to assess the real dollar value of a wage.

Table 8.1 provides a fictional example of how the CPI can be used to track the effects of inflation. The first row shows the percentage increase in inflation (i.e., the cost of goods and services) in each year. The second row shows the cumulative increase over time in the form of an index (where 100 is the base). The third row shows a worker's hourly wage in nominal dollars (i.e., how much the worker is paid), which remains at a steady rate of $15 per hour. The final row shows the real dollar value (what that wage can buy in base year prices after accounting for the erosive effect of inflation in purchasing power).

Table 8.1 Sample inflation index

	Base year	Year 1	Year 2	Year 3	Year 4	Year 5
Annual inflation	n/a	3.4%	2.0%	1.7%	4.6%	8.5%
CPI	100.0	103.4	105.5	107.3	112.2	121.7
Nominal hourly wage	$15.00	$15.00	$15.00	$15.00	$15.00	$15.00
Real dollar hourly wage	$15.00	$14.49	$14.18	$13.91	$13.17	$11.75

This table shows that the rising cost of goods reduces the worker's purchasing power (the real dollar value of the wage) over time. The year-to-year loss of purchasing power is usually small, but these losses compound over time. A single year with high inflation (e.g., the fifth year in this example) can have significant effects on real dollar wages.

For low-wage workers, the rising costs of food, shelter, and transportation can be very difficult to manage. A worker who faces stagnant nominal wages might be forced to make difficult choices (e.g., do I buy food, or do I pay rent?). Not surprisingly, workers often seek a **cost-of-living adjustment** in their wages to maintain their purchasing power. Those unsuccessful in receiving such increases might respond individually by seeking a new job and/or reducing their effort at work.

Workers can also band together to increase their bargaining power. This can occur formally (e.g., they might seek to unionize the workplace; see Chapter 10), such as recent efforts to unionize Starbucks locations and Amazon warehouses across North America. It can also occur informally through actions such as engaging in slowdowns, using sick-outs, or refusing to perform certain duties or work overtime. Workers can also act together beyond a single workplace, such as the Fight for $15 movement, which sought to raise all wages to at least $15 per hour.

Organizational factors can also affect pay structures. For example, total organizational revenue creates an absolute limit on what an organization is able to pay workers. Compensation must also be sensitive to the price and cost structure of an organization's products or services. Compensation usually comprises a large portion of overall production costs and can affect the ability of an organization to compete on price. As shown in the opening vignette, however, there are multiple aspects of the cost of labour. An increase in wages can drive down other costs (e.g., turnover) as well as increase productivity.

An organization's business and functional strategies can also affect the pay structure that the organization adopts (i.e., what it is willing to pay). For example, an organization that aims to compete on the basis of cost might be unwilling to increase compensation even if it could. An organization that has adopted a market-dominance business strategy might be prepared to pay more in order to attract the "best and brightest" (thereby denying these workers to its competitors). In this way, pay structures send messages to workers about whom and what the organization values, thereby shaping the workers' behaviours.

Developing a Pay Structure

The external and internal factors help to establish the broad parameters of a pay structure. Constructing a pay structure starts with an HR practitioner's determination of the value of each job in the organization relative to other jobs. This process is distinct from that of assigning a wage rate to each job, which happens later. The relative value of each job is determined by performing a **job evaluation**. It establishes a hierarchy of job values. There are three basic ways to perform a job evaluation.

- *Job ranking system*: The value of each job in the organization is assessed, and jobs are then ranked from highest to lowest. A person or people knowledgeable about all jobs in the organization systematically review each job, compare it with other jobs, and rank it accordingly. This is the easiest and cheapest method of determining the hierarchy because it evaluates each job in its entirety. However, this approach also lacks nuance and is susceptible to personal bias. This method is most common among small employers with fewer employees and simple organizational structures.
- *Job classification system*: This two-part process begins by grouping jobs with similar duties, responsibilities, or subject matter (e.g., administrative, IT, managerial) into classes. Then, within each class, the jobs are evaluated and assigned classifications based on degree of skill, responsibility, complexity, and experience required. For example, the administrative class might have four levels to reflect different responsibilities. This approach handles complexity well but still evaluates whole jobs, and it is susceptible to bias, in particular along equity lines, since jobs are clustered with "like" jobs rather than across classes. This system is common in large organizations (e.g., government agencies) with large numbers of job types and complex structures.
- *The point method*: This system breaks down each job into its key characteristics (e.g., experience needed, decision-making authority,

working conditions), and each characteristic is assigned a score. All of the scores are summed up to create an overall point score for the position. The scores are then used to order jobs based on their perceived values. Feature Box 8.3 provides an example of the point method. It is more complex to establish and requires more in-depth knowledge of each job, but it can provide a more nuanced assessment of each job because it breaks jobs into their components. This extra rigour helps to control for but does not entirely eliminate bias.

Feature Box 8.3 Example of the Point Method

There are four basic steps in completing the point method of job evaluation. Initially, designing the plan can be time consuming, but once the scoring matrix is in place evaluation of each job proceeds efficiently.

Step one involves identifying key characteristics. The method begins by identifying the characteristics (or factors) of jobs relevant to compensation. Four factors are widely recognized: skill, effort, responsibility, and working conditions. There can be relevant sub-factors within each factor.

- Skill: education, work experience
- Effort: physical effort, mental effort
- Responsibility: supervisory, planning/directing, budgeting
- Working conditions: physical environment, travel, stress

Step two involves determining factor weights and degrees. The importance of each factor to the jobs is indicated by assigning it a weight (usually as a percent).

- Skill: 30%
- Effort: 30%
- Responsibility: 30%
- Working conditions: 10%

For each sub-factor, determine the number of "degrees" (or levels). The degree is the frequency that a factor occurs or is required in a job. For example, travel might have four degrees: never (0% of the time), occasional (less than 30% of the time), frequent (from 30% to 60% of the time), or continuous (more than

60% of the time). Sub-factors can have differing numbers of degrees and descriptors.

Step three involves assigning points to each degree. These points are usually assigned by an HR practitioner (perhaps in consultation with other organizational actors) and often informed by a job analysis to represent the value of each factor to the organization. This process will result in a matrix that can be used to evaluate each job. It might look like the example in Table 8.2.

Table 8.2 Weighted point matrix

Factor	Degrees 1	2	3	4	Maximum points	Weight
Skill					300	30%
Education	50	100	150	200		
Work experience	25	50	75	100		
Effort					300	30%
Physical	25	50	75	100		
Mental	50	100	150	200		
Responsibility					300	30%
Supervisory	25	50	100			
Planning/directing	25	50	100			
Budgeting	25	50	100			
Working conditions					300	10%
Physical environment	20	50	100			
Travel	5	15	30	50		
Stress	15	75	150			
					1,200	100%

Step four involves evaluating the jobs. Once a matrix has been constructed, each job in the organization (or unit) can be scored according to how much of each factor is required for that job. Here in-depth knowledge of each job is necessary to provide an accurate score. Also, this step can be susceptible to bias and stereotypes about what is required for different kinds of jobs (for example white collar vs. blue collar jobs).

Table 8.3 Example of point awards

Factor	Teacher	Principal	Custodian	Secretary
Skill				
Education	150	200	50	100
Work experience	50	75	25	50
Effort				
Physical	25	25	75	50
Mental	100	150	50	100
Responsibility				
Supervisory	50	100	25	25
Planning/directing	50	100	25	25
Budgeting	25	100	25	25
Working conditions				
Physical environment	50	20	100	50
Travel	5	15	5	5
Stress	75	75	15	15
TOTAL SCORE	580	860	395	445

The example above reveals some of the challenges in applying values to jobs through the point system. Certain characteristics are perceived as more valuable than others. For example, mental effort is awarded twice the points as physical effort in Table 8.2, which might or might not be accurate. Similarly, certain types of work are deemed more demanding or intense. For example, in Table 8.3, the principal is seen as having more supervisory responsibilities than a teacher, and the two are scored as experiencing similar levels of stress. It is fair to ask whether the principal's supervision of teachers should be rated as twice the supervisory effort of teachers, who must supervise a classroom of 30 young children. When conducting a points evaluation, it is important to be aware of implicit bias and stereotypes among those who create the points system regarding different forms of work.

All of the job evaluation systems are vulnerable to bias, both explicit and implicit. Whenever a person or group of people is tasked to evaluate and rank jobs based on perceptions of their characteristics, stereotypes and biased assumptions can influence the process. Common biases include downgrading the difficulty of work more likely performed by women than men since it is perceived as less demanding or less complex, such as the emotional labour discussed in Feature Box 3.5. Similarly, blue-collar (i.e., manual) work is often seen as of lower value than white-collar work because it is perceived as requiring physical strength or endurance rather than "intelligence." Often organizations value jobs more directly associated with the product or service (i.e., working "on the tools") more than they do the indirect support positions that keep the organization operating. These stereotypes entrench existing inequities in the workplace. To escape bias, evaluators consciously need to build equity into the process, challenging presuppositions about a particular job's value or difficulty.

Once a job hierarchy has been completed, it is necessary to determine the pay for each job. The external factors (e.g., competitor salaries) and internal factors (e.g., business strategy, ability to pay) will affect the pay for each position. Feature Box 8.4 offers an example of how the job evaluation can be translated into a pay grid.

Feature Box 8.4 Example of Determining Pay for Jobs

Continuing with the elementary school example from Table 8.3, an organization can use the points system to help it establish the pay rate for each job. It might select teachers as the classification that it uses to establish a base pay rate because there are more teachers than there are any other type of worker.

A quick review of government wage data tells the organization that the average salary for an elementary teacher in Alberta is approximately $77,000. It might also be able to find minimum and maximum pay rates, but to keep this example simple we will look just at average pay.

Assuming that the organization wants to pay teachers the average salary for the region, it can set the targeted average pay for them at $77,000. To set the average wages for the other jobs, it could use the points award in Table 8.2 to calculate proportionate salaries.

The teacher job is awarded 580 points. Dividing the average teacher salary of $77,000 by 580 tells us that each point is valued at $133. The organization can then multiply the points awarded to other jobs by $133 to establish a target for average pay for the job (figures are rounded off for simplicity).

- Teacher, 580 points x $133/point = $77,000
- Principal, 860 points x $133/point = $114,380
- Custodian, 395 points x $133/point = $52,535
- Secretary, 445 points x $133/point = $59,185

Interestingly, in Alberta, the actual average salaries for these positions in 2021[6] were as follows.

- Teacher, $77,000 (index position)
- Principal, $109,000
- Custodian, $39,000
- Administrative assistant, $46,000

Overall, the ranking of the salaries in the example and in real life are the same. The dollar-value differences between the calculated and real salaries likely reflect a combination of different weightings and contextual factors (e.g., job tenure of real staff, long-term public sector wage freezes) not visible in this approach.

Commonly, organizations establish a **pay range** for each job or classification. A pay range sets out the minimum and maximum wage rate for that position. Each worker is placed within the range based on seniority, experience, education, and other factors. Larger organizations might establish more complex systems, and in a unionized workplace these pay ranges would be negotiated with the union. Table 8.4 illustrates how an organization might use minimum, average, and maximum wages to develop a pay range for jobs at our notional elementary school.

Table 8.4 Example of pay ranges

	Starting salary	Average salary	Maximum salary
Teacher	$50,000	$77,000	$100,000
Principal	$95,000	$114,380	$150,000
Custodian	$35,000	$52,535	$60,000
Secretary	$50,000	$59,185	$75,000

The utility of a pay structure is that it makes determining what to pay a particular worker more transparent, fair, and straightforward. The two main risks associated with developing pay structures are the possibility of entrenching inequities (e.g., undervaluing the work of women) and diminishing the efforts of workers by making transparent the employer's valuation of a particular job. When developing a pay range, it is also necessary to contemplate how pay increases will be awarded. Will an annual increase to offset the impact of inflation be offered? Will workers' salaries increase annually by a certain amount (e.g., 2.8%) to reflect increased experience and value? If so, then on which criteria (if any) will the increase be conditional? The answers to these questions can be influenced by an organization's overarching strategy as well as industry norms.

The issue of determining the value of a position becomes more complicated when addressing senior management or positions requiring rare skills or abilities. It can be difficult to determine how much more valuable a senior executive's position is compared with that of their subordinates. The standard points method might not work as well in these situations. Often at higher levels of an organization, value is determined by how well the executive can negotiate and what they could get working elsewhere. Over the years, this has created a situation of executive pay inflation, in which the pay of CEOs and other senior executives vastly outstrips the pay of anyone else in the organization. Feature Box 8.5 discusses this issue in more depth.

Feature Box 8.5 Executive Pay

In the fall of 2019, Japanese auto manufacturer Nissan Motor was plunged into crisis when it was revealed that the CEO and other senior executives had secretly paid themselves hundreds of millions of dollars more than their contracts had stipulated.[7] The company had no system of checks and balances to ensure that senior executives, ostensibly the people in charge of the finances, were not using their power for their self-interest. The story provides a rare inside look at the world of executive pay at large corporations and the challenges in holding executives accountable for their compensation.

According to a study by the Economic Policy Institute, CEO compensation in the United States has increased 940% since 1978.[8] In that year, the average CEO earned about $1.5 million (in 2018 dollars). Forty years later that salary had ballooned to over $14 million. At the same time, average worker wages in the United States had increased only 12%. The situation is not much different in Canada. The top 100 CEOs in Canada made an average of $14.3 million in 2021, more than 243 times higher than the average Canadian worker.[9] Table 8.5 lists Canada's highest-paid CEOs.

Table 8.5 Top 10 Canadian CEO salaries (2021)

Philip Fayer	Nuvei	140,778,515
Patrick Dovigi	GFL Environmental Inc.	43,440,598
Joseph C. Papa	Bausch Health Companies Inc.	28,691,533
Jean Paul Chauvet	Lightspeed POS Inc.	27,707,758
Joe Natale	Rogers Communications Inc.	27,380,319
Keith E. Creel	Canadian Pacific Railway Ltd.	26,728,981
Mark J. Barrenechea	Open Text Corp	26,276,655
Tobias Lutke	Shopify Inc.	25,070,574
Chuck Magro	Nutrien Ltd.	23,166,435
Sebastien de Montessus	Endeavour Mining Corp.	22,717,768

Why has compensation for executives increased so much? The common defence is the value that they bring to a corporation and the unique skill sets that they possess. However, this argument is disputed since executive compensation is not correlated to the financial success of a company or to the education and qualification levels of senior executives.[10]

Some business analysts and economists argue that CEO salary inflation is linked to rising stock prices,[11] but that claim is also disputed since CEO salaries have outstripped stock market values.[12] A more likely cause is the disproportionate power of executives within organizations and the lack of structural accountability within most organizations to keep oversized pay increases in check. A similar power dynamic played out regarding hiring in the opening vignette in Chapter 1.

Why should HR practitioners care about executive pay? Beyond the symbolism, excessive executive compensation legitimizes extreme inequality. Many argue that high executive pay is economically unsound. Specifically, giving CEOs lucrative stock options incentivizes short-term thinking by executives at the expense of long-term consequences. Some also argue that high executive pay is part of a broader societal concern by feeding division and mistrust and undermining social solidarity.[13] Is an hour of work by a CEO really worth 220 times an hour of work by an average worker in a coffee shop, feedlot, or government office?

Establishing the Wage Structure

Once a pay structure is established, an organization must determine which form that payment will take. The wage portion of compensation (in contrast to benefits, discussed below) can take different forms, including base pay and variable pay. Which form of payment is most appropriate depends on the nature of the work and the organization's strategic goals. Issues of pay equity also need to be considered.

Base pay is the permanent, non-varying core wage provided for work performed. It can take the form of an hourly wage or a fixed salary (weekly, monthly, or annual). It generally does not vary according to performance, finances, or any other criteria. It is the most common form of wage payment because it is predictable (for workers and employers) and is easy to administer. Base pay is easily increased over time (e.g., as workers' performance or job tenure increases or to offset inflation) but is much more difficult to reduce. As discussed in Chapter 9, reducing a worker's base wage is often considered a breach of the employment contract and gives the worker the right to sue for wrongful dismissal. For this reason, employers need to take great care in establishing the original rate of pay since they cannot go back and correct it if they believe later that they are paying too much.

To link workers' pay more closely with their performance or the organization's financial situation, some organizations utilize **variable pay**, either as an alternative or as a supplement to base pay. Variable pay is compensation linked to a measure of worker or organizational performance. Unlike base pay, it can increase or decrease (or not be paid at all) over time. Changing variable pay is legally permitted because the employment contract stipulates that it will vary, and usually it is in addition to base pay.

Variable pay takes several forms. Some types are designed to be a supplement to base pay, whereas others are an alternative form of core compensation. Some are sporadic in timing (e.g., annual bonuses), whereas others are more consistent (e.g., commissions). The forms of variable pay can be sorted into six groups.

1. **Pay for performance**: Payment is linked explicitly to and varies based on measures of a worker's performance. For example, commissioned retail salespeople receive a percentage of the sales that they make. Piecework pay is another example: workers are paid a predefined amount for each unit that they produce or service that they perform. Sometimes a worker's entire income is performance based. Other times an employer might establish pay for performance on top of a lower base rate.
2. **Bonuses**: One-time or semi-regular payments are given to workers or groups of workers based on their performance. Bonuses can be periodic and based on overall performance (e.g., a year-end bonus), or they can be given to reward a specific achievement (e.g., landing an important client). The key quality of bonuses is that they are an after-the-fact recognition of achievement.
3. **Incentive pay**: This form of variable pay provides workers or groups of workers with supplemental compensation when agreed-on performance standards are met. Often these standards take the form of targets or quotas, such as reaching specific sales or production figures. Sometimes they can be tied to other aspects

of performance, such as the number of days without a workplace injury or a reduction in product waste.

4. **Merit increases**: Some employers link increases to base pay to workers' performance. For example, a raise might be provided, or the amount adjusted, only if a worker meets performance criteria. Often merit pay is granted after a formal review of performance over the past year.
5. **Profit sharing**: Some employers create programs in which workers receive a share of the organization's profits each year. This form of pay ties compensation to the overall health of the organization without the need for complicated performance assessments.
6. **Stock purchase**: Variable pay can take the form of offering shares in a private company to workers as part of their compensation. This practice is most common for senior executives, but some organizations have established employee stock ownership plans in which a portion of the organization's shares are allocated to workers based on years of service or some other formula. The financial benefit for workers occurs only when they sell their shares and is highly dependent on the price at the time of sale.

Employers like variable pay because it links compensation to performance, to a greater or lesser degree. They believe that this incentivizes workers to improve their performance either individually or collectively. Variable pay can also be more sensitive to external considerations, such as the organization's financial situation. Workers' reactions to variable pay are mixed. Some workers appreciate the opportunity to earn more by working harder, and profit sharing and stock purchase can make them feel like they share in the organization's prosperity. Other workers resent the contingent nature of payment (i.e., the employer has shifted risk onto them) and that their pay is dependent on things beyond their control (e.g., they do not control economic conditions). The lack of a predictable wage is also a downside for workers.

A further concern for them is that it is usually the employer who sets the criteria and establishes the target. There are opportunities for the employer to set bonus targets at unachievable levels or to construct an incentive pay scale that undervalues workers' performance. If variable pay is part of the employment contract, then the criteria cannot be easily changed, for the same reasons that base pay cannot be reduced. Many employers construct variable pay as a discretionary payment that provides greater latitude in changing the rules of how or when the pay is awarded.

Variable pay has pitfalls for employers as well. They need to take care in selecting the measures to which they index variable pay because those measures can create unexpected outcomes. For example, if workers are rewarded for increasing production, then they might shift their focus from quality to quantity. The structure of sales commissions can trigger similar gaming behaviour from salespeople, who might target their efforts on customers whom they think will be big buyers, ignoring other customers and potentially damaging the organization's reputation. Safety incentives (in which rewards are provided for remaining accident free) are more likely to reduce the reporting of incidents than the occurrence of incidents.[14] Incentive pay, ironically, can also decrease performance: once a worker reaches the reward target, the motivation to keep working can decline since there is no additional reward for extra effort.

Benefits

Benefits are indirect forms of pay provided to employees as part of the overall compensation package. They commonly include supplementary health insurance, pension plans, vacation and other forms of leave, and other monetary and non-monetary allocations. Benefits offset the cost of expenses that normally would come out of workers' pockets (e.g., prescription drug and eyewear costs, time away from work) and thus are a form of compensation that can be attractive to workers. A good benefit package can also increase productivity. Workers who can access dental care, supplementary health care, reasonable vacation time, and so on are healthier workers who will miss less time because of illness and be more productive because of lower levels of stress and better mental health.

When establishing an overall compensation package, organizations must consider which benefits they have to provide by law as well as the cost of providing and administering benefits. **Mandatory benefits** are indirect forms of pay mandated by the government. Unless legally exempted, all employers are required to provide or participate in mandatory benefit programs. In Canada, there are four basic mandatory benefits.

- *Employment Insurance (EI)* is a federal program that provides temporary income and training support to workers who experience an interruption of employment income. EI is funded by employer and worker premiums collected by employers. EI also provides income support for workers on parental and compassionate care leave. Over time, changes to the eligibility rules have made it more difficult for unemployed workers to collect these benefits. In 2017, only 42% of unemployed Canadians and 28% of low-wage (under $15 per hour) unemployed workers received EI payments.[15]
- The *Canada/Québec Pension Plan (CPP/QPP)* is a federal program that provides retirement income support to workers as well as disability income support and benefits to surviving dependants of a deceased worker. Like EI, CPP/QPP is funded by employer and worker premiums collected by the employer. Upon reaching retirement age (65 years for full benefits), workers receive a monthly pension calculated based on their contributions.
- As explained in Chapter 2, each province and territory operates a *workers' compensation board (WCB)* that provides wage loss and medical benefits and vocational rehabilitation support to workers who have been injured or become sick because of work. Workers' compensation is funded by employers' premiums calculated based on an employer's payroll and injury costs. In exchange, employers are indemnified (i.e., cannot be sued) when workers are injured or killed on the job. WCB eligibility and benefit levels are ongoing sites of contention between employers and workers. Employers' premiums are driven, in part, by the costs of injuries incurred by their workers. Some employers seek to minimize these costs by encouraging workers not to file claims and/or disputing whether injuries are compensable.[16]
- As shown in Chapter 2, governments mandate paid forms of leave for workers. They include **statutory holidays** (i.e., government-assigned days off with pay), **paid vacation**, and daily rest breaks.

The required leaves as well as the rules on entitlement and methods of payment vary between jurisdictions.

Most employers also choose voluntarily to provide other benefits to their workers. These benefits are often detailed in an employment contract, employer policy, or collective agreement. Benefit packages are often purchased from and administered through insurance providers. Some employers offer a standard package to all workers, whereas others might offer workers some degree of choice in the benefits that they receive.

The most common forms of voluntarily provided benefits include the following.

- **Supplementary health benefits** provide paid or subsidized access to a range of health services not covered by government health plans, including dental care, prescription medication, optical care and eyewear, counselling and therapy, and other paramedical services, such as physiotherapy and therapeutic massage.
- **Life insurance** provides a set payment to family members in the event that a worker dies. This is often set as a percentage of the annual salary.
- **Sick leave** provisions allow workers to be absent a set number of days per year without losing pay.
- **Short-term disability** *plans* provide part or all of a worker's pay when that worker cannot work because of illness or disability unrelated to work (a work-related injury would be covered by workers' compensation). Most often short-term disability starts after any sick leave days are exhausted and continue for a set period of time, such as two to six weeks.
- **Long-term disability** *plans* provide income support for workers who cannot work because of disability for a long period of time. Long-term disability benefits typically begin when short-term disability benefits are exhausted and can last until retirement. They usually provide a reduced payment to the recipient, ranging from 50% to 75% of pre-disability wages.
- **Top-up benefits** supplement existing mandatory benefits. A common example is parental leave top-up, in which the employer pays the difference between EI payments for parental leave and the

worker's existing salary. Employers can also provide additional time away from work beyond what is required under law (e.g., additional vacation leave).

- **Wellness programs** are benefits designed to assist workers to improve their physical and mental health. Such programs can be as simple as providing a subsidy for a gym membership to elaborate incentives for healthy living. Feature Box 8.5 discusses the dynamics of wellness programs.
- **Employee and family assistance programs** *(EFAPs)* provide access to counselling services and referrals to workers who experience mental health or other difficulties, including substance abuse, marital conflict, and financial difficulty. Employers' willingness to bear the cost of such a program is based on the business case that it minimizes loss of productivity.
- **Dependant-care benefits** provide support to workers in addressing their specific family needs, including child care and compassionate care. These benefits can include providing extended time off (with or without pay) to workers who have a sick or dying loved one to care for. Employers can also accommodate child-care needs by altering work schedules, subsidizing child-care expenses, or providing workplace child care.
- **Work arrangement accommodations** alter standard work arrangements, such as hours and days of work or locations of work, to accommodate workers' needs. Examples include **flex-time** (i.e., varying start and end times), **compressed work weeks** (i.e., working longer hours per day but fewer days per week), and working from a remote location, such as home (sometimes called teleworking). Since the COVID-19 pandemic, working from home has become a hot topic with workers calling for more flexibility in terms of where they perform their work. Although working from home is popular with workers, the benefits of doing so are not evenly distributed.[17] Women and workers with children experience more negative impacts from working at home,[18] and the gains from working there are often offset by increased work hours, greater stress, and struggles to create boundaries between work life and home life.[19]

- **Education assistance** entails subsidizing tuition and/or paid time off. Often these benefits will be linked to the worker's job responsibilities and contingent on the worker's achievement of a certain minimum grade in the course. Employers might also require workers to agree to maintain their employment for a period of time following the training. Quitting during this period of service might require the worker to reimburse the employer for the training costs.
- **Personal benefits** are small amenities provided to workers to boost morale or increase productivity. They might include employer-sponsored meals or social events and worksite amenities (e.g., recreational spaces and equipment and refreshments).

Benefits are often expensive. Employers typically offer them for two reasons: to attract and retain qualified workers and because there can be a positive rate of return on some benefits. For example, research has found that, for every dollar spent on EFAPs, employers earn $8.70 in productivity gains and reductions in time away from work.[20] Employers might seek to reduce the costs of benefits by limiting claim values (e.g., setting annual maximum benefit values, such as $700 every two years in vision care costs) and/or having workers pay some portion of the premiums associated with their benefits. In estimating the costs of benefits, it is important to be mindful that workers might not access all of the benefits available to them. For example, only 7% of eligible workers access EFAP services.[21]

Feature Box 8.6 Wellness Programs

Wellness programs have become ubiquitous at organizations around the world; 90% of companies have implemented at least one form of wellness initiative, and almost 60% have dedicated "wellness budgets."[22] One reason for these high numbers is the loose definition of what constitutes a wellness program. For example, here is the definition used by the US government: "A program intended to improve and promote health and fitness that's usually offered through the workplace, although insurance plans can offer them directly to their enrollees. The program allows your employer or plan to offer you premium discounts, cash rewards, gym memberships, and other incentives to participate. Some examples of wellness programs include programs to help you stop smoking, diabetes management programs, weight loss programs, and preventative health screenings."[23] The definition can encompass a wide range of initiatives, basically anything designed to "promote health." Passive options—such as gym memberships, on-site workout facilities, or healthy food options in the cafeteria—provide opportunities for employees to make healthy choices. Other offerings are more active. Initiatives such as providing lower health plan premiums or cash bonuses for certain behaviours try to incentivize workers into the kinds of behaviour that the employer wants to encourage. Mandatory programs, such as health screening or compulsory education classes, can verge on being coercive since the employer uses its power in the workplace to direct workers' behaviour regarding their private lives.

This raises two questions. First, why do employers implement wellness programs? Although they might be genuinely concerned for workers' health, they are also likely to consider how healthier workers increase productivity and profit. In theory, healthier workers are less likely to miss time from work and more productive while at work. They also utilize health-care services less frequently, reducing other benefit premiums and WCB costs. In other words, employers make a cost-benefit calculation.[24] Some commentators argue that the health outcomes for workers are of secondary, almost passing, concern for employers.[25]

Second, do wellness programs work? Advocates argue that successful programs ensure strong communication, create the right incentives, avoid penalizing non-participation, and measure the right outcomes.[26] However, recent studies have cast doubts on their effectiveness, finding few positive health outcomes for workers who participate in wellness programs.[27] One study, involving over 30,000 workers, found increased reporting of healthy behaviour such as exercising, but "the program did not generate differences in clinical measures of health, health care spending or utilization, or employment outcomes after 18 months."[28] Research suggests that the lack of results might be self-selection: wellness programs are more likely to attract already healthy workers and might even turn off workers with physical or mental health struggles, removing the potential for gains.[29] It is noteworthy that the research points to a lack of benefits for either workers' health or employers' financial situations.

Retirement Benefits

Retirement benefits are an arrangement to provide post-retirement income support to workers. These benefits are often highly valued by workers because they provide financial security in old age. For employers, retirement benefits can be expensive to administer and entail commitments that extend significantly beyond the duration of the employment relationship. The most commonly discussed form of retirement benefit is a pension plan. In Canada, employment-based pension plans are structured as supplements to the universal pension payment that every citizen receives—called Old Age Security—and the government-administered CPP/QPP (governments also provide income-tested supplementary benefits to seniors). Some employers offer additional retirement benefits in the form of a pension plan. There are three main types of employer-offered pension plans.

- *A defined-benefit pension plan (DBPP)* provides a predetermined benefit to retirees, usually calculated based on years of service, age, and income. The worker is "guaranteed" a certain monthly or annual amount for the pension until death. Contributions to a DBPP are calculated to ensure that the plan is fully funded overall.
- *A defined-contribution pension plan (DCPP)* entails fixed contributions to an employer-managed pension fund or a Registered Retirement Savings Plan (RRSP) controlled by the worker. Upon retirement, the worker receives a benefit determined by the value of the fund at that time. Either the DCPP administrator will calculate the amount to be paid out, or, in the case of RRSPs, the worker will make decisions about how much to withdraw each year.
- *A hybrid pension plan (HPP)* (sometimes called composite plans) possess characteristics of both DBPPs and DCPPs and take a range of forms. For example, they might stipulate a stable contribution rate and allow benefit levels to fluctuate within a range based on the financial health of the plan. Or they might provide a core defined benefit with a supplementary benefit based on defined contributions.

All pension funds have three potential funding sources: employer contributions, worker contributions, and returns earned from investing the employer and worker contributions (usually in the stock market). All pension funds also have a single recipient of benefits—retired workers (and their families if they pass away). The revenue sources must meet the financial obligations to current and future recipients (and administrative expenses, which make up a small percentage of plan obligations). Complex actuarial calculations involving life expectancy, inflation, and payroll estimates tell plan managers how much money the plan needs to have available to pay for all of its obligations. If there is a calculated shortfall, then the plan is said to have an unfunded liability: the present shortfall in funds in the plan (accounting for future investment growth) necessary to meet the expected future cost of the plan's obligations.

A key difference among the three types of plans is how they manage to balance funding and financial obligations. DBPPs opt to allow contribution rates to vary to ensure a stable and guaranteed level of benefit. DCPPs vary benefit levels to match the funds available from stable contributions. HPPs offer a bit of each option. This difference leads to a shift in who carries most of the risk associated with the third funding source (i.e., investment returns, which can be volatile). In DBPPs, employers and current/future workers share the risk of investment volatility through variable contributions to ensure a stable benefit. Workers' risk is pooled across all workers who pay into the fund. Also, for most private sector pension plans, the employer bears legal responsibility for ensuring the solvency of the pension fund, meaning that they are responsible for any shortfall (often in the public sector plans are jointly managed, meaning that both parties carry that fiduciary responsibility).

With DCPPs, the risk lies with individual workers. Since only contributions are predetermined, the value of the worker's benefit can be determined only at retirement. If the worker retires at a time when investment income is low, for example during a stock market crash, then the retirement fund will be valued substantially less than if the worker retired when investment income was good. In particularly bad times, it is possible for workers to receive less than the sums of what they and their employers contributed. This means that two workers in a DCPP with the same pre-retirement income and years of service could receive wildly different pension payouts if they retire at different points in the economic cycle.

The difference in risk is why debates over retirement benefits are some of the most heated. In recent years, employers in many industries have pushed to transform DBPPs into DCPPs. Employers have a preference for DCPPs since they shift the risk of financial instability entirely onto workers. Most workers prefer DBPPs for the income security that they provide. However, some workers believe that a DCPP might be preferable since they have more control over how the money is invested. In most cases, institutional pension investors perform better than individual members because they have access to greater pools of money (creating investment opportunities not available to individuals) and better access to information. A worker who advocates for a DCPP might be considered an example of a worker who argues against their own self-interest.

The percentage of Canadian workers who have pension plans as part of their compensation has been shrinking over the past 30 years, as has the share of DBPPs. One growing trend is toward hybrid or composite plans, which adopt elements of both types of pension. Feature Box 8.7 provides some facts about pension coverage in Canada.

Feature Box 8.7 Pension Plan Coverage in Canada[30]

In 2019, 37.5% of Canadian workers were covered by a pension plan. That was down from 40.6% in 1998. However, pension plan coverage was not equal among all workers. Some groups of workers were more likely than others to have retirement benefits.

- Women were more likely to have pension coverage than men (39.5% to 35.6%).
- Among public sector workers, 88.0% had a pension (up from 87.3% in 1998).
- Among private sector workers, 23.0% had a pension (down from 27.7% in 1998).

The majority of workers with pension coverage work in the public sector. Women have a higher rate of pension coverage because more women work in the public sector.

The type of pension plan coverage also differs. Among workers with pension coverage, the proportion in each type of plan breaks down as follows.

Public sector
DBPP: 91.0%
DCPP: 4.5%
HPP: 4.5%

Private sector
DBPP: 41.3%
DCPP: 32.6%
HPP: 26.0%

Higher rates of unionization in the public sector are likely an important factor in explaining why public sector workers are more likely than private sector workers to have defined benefits plans (in which risk is borne mostly by the employer).

Conclusion

Wages and benefits are a crucial element of any organization's human resources strategy. Compensation affects competitiveness, productivity, worker morale, employee recruitment and retention, and many other aspects of organizational effectiveness. Careful planning is required to ensure that the overall compensation package fits both specific positions and workers and the organization's strategic goals. Wages and benefits, however, are not a simple cost-benefit calculation. Determining the optimal wage level or benefit offering is not just about offering the required package at the lowest cost. The dynamic between costs and outcomes is complex. Minimizing compensation costs can lead to additional costs elsewhere, including turnover and poor performance. Implementing initiatives in a non-strategic way might not result in intended outcomes.

Finally, compensation decisions entail a tension between the positive intentions of wages and benefits and their financial costs. Employers are engaged in a never-ending struggle to ensure that workers are paid adequately (and perceive themselves to be paid fairly) and to keep costs controlled. In recent years, employers have focused increasingly on cost containment and sought reductions in pay and benefits. This shift leads to increased conflict in the workplace as workers resist the reductions. The Page the Cleaner vignette at the beginning of this chapter shows us that too much focus on cost, and not enough attention to the long-term consequences of a low wage and benefit strategy, can be an unsuccessful business strategy.

EXERCISES

KEY TERMS

Define the following terms.

- Base pay
- Benefits
- Bonuses
- Compressed work week
- Cost-of-living adjustment
- Defined benefit pension plan
- Defined contribution pension plan
- Education assistance
- Employee and family assistance program
- Flextime
- Incentive pay
- Inflation
- Job evaluation
- Life insurance
- Living-wage market-basket indicator
- Long-term disability
- Mandatory benefits
- Merit increases
- Paid vacation
- Pay equity
- Pay for performance
- Pay range
- Pay structure
- Personal benefits
- Profit sharing
- Retirement benefits
- Short-term disability

- Sick leave
- Statutory holidays
- Stock purchases
- Supplementary health benefits
- Top-up benefits
- Total compensation
- Variable pay
- Wage discrimination
- Wage survey
- Wellness program
- Work arrangement accommodation

DISCUSSION QUESTIONS

Discuss the following questions.

- When designing a compensation package, why is it important to consider more than just the base pay?
- Why might increasing total compensation sometimes lead to lower overall costs for the employer?
- What are the pitfalls in evaluating jobs for the purposes of establishing pay structures?
- Why might some workers prefer variable pay structures? Why might some oppose them?
- What are the key differences among DBPPs, DCPPs, and HPPs?

ACTIVITIES

Complete the following activities.

- Look up the employment standards in your jurisdiction for the following areas of compensation: minimum wage, overtime rules, statutory holidays, and paid vacation. How do they compare to the compensation at your workplace or that of a friend or loved one?
- Look up the Canadian starting and average salaries for Walmart and Lee Valley, a specialty gardening and tool retailer (many sites publish

publicly known wage rates). What does the difference in these rates suggest about the companies' respective business models?

- Search for the CEO salaries for Walmart and Lee Valley. What do they say about the relative value of senior executives at each company?
- Go to alis.alberta.ca/occinfo/ and search for the average salaries for the following occupations: early childhood educator (daycare worker), refuse (garbage) collector, paralegal, lawyer, licensed practical nurse, automotive service technician. What do the respective salaries say about the values assigned to these jobs in the labour market?

SELF-REFLECTION QUESTIONS

Write self-reflections of 200 to 500 words on the following topics.

- In a previous or current job, how important was the non–base pay compensation package to you? Which elements or benefits mattered the most to you?
- In your opinion, is it more important to incentivize workers through variable pay or to provide them with a steady income?
- Which steps, if any, should be taken to address bias in job evaluation and determination of pay structures when it comes to issues of gender, ethnoracial background, and disability?
- Who should carry the risk of volatile investments when addressing retirement benefits?

9 Performance Management, Discipline, and Termination

Donald Babcock worked for 12 years as the inventory control manager at a Canadian Tire franchise owned by his father in Bedford, Nova Scotia. Upon his retirement, Babcock's father sold the franchise to Donald Weickert. Weickert promoted Babcock to the position of general manager on the recommendation of Babcock's father. Babcock did not receive a job description. He performed his duties for seven months without incident. He did not receive a performance review during that time. Because of a concern about internal theft unrelated to Babcock, Weickert hired an investigator to determine the source of the problem. In the report on the theft issue, the investigator also noted that department managers did not have confidence in Babcock, and this was a serious issue in the store.

Weickert met with Babcock to discuss the severity of the concern and instructed him to meet with the managers, who were to advise Babcock on how to improve his performance. He was told to report back to Weickert with a plan and timeline to fix the issues, which he did. Weickert responded that he would keep an eye on the situation. Shortly after, Babcock went on vacation. While he was gone, Weickert met with the department managers, who agreed that Babcock was not performing his duties adequately. The group decided to give him 45 days to demonstrate his ability to perform the job satisfactorily. Nevertheless, after Babcock returned from vacation, Weickert, on the advice of his lawyer, instead dismissed Babcock for cause. Babcock sued and, on appeal, won. The court ruled that Weickert had not provided sufficient opportunity for Babcock to improve his performance and awarded Babcock the equivalent of five months of salary and his legal costs.[1]

On the surface, this appears to be a story of an employer acting too quickly to terminate an employee with poor performance. But it was more than that. Weickert's mistakes started much earlier than his decision to dismiss Babcock. At the outset, Weickert failed to conduct an appropriate selection process (Chapter 6) before he promoted Babcock. He also failed to establish a clear job description (Chapter 3) and performance review system. That system would have monitored Babcock's performance and identified shortcomings earlier, thereby preventing concerns from festering and increasing the chances for performance improvement. If Babcock's performance did not improve, then such a system also would have provided evidence that the employer could have relied on to justify the termination. Finally, as the court pointed out, Weickert did not provide Babcock with sufficient opportunity to correct his unsatisfactory performance.

This case highlights the importance of properly managing workers' performance. As stated in Chapter 2, in an employment relationship, workers agree to give their time to do work directed by the employer in exchange for pay. How productive workers are and how well they perform their work depends, in large part, on the degree to which employers provide effective direction, support, supervision, and evaluation. **Performance management** is the process by which organizations maintain and improve employee performance through an integrated set of actions, including setting expectations, providing feedback, evaluating and correcting performance, and, if necessary, imposing discipline. As the Weickert case demonstrates, this should be an ongoing process that begins at hiring and involves multiple forms of engagement. Only at the end of the process, if other actions have not succeeded, do questions of discipline and termination come into play. In this chapter, we examine the performance management process and discuss the difficult area of discipline and termination.

Performance Management Purposes, Processes, and Systems

There are three purposes of engaging in performance management:

- *Strategic*: Managing performance helps organizations to achieve the goals set out in their overall strategic plans. Aligning workers' performance with overall organizational strategy requires establishing clear expectations and feedback systems.
- *Administrative*: Performance management and, in particular, evaluation inform many organizational decisions, including the allocation of pay increases, promotions, and variable pay as well as restructuring, discipline, and termination.
- *Developmental*: Performance management should help workers to improve their performance and develop their skills and abilities to increase their job satisfaction and effectiveness. This can include identifying areas requiring additional training.

Organizations often use performance management only for administrative purposes. A more effective approach integrates the three purposes into an ongoing process. It is useful to view performance management as a five-step process (see Figure 9.1).

1. *Define expectations and goals*: Identify and convey which behaviours and outcomes are expected from workers and how their work fits into the organization's goals. This step should be in alignment with overall organizational strategy.
2. *Provide ongoing feedback*: Provide immediate and informal feedback and coaching during day-to-day supervision to shape day-to-day performance.
3. *Undertake performance appraisal and evaluation*: Conduct periodic formal evaluation of worker performance to identify strengths and areas that need improvement.
4. *Determine outcomes*: Allocate rewards (e.g., performance bonus), consequences (e.g., warning letter), or future actions (e.g., training) to recognize, correct, or improve performance.

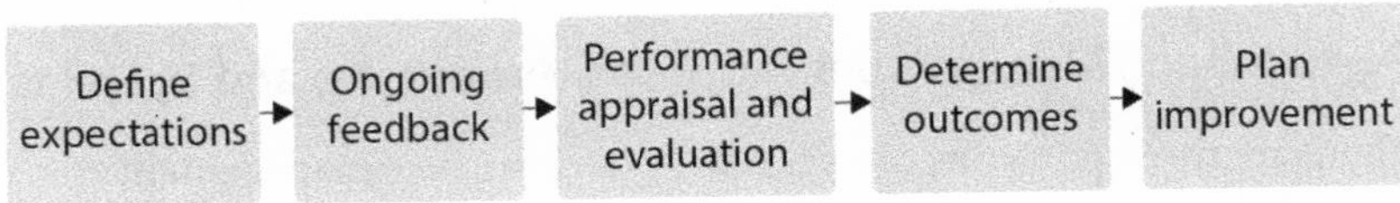

Figure 9.1 Performance management process

5. *Plan improvements*: Discuss workers' future development and include planning for career advancement, achieving personal goals, or improving effectiveness and satisfaction.

It is important to keep in mind that, while these steps usually occur in a sequence, they can overlap one another. Each step addresses a different purpose in performance management. In any particular context, one or more of the steps can take on a larger or smaller significance, but it is a mistake to omit or skip any of the steps since together they create a complete process of performance management.

This five-step process can be integrated into organizational processes by establishing a performance management system. This entails developing policies and practices, providing resources, and actively managing the processes necessary to make performance management effective. A performance management system is most effective when clearly linked to the organizational strategy such that, if strategic goals shift, the new expectations will be reflected in the system. It also includes developing and communicating new expectations to workers, ensuring that their behaviours and outcomes change, and updating evaluation criteria and processes to reflect the new goals.

An effective performance management system should recognize the needs of employees as well as those of the organization. Not recognizing employees' needs can result in workers who ignore or sabotage the system. For example, if workers think that they cannot possibly meet the standards on which they are to be evaluated, then they might choose to ignore the goals implicit in a system of evaluation. Or they might choose to game the performance system. For example, if advertising salespeople are monetarily rewarded based on gross sales and the target is set too high, then they might sell ads to clients whom they suspect or know will not pay their bills. This behaviour lets the salespeople hit the sales target but does not contribute to the underlying organizational goal (probably related to increasing revenue). This possibility also suggests that performance management processes need to be periodically evaluated to ensure that they are working as designed. Performance management systems also need to respect whatever workers' rights exist in common or statutory law or have been negotiated in a collective agreement by a union.

Defining Expectations

Workers can perform satisfactorily only if they know which behaviours and outcomes their employer seeks. There are two main types of expectations.

- **Task expectations** focus on the specific functions, outcomes, and demands related directly to a worker's job. They can consist of quantitative goals (e.g., sales targets expressed with a dollar value). They should focus on elements of a job within a worker's control and be achievable. Task expectations should be informed by organizational goals but need to speak specifically to the worker's job.
- **Contextual expectations** address aspects of a worker's job performance that contribute to broader organizational goals, such as fostering better teamwork, improving interdepartmental communication, or achieving better work-life balance. Contextual expectations should reflect a worker's relative position in the organization. For example, a front-line worker is unlikely to be able to influence corporate-level behaviour (e.g., work-life balance) but can contribute to how clients experience an organization's service.

Performance management systems flounder when expectations are not communicated clearly. For example, workers might be expected to "just know" what is important to do. Yet, if no one has told them the importance of being a team player or exercising discretion to make every customer happy, then it is not surprising that they might simply focus on doing their jobs well or carefully following organizational rules. Feature Box 9.1 discusses how to create a well-developed set of expectations.

Feature Box 9.1 Developing a Set of Performance Expectations

The underlying logic of performance management systems is that organizations can influence how workers act by identifying important behaviours and outcomes. A major challenge in developing such systems is focusing workers' attention on the right behaviours and outcomes in the right ways. For example, as shown in the sales target example above, targets set too high focus workers' attention but do not necessarily generate desirable behaviour. Developing a set of expectations that results in the kinds of performance that organizations desire is tricky work.

A good place to start this process is by identifying the outcomes or behaviours specific to a job that help an organization to meet its goals. For some jobs, this is a straightforward task. For example, an organization that operates an assembly line might require assembly line workers to (1) attend work punctually every day and (2) meet a daily production quota with (3) no defects. Such work performance is relatively easy to understand and assess.

It can be more difficult to identify desired behaviours in jobs with greater scope, complexity, or variability. For these jobs, it can be useful to emphasize general outcomes that the organization wants workers to achieve. For example, a labour relations officer (LRO) for an organization might need to make decisions on which grievances to settle and which to advance to arbitration (see Chapter 10). This decision can involve complicated trade-offs, all of which entail costs to the organization. An organization might evaluate an LRO's performance (in part) by assessing how well the worker "managed grievances to minimize costs." This gives the LRO clear direction (keep costs low) and a basis on which to assess performance. But it also gives the LRO discretion to advance or settle grievances based on the specifics of each case. For example, it might be worthwhile for an organization to spend $30,000 to settle a grievance rather than spend $80,000 to fight it (and potentially still lose and have to pay a settlement).

Sometimes it also makes sense to consider outcomes that organizations want to avoid. For example, a personal care attendant (PCA) in a long-term care centre might be assigned a variety of duties (e.g., attending to the feeding, toileting, and dressing needs of residents on a floor). But these demands sometimes might compete with the worker's attention (i.e., cleaning up residents who have soiled themselves when all residents must be brought to the dining area for lunch). The complexity caused by competing priorities can make it difficult to specify the outcome or behaviour that a worker must meet. In these situations, it might make more sense to give workers the flexibility to juggle the demands and provide them with guidance on how they should prioritize the work. For example, PCAs might be directed to prioritize work as follows: toileting, feeding, and dressing residents. But this set of priorities can come with some caveats about outcomes to avoid. For example, PCAs should organize their work such that no resident's feeding is delayed longer than one hour past normal meal times unless other residents have soiled themselves.

A second challenge with developing performance expectations is the tendency to ignore **citizenship behaviours** in the workplace. Such behaviours are enacted by workers to maintain the physical and psychological environment necessary for effective organizational functioning.[2] Often, but not always, these behaviours fall outside official job descriptions and performance management systems. In fact, citizenship behaviours often can be identified by asking which tasks in the workplace need to be done but are no one's responsibility. For example, dealing with dirty dishes and counters in a staff lunchroom, providing emotional support, and replenishing toner and paper in printers are important tasks that are often no one's responsibility. As discussed in Feature Box 3.5, these sorts of citizenship tasks are often performed by women.

Citizenship behaviours are relevant to performance expectations because workers have a finite amount of time and energy to allocate among job demands. Identifying certain behaviours and expectations can cause workers to reallocate their efforts. Assuming that workers are not willing and able to work harder, they might choose to reduce their citizenship behaviours (often not even a part of their jobs). This withdrawal of effort can create operational and interpersonal friction. Consider, for example, the impact that removing necessary supports might have, whether it be an empty stapler with no spare staples available or no one with whom to talk through problems and frustrations.

A similar dynamic can occur with tasks in a job description but left out of an assessment. For example, as set out in Chapter 2, clear and thoroughly documented OHS paperwork (e.g., a hazard assessment) might meet important organizational needs (demonstrating due diligence). But the completion of a hazard assessment might be burdensome and seen by workers as unnecessary. If an organization implemented a performance management system that ignores such tasks, then workers might rationally choose to expend less effort on this task. This can open the employer to liability should there be an injury or OHS inspection.

In this way, performance management can have unintended consequences as different organizational actors adjust their behaviour in response to it. For this reason, HR practitioners need to consider the potential risks and rewards of altering existing performance management systems. This is particularly the case when material rewards are attached, changed, or eliminated. An important question to ask is whether the potential reward from a change outweighs the risks created by making the change.

Ongoing Feedback

Providing workers with ongoing feedback about their performance means that concerns can be addressed in a timely manner. Such feedback is often provided by supervisors engaged in day-to-day observation, engagement, and direction of workers. The resulting discussions can identify areas for improvement as well as recognize accomplishments and identify paths for further development. The strength of ongoing feedback is its immediacy. It takes place on the spot, close to the moment when a worker exhibits a behaviour or achieves an outcome. This makes feedback concrete and prevents the development of undesirable work habits. This immediacy can also create challenges. Supervisors and workers might find it difficult to provide or receive feedback effectively if emotions are running high. Ongoing feedback is also a useful source of information for later formal performance assessment and evaluation and can be understood usefully as an informal version of this subsequent step in the performance management process.

Supervisor feedback is commonly called coaching. The term **coaching** emphasizes the importance of teaching and encouraging workers to improve their performance. It is noteworthy, however, that coaching tends subtly to assert that everyone is on the same team and has the same interest in "winning." This can obscure legitimate conflicting interests between workers and employers as well as the power dynamic in a supervisor-worker relationship. Workers might not want to "improve" their performance (e.g., produce more) if such an improvement makes their day-to-day experience worse (e.g., tires them out, increases their risk of injury, raises long-term expectations).

Another challenge with informal feedback is that supervisors are often inadequately trained on how to provide ongoing feedback. Often individuals are promoted to supervisory tasks based on their experience or performance in a job, not on their skill as a supervisor. Supervisors might be reluctant to engage in conflicts with their subordinates over their performance. Organizations might also have too few supervisors for them to provide an adequate level of oversight and feedback. As a result, supervisors can be either too passive or too aggressive in their supervision and provide feedback that is either too detailed or insufficient. It is important to be mindful that supervision can also be abusive. This can reflect an innocent error, be wilful, or even be a management strategy (see Feature Box 9.2).

Feature Box 9.2 Bullying as a Management Strategy

There is a power imbalance between a worker and a supervisor. That power imbalance can result in supervisors making observations, criticisms, and demands that workers might find unreasonable or even harassing. As shown in Chapter 2, harassment and bullying from supervisors are significant health, safety, and human rights issues.[3]

Bullying is usually seen as acts or verbal comments that could "mentally" hurt or isolate a person in the workplace. Sometimes bullying can involve negative physical contact as well. Bullying usually involves repeated incidents or a pattern of behaviour intended to intimidate, offend, degrade, or humiliate a particular person or group of people. It has also been described as the assertion of power through aggression.[4]

Key in the definition of bullying is the use of power to inflict harm on someone. This means that bullying is often perpetrated by those who hold power in the workplace, such as managers, supervisors, or employers. It is important to recognize that, like violence and harassment generally, power is at the centre of the issue. Bullying can take many forms. Some forms—such as insults, threats, and violence—are obvious. Other forms of bullying can be more insidious, such as the manipulation of work schedules, the assignment of tasks, or evaluations to make a worker's work life more difficult. The effects of bullying on the victim can be severe, causing significant mental, physical, and emotional distress.

It is tempting to perceive bullying as an individual problem attributable to the occasional "bad actor" in the workplace. Bullying, however, can become part of an HR strategy and thus embedded in a workplace culture. Historically, bullying was a common method that employers used to control workers and maximize profits.[5] Today's employers can also benefit from systematic bullying if it increases productivity. A study of workplace bullying suggests that strategies aimed at cost containment and productivity boosts can lead to increased bullying: "Rapid and radical management-led and cost- and productivity-driven change may create workplace climates that are conducive to and may be aided by increased workplace bullying by managers."[6]

Although anyone can become a target for bullying, certain groups in the workplace are more likely to be subject to bullying behaviour. In particular, women and workers of colour are more vulnerable to bullying because it can weaponize long-standing stereotypes and prejudices.[7] Consider the popularity of crude jokes aimed at women and visible minorities (mean-spirited, targeted humour can be a form of bullying). These groups are not only more likely to experience bullying, but research also shows that multiple forms of harassment lead to compounded negative health effects for the victims.[8]

Effective ongoing feedback focuses on worker improvement and development and avoids attributions of blame or too much focus on errors or mistakes. There should be opportunities for workers to express their perspectives on what has happened and suggest ways that their performance can improve. These suggestions can reveal barriers to performance outside the worker's control. Ongoing feedback can also be varied based on a worker's mastery of job tasks. A supervisor might need to be very hands on to walk the new worker through job tasks. As the worker learns them, the supervisor can become less involved and more passive in making observations. This change is intended to ensure that the worker feels supported when learning and trusted when performing adequately.

Training supervisors how to provide feedback effectively can improve how they handle these daily interactions.

Large organizations can become focused on the formal aspects of performance management, such as annual performance appraisals. Too much attention to the formal aspects of the process can cause organizations to overlook the importance of day-to-day interactions between supervisors and workers in improving worker performance. If handled appropriately, then ongoing feedback can offer significant benefits to both the worker and the employer.

Performance Appraisal and Evaluation

Many organizations regularly and formally evaluate the performance of their workers. This might entail quarterly, bi-annual, or annual performance evaluations. There are several approaches to performance appraisal. Selecting among them requires considering the nature of the work being evaluated, the workplace structure, and an organization's strategic goals as well as any provisions negotiated in a collective agreement by the union. Many organizations utilize more than one approach. Regardless of which approach is taken, the criteria by which workers are evaluated should be linked to established expectations and organizational goals as discussed in Feature Box 9.1.

The simplest approach to performance appraisal is to compare workers with each other to determine their relative ranking from best to worst. This comparative approach can be done in several ways. Supervisors or managers can simply examine the performances of all workers under their supervision and rank them from top to bottom. Slightly more complicated approaches include the following.

- **Alternation ranking**: A supervisor alternates between identifying the best and the worst performers. These workers are then placed at the top and bottom, respectively, of a ranked list.
- **Forced-distribution ranking**: The supervisor allocates each worker into one of several categories (e.g., above average, average, and below average). There is a fixed number of spots in each category, which forces the supervisor to differentiate among the workers (even if the actual differences between any two workers are minimal).

- **Paired comparison**: Workers are compared with every other worker in pairs and given a point every time they are determined to be higher performers. The workers are then ranked based on the number of points that they earn.

The strengths of a comparative approach are its simplicity and directness. The process is easy to implement and forces the manager to make clear decisions about performance. The result is a clear picture of relative performance within the organization. The weaknesses of a comparative approach are that it is highly subjective and can be perceived as unfair. Decisions can be shaped by supervisors' prejudices and opinions unrelated to job criteria, meaning that this approach can perpetuate inequalities and encourage favouritism. Comparisons can also create divisions within an organization since workers see each other as competitors rather than teammates.

The comparative approach also might not adequately account for intergroup differences. For example, the worst-performing member of a well-performing work group might still be performing better than the best-ranked worker in a different and dysfunctional work group. This approach also, by design, requires someone to be the worst performer in a group, even if that person is working at or above the expectations required of the position. The comparative approach is best utilized in settings where the performance expectations are easily quantified, such as sales figures or production quotas. The criteria used to rank workers should also be transparent to all workers such that everyone is clear on what basis they are being ranked. It is also more effective in smaller work settings since ranking becomes cumbersome and imprecise as group size increases.

An alternative to performance evaluation is the **attribute approach**. It measures the extent to which a worker possesses certain characteristics or traits desired by the employer. For example, an organization might identify attributes important for a job and in achieving its goals (e.g., leadership, teamwork, independence, interpersonal skills, creativity, problem solving), and supervisors can then rate workers on how well they exhibit each trait. The result is a **graphic rating scale**, which visually lays out each attribute and the worker's score on it, usually on a five-point scale (e.g., 1 for poor, 5 for excellent). The scale can be supplemented with qualitative comments. The attribute approach works best in situations in which outcomes are hard to measure or define and the job emphasizes the so-called soft skills required with human interaction. This approach also requires a high degree of one-on-one discussion to place the attributes and the scores in context.

The strength of this approach is that it is individualized, and the worker can easily see areas of strength and weakness. Workers are evaluated on their own terms and not rated compared with others. However, using attributes means that the evaluation is based not on what the worker does but on which personality traits or behaviours the worker displays. The link between possessing an attribute and a worker's job performance can sometimes be tenuous. For example, someone might display good interpersonal skills but not make much of a contribution to achieving organizational goals. The approach can also become subjective. Attributes are usually vague and the differences between scores hard to define. Considerations unrelated to the job can also creep into the evaluation, creating issues similar to those of comparative approaches. If the attributes are not clearly linked to the job, then the process can lose credibility among workers.

The **behavioural approach** attempts to overcome the issue of vagueness in the attribute approach by identifying specific desired behaviours and actions. They should be those central to strong performance. Workers' performance is then evaluated on those behaviours. At its simplest, a behavioural performance appraisal involves the evaluator identifying and recording specific examples of desired (or undesired) behaviours by the worker. This technique, often called critical incidents, provides direct and relevant evaluation and is effective at offering feedback for performance improvement.

Building upon critical incidents are **behaviourally anchored rating scales** (BARS). Clusters of critical incidents are compiled to create behavioural anchors that define different elements of performance. The BARS process has three key steps.

1. The evaluator identifies the key performance dimensions of the job (e.g., interactions with customers, store cleanliness, timeliness, etc.) from gathered critical incidents.

2. The behaviours most representative of good and bad performance on each dimension are identified as behavioural anchors.
3. The evaluator rates the worker on a seven- or nine-point scale for each dimension based on the behavioural anchors.

An example of a behaviourally anchored rating scale is provided in Table 9.1. This BARS focuses on a worker's attention to store cleanliness. The worker would be rated on this scale and several other scales addressing key performance dimensions. The worker's overall performance score is the total of the ratings for all of the scales on which the worker is rated. The ratings for several workers can then be easily compared, either on specific dimensions or overall.

Table 9.1 BARS for store cleanliness

Score	Performance anchor
7	Regularly tidies stock, reshelves material, mops floor, and throws away garbage throughout the shift
6	A few times a shift will tidy, reshelve, and clean store floor
5	When there are no customers will tidy stock and reshelve items
4	At beginning and end of shift will perform specific cleaning tasks
3	During some shifts will perform some cleaning tasks
2	When asked by supervisor will perform cleaning tasks
1	Does not address untidy stock and ends shift without performing cleaning tasks

The advantage of BARS is the close association between the evaluation and the tasks and functions performed in the job. Workers can clearly see expectations against which their behaviour is rated. BARS can also lead to specific feedback on improving performance. There is a risk of disagreement emerging if the worker does not agree with the rating or believes that the behavioural anchor is not reflective of the job duties. Also, this method can only rate directly observable elements of the job. Attitudes, thinking work, and other non-observable behaviours and actions cannot be effectively evaluated so are not considered. Behavioural approaches are best used with jobs that require tangible, explicit behaviours not prone to misinterpretation.

The final approach to performance review is the **results approach**, which focuses on measurable results of a job or group of jobs. **Management by objective** (MBO) links performance evaluation to previously established performance goals. At the beginning of the process, the organization's senior managers establish a set of goals for the organization to achieve. These goals are then translated by lower levels of managers into goals for their departments that will help to achieve the broad organizational goals. These goals are then communicated to individual workers expected either to accomplish individual goals or to work toward departmental goals. Periodically (usually annually), workers' performance is measured to determine if and how well the workers have met the goals.

The **balanced scorecard method** evolved out of MBO. It places goals into four categories of performance: financial, customer, processes, and learning. A similar process of goal setting and evaluation takes place. The balanced scorecard aims to be a more refined approach to setting goals by requiring managers (and workers) not only to identify productivity or financial goals but also to consider multiple dimensions of organizational performance. Results-based performance evaluation is best suited to larger, more complex organizations in which aligning the work of different parts of the organization is important. It might also be more appropriate for jobs that have a high degree of complexity or aspects that are difficult to observe directly.

Results-based performance evaluation methods were developed with the goal of creating a more objective, error-free process of review. Clear articulation of and agreement with goals establish a clear basis for evaluation. This approach has the advantage of including aspects of performance not easily observed. It also directly links individual performance to the organization's broader strategic goals, which should improve organizational performance. The key challenge with this approach is that it can be very top down because senior managers set the goals that start the process. If the goals are set without consultation with workers, then they might not buy in to the process. A second challenge is setting the appropriate goals. If they are too easy to achieve, then the evaluation is meaningless. Conversely, if the goals are too hard to achieve (or their achievement is not within the control of the workers), then they might give up or exhibit gaming behaviours.

Gathering Performance Information

All performance evaluation approaches require accurate information about workers and what they have done. There are five primary sources of performance information.

- **Supervisors**: The most common sources of information are observations made by a worker's direct supervisor. Supervisors understand the job requirements, observe the worker performing the job, and typically keep and/or have access to records of the worker's performance.
- **Co-workers**: Other workers performing the same job or working at the same level in the organization might have more opportunities to observe a worker in action regularly and have the benefit of interactions not available to a manager. Peers have excellent knowledge of the job and its requirements, but they also understand the challenges and barriers that someone might confront in the job.
- **Subordinates**: Subordinates are well positioned to provide insights into how a supervisor interacts with workers as well as other aspects of their performance. Using feedback from subordinates can incentivize supervisors to prioritize employees' satisfaction over other aspects of their jobs, such as productivity.
- **Workers**: Asking workers to self-evaluate their performance can reveal useful insights into why they are performing at a specific level. Self-assessment can increase workers' engagement and offer workers the opportunity to identify personal strengths, weaknesses, and areas to improve.
- **Customers or clients**: For workers who interact with others as a part of their jobs (e.g., retail or health-care workers), it is possible to solicit feedback from those whom they serve. Satisfaction can highlight both areas of strength and areas for improvement. Some organizations also solicit feedback for so-called internal customers (i.e., parties within an organization who utilize the services of a specific unit or department). That said, customers often lack

important information about the job, and their perceptions can be shaped by factors outside the worker's control (e.g., long lines, high prices).

- **Technology**: Some organizations might have the ability to gather performance-related information from the equipment that workers use. For example, delivery drivers might use GPS-enabled, hand-held devices that track parcel deliveries. This information can be used to assess how productive workers are as well as to monitor their locations. Similarly, call centre technology can produce data tracking the speed of call resolution as well as recording the interaction for subsequent analysis.

Increasingly, organizations are choosing to gather performance information from multiple sources in an effort to gather the most accurate information and to minimize the impact of bias or error. A 360-degree feedback process, discussed in Feature Box 9.3, has become a popular approach to using multiple sources. Whether using just one source or multiple sources, it is important that the selected sources are appropriate for the job being evaluated.

Feature Box 9.3 360-Degree Evaluation

The **360-degree feedback** process is designed to draw performance data from multiple sources to create a "full view" of a worker's performance. The worker performs a self-review using a survey (which can be trait based, behaviour based, results based, or a combination). The same survey is provided to the worker's supervisor, subordinates, peers, and other relevant parties (e.g., customers or vendors), who submit their feedback anonymously. The results are compiled and shared with the worker, along with recommendations for improvement.

Originally, 360-degree evaluation was intended for use with senior managers for the purposes of career development and self-improvement. Over time, its use has expanded to a wide range of positions and is now often utilized for administrative and HR decisions. Advocates identify several advantages of 360-degree feedback, including increasing worker self-awareness of strengths and weaknesses, using multiple sources of data to understand a worker's performance, increasing productivity, identifying gaps in training, and increasing organizational transparency.[9]

Although 360-degree feedback sounds like a good idea, it is useful to consider the assumptions embedded in its mechanisms. The most obvious assumption is that everyone's feedback on a worker's performance is valid and reliable. This is clearly untrue. Research has shown that co-workers often do not know enough about those being rated, their job duties, or the circumstances in which their duties were carried out to offer valid evaluation.[10] This risk can be attenuated by carefully selecting evaluators, although doing so increases costs and might be practically difficult (e.g., how would a supervisor know if co-worker X is qualified to assess co-worker Y?).

A second assumption is that anonymously given feedback is an effective way to change behaviour in a positive way. In order to be anonymous, much of the detail and context of the feedback has to be stripped away. This can leave workers struggling to understand when or how they should behave differently. Vague feedback might not be very effective in motivating behavioural change that improves organizational performance. It might also incentivize workers to behave in ways that they expect to result in positive feedback rather than in ways that might achieve organizational goals.

For their part, those who give feedback can be skeptical about whether it is actually anonymous, particularly in smaller organizations or work groups. This can make them less forthright in their evaluations. There is also a tendency, when workers are not held accountable for their feedback, to provide overly negative ratings.[11] In general, 360-degree evaluation appears to work best when used only for developmental purposes. Its shortcomings become amplified when applying it to pay raises, promotions, and other administrative matters.

Error in Performance Review

Every method of measuring performance is vulnerable to error. The consequences of error in performance assessment are that our evaluations are inaccurate. This can lead us incorrectly to take (or to refrain from taking) action, which in turn might result in serious consequences for an organization. For example, if a supervisor fails to notice poor performance, then it is unlikely that the worker's performance will change, and thus organizational performance will be lower. Other workers can also be demotivated by poor performance that is not remedied. Conversely, if a supervisor fails to notice good performance and thus fails to allocate expected rewards (e.g., praise, bonuses), then a worker can become demotivated, cease the desirable behaviour, and possibly begin to look for work elsewhere.

There are many potential sources of error.

- *Validity or reliability error*: As discussed in Chapter 3, validity and reliability are important aspects of any organizational decision-making process. A valid measure of performance considers factors relevant to performance. A reliable measure of performance consistently measures the same thing across different workers, jobs, and times. Issues with reliability and validity can occur when HR practitioners do not adequately operationalize the concepts that they are trying to measure. For example, a worker's ability to operate effectively in a team might be measured by assessing that worker's contributions to the team's performance. In contrast, asking whether the worker "gets along well with others" is not a valid measure of that worker's teamwork ability. Similarly, assessing revenue generated by workers from sales against historical revenues might be an appropriate measure normally but would not be a reliable measure during a pandemic (when sales are affected by factors unrelated to workers' performance). Sometimes measures are appropriate for one purpose but not for others, as shown in Feature Box 9.4.
- *Lack of clarity*: One of the most common errors is establishing standards or creating measures that are not clear. The "gets along well with others" example above is an unclear standard or measure. What does "gets along well" mean in this context? A more precise phrase (e.g., "offers constructive criticism") can measure more accurately the desired behaviour. Clarity in scales is also important. What is the difference between "good" and "fair" performance? Terms should be well defined and differentiated. The BARS example in Figure 9.2 shows clear criteria.
- *Halo and horns effect*: This effect is the tendency to allow an assessment of one trait to influence the rating of other traits. For example,

someone who does not "get along well with others" might also (and undeservingly) be rated more negatively by a supervisor on other traits, such as productivity or attention to detail, because the initial negative rating affects the supervisor's judgment.

- *Recency effect*: Weighting more recent observations more heavily than older experiences, whether positive or negative, is another common error. For example, a poor performer who does a great job immediately before an assessment might receive a more positive rating than warranted if behaviour during the entire assessment period is weighted equally.
- *Central tendency*: Psychologists have found that people are more reluctant to score on the extremes of a scale and more likely to cluster their scores in the middle.[12] This tendency can affect performance evaluation, with supervisors clustering their ratings in the middle of the scale to avoid being perceived as overly generous or harsh.
- *Bias*: Often evaluations can be shaped by a supervisor's views about workers' characteristics unrelated to performance, such as gender, ethnoracial background, or age. These biases can seriously impair the accuracy of an evaluation. Some researchers have found that fewer than half of ratings are related to performance, with most based on idiosyncratic factors.[13] If these biases remain consistent, then over time they can become apparent to others and give rise to a human rights complaint. Often supervisor bias is related to a *similar-to-me bias* (discussed in Feature Box 9.5).
- *Intentional error*: The stakes associated with performance assessment are often material (e.g., wages, promotions). This can result in intentional efforts to distort the results of performance evaluation. Managers might alter their assessment to help a friend, to punish a worker whom they do not like, or to make themselves look good. Workers might work together to "game" a peer review process, giving each other positive scores to subvert management's efforts to rank them.

Reducing the potential for error in performance assessment starts with carefully designing the evaluation instrument(s). Using quantifiable and objective measures of behaviour and outcomes whenever possible can limit some forms of error. Training supervisors to spot bias and avoid error-creating tendencies helps to reduce error, as does using multiple independent raters. Finally, creating a process of feedback, in which the process of evaluation is regularly assessed, can help to improve the process over time and reduce the likelihood of persistent errors.

Feature Box 9.4 The Promotion Dilemma

In 2019, a study was published that examined the promotion practices of 131 sales firms. The study evaluated sales performance of sales teams before and after a promotion.[14] The researchers found that, when firms promoted their best-performing salespeople into management (a logical basis for promotion), the performance of the rest of the team dropped in the months following the promotion.

The researchers theorized that there is a mismatch between the criteria used to evaluate candidates and the job. Essentially, the skills that make a good salesperson do not necessarily make a good manager. They also found that, if the company promoted a worker on the basis of other characteristics, such as friendliness or ability to work collaboratively, then overall sales increased by up to 30% more than teams that promoted the best performer. Interestingly, in those situations, the sales performance of the best salespeople (who were not promoted) dropped significantly. These salespeople were also more likely to leave the company in the months following the promotion because they felt snubbed by being overlooked for promotion.

This study highlights how HR practitioners need to consider whether a performance measure is valid and reliable each time it is applied. Although the level of sales is likely a valid and reliable measure of a salesperson's performance as a salesperson, it is not necessarily a valid measure of that person's ability to manage a sales team. And, because of the different context, it is not a reliable predictor of workers' likely success in a managerial position.

The study also highlights a dilemma for HR practitioners. Although selecting a worker on the basis of past performance (e.g., strong sales numbers) does not necessarily predict success in a new position going forward, workers might not agree with decisions based on more valid criteria. In this example, it appears that salespeople expected that good sales performance would be rewarded with promotions. If promotions are allocated on the basis of other (more valid) criteria, then these workers might perceive the process to be unfair and reduce their performance. This problem can be countered with more effective communication of expectations and the criteria for promotion. To some, this conundrum might seem to be unresolvable. Indeed, the study authors conclude that promotions contain an inherent "trade-off": that is, each metric used to make the decision has unintended consequences.

Feature Box 9.5 The Similar-to-Me Bias

Research has found that supervisors give higher or more positive ratings to workers with whom they have something in common.[15] This reflects the tendency for individuals to be more empathetic and lenient toward those with whom they think they share values, habits, beliefs, and demographic characteristics, such as sex, ethnoracial background, and age.[16] This form of bias can result in inaccurate performance assessments. To the degree that these assessments shape future worker behaviour, they can degrade organizational performance.

Similar-to-me bias can also result in structural inequities in the workplace. Those more like the boss are more likely to get raises and promotions. White men make up a disproportionate share of senior managers in many industries. Similar-to-me bias can perpetuate this inequity by rewarding workers who are like the boss and penalizing workers who are not. Those who persist and advance in the organization tend to be those who are most like their bosses, in turn reinforcing the similar-to-me bias. Workers who are not part of the privileged group might reduce their efforts or depart.

It can be difficult for organizations to mitigate the effects of similar-to-me bias. Organizational tasks—such as hiring, promoting, and assessing performance—tend to give actors a degree of decision-making discretion. It reflects that often these decisions are not clear cut and require judgment to be exercised. For example, is Kelly abrasive and difficult to work with? Or is Kelly hard-charging and driven to succeed? These sorts of decisions can be shaped not only by our biases but also by our well-reasoned conclusions.

To reduce the impact of similar-to-me bias, organizations need to structure performance evaluations such that they measure job performance only. This is easier said than done. The key is not to make performance "blind" to identify factors such as sex or ethnoracial background since that actually perpetuates similar-to-me bias. Instead, the problem of racism, sexism, ableism, and ageism in the workplace needs to be tackled openly and directly. Organizations need to acknowledge openly that bias is an ongoing and structural problem, raise awareness of it among managers and workers, and establish clear rules and procedures to minimize its impact.

Although this goal is laudable, it can threaten the power of existing organizational cliques. It is axiomatic that those with power typically want to keep it because it benefits them. For example, an organization with an old boys' club (i.e., men who have risen to positions of power and have long-standing relationships of mutual reciprocity) might use its formal and informal power to deflect or sabotage organizational efforts (e.g., more transparent performance assessment) that threaten it.

Analyzing Performance and Providing Feedback

Once the performance assessment has been completed and a score/evaluation has been assigned to a worker, a supervisor must decide how to translate the results of the assessment tool into tangible feedback and a preliminary action plan. For workers at the extremes, the conclusion might be clear. For a strong performer who gets high evaluations on every metric, the feedback will be highly positive, and the discussion might focus on finding routes for advancement or more challenge and responsibility. For a consistently weak performer, the focus will be on strategies for improvement or discipline (discussed below).

It is more challenging to develop a plan to provide feedback to a worker who receives a mixed evaluation. A good place to start is for a supervisor to develop a preliminary explanation for any performance that falls below expectations. Figure 9.2 identifies a series of questions that supervisors can ask themselves about the factors driving a worker's performance prior to meeting with the worker to discuss the performance.

The questions in Figure 9.2 reflect the various barriers that can exist to impede acceptable worker performance. It is easy to attribute poor

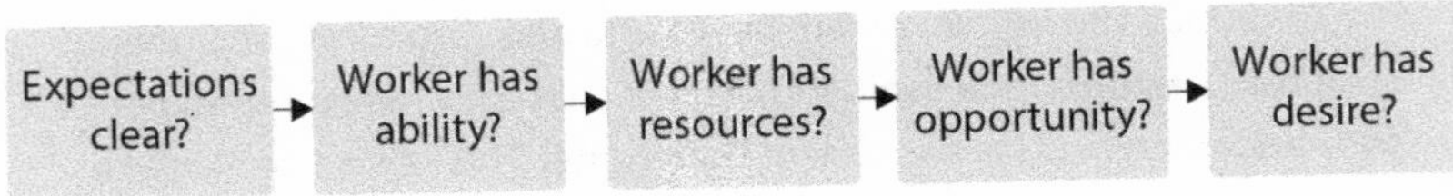

Figure 9.2 Process for assessing performance problems

performance to a lack of effort by a worker (a version of blaming the worker mentioned in Chapter 2). A lack of desire is rarely the full explanation for poor performance. The range and sequence of the questions in Figure 9.2 are designed to identify all of the barriers that can contribute to poor performance. The remedies to each barrier are different.

- *Expectations*: Workers can fail to meet expectations because they are unaware of them or do not fully understand them. Clarifying expectations, policies, and processes can eliminate this barrier.
- *Ability*: A worker might lack the knowledge, skills, or abilities to perform work. If this is the case, then training can eliminate this barrier.
- *Resources*: A worker might lack particular resources necessary to perform work adequately. This issue can be resolved by providing resources, such as tools, authority, staff, or funding.
- *Opportunity*: A worker might not have the opportunity to meet the performance expectations. This might reflect a lack of time to perform the work. Or a worker might face uncooperative co-workers or a change in external conditions, such as a recession. All of these circumstances are barriers over which workers have little control.
- *Desire*: A worker might not be interested or sufficiently motivated to perform a job acceptably. This barrier can be addressed by attaching rewards or penalties to a worker's behaviour. It might also require considering the worker's personal circumstances and how they are affecting job performance. A temporary or ongoing personal issue might require accommodation or other action by the organization. A job designed in a way that makes it unpleasant to perform or that is poorly compensated can also negatively affect a worker's motivation.

This preliminary diagnosis of the causes of unacceptable performance can be useful in framing any discussion with a worker. It also allows an HR practitioner to give some initial consideration to which remedial actions are cost effective for the organization and which are not.

Once supervisors have gathered and analyzed performance data, they must communicate the results of the performance evaluation to affected workers as well as other organizational actors. Most of the time, workers receive feedback during a formal meeting with their supervisors, although different methods (e.g., letter, email) can also be used. Feedback meetings should not be seen as a one-off activity but as part of the ongoing manager-worker relationship. Feature Box 9.6 offers recommendations on how to handle the meeting.

Feature Box 9.6 Tips for Effective Feedback Meetings

- Feedback should happen not only during the formal evaluation process but also be a regular and ongoing aspect of supervising workers.
- If self-assessment is part of the process, then ensure that you have received and read it.
- Create a back-and-forth discussion on performance. Avoid a "stand and deliver" approach to providing feedback.
- Begin with recognizing positive performance. People are better able to hear constructive criticism when it is preceded by praise or positive assessment. It also increases perceptions that the evaluation is fair.
- Minimize the number of items to criticize. To prevent a barrage of negative feedback, select the most important areas for improvement.
- Do not personalize criticism. Focus on behaviours or specific actions.
- Focus on solving problems. Encourage solutions from the worker.
- Establish clear and achievable goals for improvement. Identify specific actions that the worker can take to improve.
- Determine which additional supports the worker might need from the organization to achieve the goals.
- Follow up. Regularly check in to see how well the worker is meeting the identified goals.

If the evaluation identified areas requiring improvement, then it is important to spend time explaining to the worker which performance is of concern. Building a shared understanding of the issue can lead to a more productive discussion of the underlying reasons. Asking a worker to explain the reasons for the unsatisfactory performance is a useful way to ascertain the validity of the preliminary diagnosis (see Figure 9.2) that a supervisor has completed. This discussion can support the supervisor's initial thoughts about how to improve the worker's performance. Or it can identify barriers that the supervisor was unaware of and necessitate rethinking the actions and goals that should improve performance. This discussion can then lead to goal setting with the worker, identifying specific changes or levels of performance on which to base subsequent assessments.

Discipline

Sometimes unsatisfactory performance requires an organization to discipline a worker. **Discipline** comprises measures designed to alter a worker's behaviour by attaching consequences to undesirable behaviour. Discipline can take many forms, including verbal warnings, letters of reprimand, suspensions, demotions or transfers, and ultimately dismissal. As discussed below, the exact disciplinary options available to an organization depend on the nature of the employment relationship.

Discipline typically occurs in two circumstances.

- A worker is unresponsive to efforts to improve performance. For example, a worker might fail to meet certain performance standards or have an ongoing issue with tardiness. The employer might decide that the inadequate performance stems (at least in part) from a lack of effort by the worker and therefore might attach consequences to the behaviour in the hope of motivating change.
- A worker behaves in a way that breaches organizational policy or the employment contract in a manner that warrants some form of discipline. Discipline imposed for this sort of violation is also expected to alter the worker's future behaviour. It is important to note that discipline can be imposed for actions at the workplace and outside it, even for things posted on social media (see Feature Box 9.7).

One of the paradoxes that HR practitioners face when disciplining workers is that usually discipline is an effort to improve a worker's behaviour by both punishing the worker and (at least implicitly) threatening further punishment. Consequently, discipline can require HR practitioners to navigate and manage complicated interpersonal dynamics. Workers who disagree that their behaviour warrants punishment can be resentful, and this can reduce the likelihood of meaningful behavioural change (although they might comply in a pro forma manner) and, indeed, result in workers reducing their discretionary efforts.

Supervisors who wish to discipline a worker might see the worker's behaviour as a challenge to their authority. For example, repeated tardiness by a worker even after a supervisor has directed the worker to show up on time is doubtlessly frustrating for a supervisor and can result in anger, which can then cause the supervisor to impose discipline beyond what is likely warranted. Overdisciplining a worker can undermine the chances that the behaviour will be altered. Overdisciplining can also expose the organization to risk. For example, the worker might complain about being overdisciplined, and this can negatively affect the morale of other workers and make the organization less attractive to potential workers. Workers are also more likely to use legal means to dispute discipline that they perceive to be unfair.

Feature Box 9.7 Common Law, Social Media, and Discipline

A firefighter with the City of Toronto was fired after a series of tweets from his personal Twitter account containing racist, sexist, and homophobic material was published in a newspaper. He also sent out tweets that were derogatory toward homeless people and people with disabilities. These tweets were unrelated to his work, but he did identify himself as a Toronto firefighter on his profile page. The firefighter apologized for the tweets. The union grieved the dismissal. The arbitrator ruled in favour of the employer, stating that it is the grievor's violation of the [City of Toronto's] Human Rights policy that specifically reflects the seriousness of the misconduct. His comments denigrated women, ethnic minorities, disabled people, and people of different sexual orientations. By his disregard of the Human Rights policy, he promoted these forms of discrimination and harassment by circulating his comments, photographs and inappropriate jokes. He did this, with intention, among his followers. These included co-workers. He sent messages to at least three members of the public. He did, through recklessness, make this promotion of discrimination available to the general public.[17]

This case makes the point that workers can be fired for the things that they post on social media. In this case, the posts violated a clear policy of the employer, placing the firefighter in breach of the employment contract. But can a worker be disciplined for posting negative comments about an employer on Facebook? How about for posting images of lewd behaviour at a party? The answer to both questions is yes.

Under common law, employers have the right to impose discipline proportionate to the severity of the incident. As discussed in Chapter 2, common law relies on precedent (i.e., past court decisions) to build a body of rules surrounding legal issues over time, including employment law. One common law rule that emerged in the 1700s is the master and servant doctrine governing the employment contract. Under that doctrine, employees have a duty of fidelity, which means that they are "required to serve the employer faithfully in a manner that advances the employer's commercial interests."[18]

In practice, this duty has been interpreted to mean that employees cannot act in a manner that brings disrepute to their employer, even in their private time and space. For example, an employee convicted of a crime can be dismissed lawfully without notice for damaging the employer's reputation. There are cases in which employees have been disciplined for insulting their employer in a public space (e.g., a bar). The courts have interpreted social media platforms such as Facebook, Twitter, and Instagram as public spaces. As a consequence, workers can be disciplined (including dismissal) if they disparage their employer on these platforms. Furthermore, if social media posts depict a worker engaging in activities that are deemed embarrassing to the employer and thus damaging to its reputation, then discipline can also be imposed in those cases.

As with other forms of discipline, the repercussion must be proportionate to the wrongdoing. The firefighter's tweets warranted dismissal. A photo showing the worker playing beer pong or being too friendly with a fellow partygoer likely would not merit dismissal but could lead to other forms of discipline.

Discipline is normally preceded by an investigation. The size and sophistication of an organization will shape who performs the investigation, as will any procedural obligations that it might have under a collective agreement. In a large organization, investigations of minor issues might be conducted by a supervisor or manager, whereas more complex issues or those potentially resulting in termination (e.g., harassment or theft) might be referred to a more experienced investigator (e.g., HR practitioner, outside investigator). In smaller organizations, the owner or most senior staff member might end up handling all such investigations.

Typically, an investigator gathers information about the issue(s). This can include reviewing organizational records and taking statements from witnesses. If this preliminary work suggests that indeed there might be an issue warranting discipline or other action, then the investigator might inform the worker of the investigation and, at some point in the process, give the worker an opportunity to hear and respond to the allegations. This approach to discipline reflects broadly accepted norms associated with **natural justice**. These norms include the right to a fair hearing in which an individual can learn about the case against them and provide a response. Disciplinary processes that accord with broadly accepted notions of fairness are more likely to result in outcomes that all parties will accept.

At some point, the investigator will have enough information to come to a conclusion about whether or not a worker's conduct warrants discipline. The first step is to decide if the worker did what they were accused of doing. The usual standard for making this decision is the **balance of probabilities** (i.e., is it more likely than not that the worker behaved in a particular way?). This standard is lower than that of beyond a reasonable doubt used in criminal matters. Since discipline often can be disputed by a worker, an investigator normally creates a written record of the decision and the rationale for it, including any relevant evidence gathered.

If the worker did what they were accused of doing, then the employer must decide (1) if discipline is warranted, and (2) what discipline to impose. In theory, these are separate decisions. In practice, the line between them is blurry. An organization might engage in internal bargaining on these decisions. For example, if there is weak evidence that discipline is warranted, but a supervisor pushes hard for discipline, then the worker might be disciplined, but the penalty imposed might be modest (in the hope that the worker does not dispute the discipline). This type of horse trading reflects that discipline is both a technical process and a political one.

Most of the time, discipline is applied in a series of escalating steps called **progressive discipline**. Its logic is twofold. If the goal is to correct behaviour, then imposing the lightest possible discipline is most likely to trigger the desired change. If the light discipline is not effective, then increasingly heavy discipline can be applied gradually until the worker complies or is terminated. In this way, progressive discipline serves the goals of being both proportional and non-punitive (i.e., directed toward improving behaviour). It also provides the employer with a written record of repeated efforts to inform and assist the worker. This record can serve to justify any potential dismissal. An example of progressive discipline is found in Feature Box 9.8.

Feature Box 9.8 Example of Progressive Discipline

Incident 1: Clerk in a clothing store arrives for work 30 minutes late twice in one week.
Action 1: Provide feedback that lateness is not tolerated. Explore possible reasons for lateness.

Incident 2: Clerk is late one more time the next week.
Action 2: Provide verbal warning that discipline will occur if lateness continues.

Incident 3: Clerk is late twice the following week.
Action 3: Provide written letter of reprimand and warning of further discipline (suspension).

Incident 4: Clerk is late once the following week.
Action 4: Suspend employee for one week. Provide written warning of dismissal if behaviour continues.

Incident 5: Upon return, clerk is late once more.
Action 5: Dismissal.

Although discipline can take many forms, the law can restrict the kinds of discipline that an organization can impose. As stated in Chapter 2, the common law imposes certain rights and duties on employers. One of an employer's duties is to provide a worker with the opportunity to do the job that the worker has agreed to perform. If an employer prevents a worker from doing that (e.g., by suspending the worker as a form of discipline), then the worker can claim that the employer has breached the employment contract and seek damages for wrongful dismissal. One way around such limitations is for an employer to specify at the time of hiring various penalties that it can impose during discipline. Some organizations do this by writing an employee handbook outlining the process of discipline and penalties and then incorporating the terms of the handbook (as amended from time to time) into the employment contract. Unionized employers can also face limitations on discipline set out in the collective agreement.

Termination

Every employment relationship comes to an end, one way or another. Most of the time, termination occurs through **voluntary turnover** when an employee initiates termination by retiring or quitting. **Involuntary turnover** is when the employer decides to end the employment relationship. Under common law, employers are permitted to terminate the employment of non-unionized employees without their consent but must do so in a particular fashion. There are two basic ways to terminate an employee: with notice and for cause.

Employers can terminate an employee at any time and for any reason as long as they provide **reasonable notice** of the termination. In practice, and in lieu of notice, employers often provide a payout equivalent to the number of weeks of notice required under the common law. Reasonable notice is considered to be an implied term in all employment contracts (meaning that the contract does not have to stipulate a notice period for one to exist). What length of time is reasonable is variable and depends on the worker's occupation, age, length of service, and availability of other employment. Depending on those factors, reasonable notice can be calculated to be anything up to about 24 months. Legal advice should be sought to determine which notice period is reasonable for each situation.

Some organizations set out in their employment contracts what reasonable notice means. Doing so eliminates uncertainty for both the employer and the worker. Contracts can stipulate that reasonable notice is a fixed period of time or linked to the duration of the employment contract. The only limitation on the agreed-to period of notice is that it must be at least as long as the statutory minimum notice period set out in the relevant legislation (e.g., labour or employment standards acts) discussed in Chapter 2. Organizations that seek to minimize the period of reasonable notice might find that they must make other aspects of the employment offer (e.g., wages) more attractive to offset this potential loss to the worker.

Termination for (or with) cause allows the employer to waive the notice period and dismiss the employee immediately. This form of termination is sometimes called summary dismissal. To terminate a worker for cause, the employer must have a good reason (i.e., cause). Feature Box 9.9 outlines common grounds accepted by the courts to justify summary dismissal. A key legal principle underlying termination for cause is proportionality. The consequence (dismissal) must be proportionate to the severity of the employee's misconduct.

Feature Box 9.9 Grounds for Summary Dismissal

The rules on summary dismissal reside in the common law, meaning that they are constantly evolving and changing as judicial decisions set new precedents. Over time, some grounds for summary dismissal have become well defined and established.[19]

- *Dishonesty and conflict of interest*: Not all forms of dishonesty warrant summary dismissal, but lying to one's employer about something significant can be a ground for termination. Included here are cases of theft or fraud.
- *Gross incompetence and safety violations*: Being a sub-standard worker is not a ground for summary dismissal. Nevertheless, gross incompetence—defined as performance falling far below that of a reasonably competent worker—can be a ground for termination. An ongoing pattern of incompetence or a single act of particularly egregious incompetence would count. Putting others' safety at significant risk is also a ground for dismissal.
- *Breach of faithful service*: This ground relates to the duty of fidelity discussed in Feature Box 9.7 in that it relates to the on- and off-work responsibility to act in the employer's economic

interests. A significant breach of this duty can be considered a ground for summary dismissal. Running a competing business and revealing an organization's private information are examples of breaches of this duty.

- *Insubordination and insolence*: Employees have an obligation to obey lawful instructions of their employers. Failure to do so is considered insubordination and can justify summary dismissal. The same consideration is given to insolence or vocal defiance (insults, verbal abuse) of the employer.
- *Harassment, violence, and threats of violence*: Harassment and acts of violence, unless minor or isolated, are usually considered grounds for dismissal. Threatening violence is also considered a valid reason.
- *Absenteeism and lateness*: Not showing up for work or being late for work is not automatically considered a ground for summary dismissal. Nevertheless, persistent, repeated, or extended occurrences can elevate the issue to become a valid reason for termination.

There are other circumstances in which summary dismissal is legal. They depend on the specific facts of the case. In all cases, including those listed here, they are subject to the principle of proportionality. Termination must be deemed to be a reasonable response by the employer to the misconduct.

Workers **terminated for cause** can dispute their termination by filing a lawsuit alleging wrongful dismissal (unionized employees can have their union file a grievance). The nub of such a suit is the claim that the employer breached the employment contract by not providing reasonable notice of termination. Although the high cost to an employee of filing a wrongful dismissal suit means that they are uncommon, successful suits can entail significant monetary and reputational costs to an organization. To eliminate the risk of such suits, organizations sometimes seek to address conduct that warrants dismissal by getting workers to agree to dismissal. Such agreements (sometimes called a *buy-out*) often include a monetary settlement, a non-disclosure agreement, and a letter of reference in exchange for a letter of resignation. Such agreements attenuate the risks associated with an involuntary termination for both parties.

A special, and complex, form of wrongful dismissal is **constructive dismissal.** It occurs when an employer makes a fundamental change to an employment contract tantamount to terminating it. In other words, if a material condition of employment is unilaterally changed by the employer, then the employee can claim that the employer, in effect, wrongfully dismissed them. To make such a claim, the employee would need to quit and sue for wrongful dismissal, ostensibly arguing that they were forced to quit by the employer's change to the contract. An example is if the employer unilaterally reduced a worker's salary by 25%. The salary is part of the employment contract, and, by reducing it without specific authority in the contract to do so, the employer has violated the terms of the contract and thereby terminated it. Common situations that can give rise to claims of constructive dismissal include reductions in compensation and benefits, changes to a job assignment (including demotion), reassignment to a different location, temporary layoff, unpaid suspension, and harassment.

Conclusion

Job design (Chapter 3) and performance management are the main HR functions that help organizations to convert workers' capacity to work into actual work. In this chapter, we outlined key techniques designed to maximize workers' performance. They include defining expectations, providing feedback, and taking steps to correct deficiencies in workers' performance. We also explored the related topic of disciplining workers, including terminating them when their performance is unsatisfactory.

In the case of Donald Babcock, the implementation of a structured performance management system at the workplace likely would have prevented the legal troubles that ensued. This vignette highlights the importance of making sure that all aspects of performance management are functioning appropriately. It also shows how crucial monitoring performance is to the smooth running of an organization and the perils that organizations face if they jump too quickly past performance management to discipline and termination. Finally, it illustrates the importance of keeping clear records so that an employer can demonstrate that it took appropriate steps and met its obligations to a worker.

EXERCISES

KEY TERMS

Define the following terms.

- 360-degree feedback
- Alternation ranking
- Attribute approach
- Balance of probabilities
- Balanced scorecard method
- Behavioural approach
- Behaviourally anchored rating scale (BARS)
- Citizenship behaviours
- Coaching
- Constructive dismissal
- Contextual expectations
- Discipline
- Forced-distribution
- Graphic rating scale
- Management by objective (MBO)
- Natural justice
- Paired comparison
- Performance management
- Performance management system
- Progressive discipline
- Reasonable notice
- Results approach
- Similar-to-me bias
- Task expectations
- Terminated for cause
- Voluntary turnover

DISCUSSION QUESTIONS

Discuss the following questions.

- What are the reasons for conducting performance management?
- What are the key steps in the performance management system?
- Why is it important to train supervisors how to provide ongoing feedback?
- What are the different approaches to conducting performance appraisal?
- Which strategies can make feedback meetings more effective?
- When is dismissal an appropriate disciplinary action?

ACTIVITIES

Complete the following activities.

- Select a job that you are familiar with. Identify the tasks and contextual expectations that will serve as the basis of performance appraisal.
- Using the same job, identify which performance appraisal approach would be most appropriate given the expectations.
- Using the same job, create BARS for three performance anchors central to the job.

SELF-REFLECTION QUESTIONS

Write self-reflections of 200 to 500 words on the following topics.

- Think about your current/recent job. How effective was the performance evaluation process? What would have made it more effective?
- Have you ever had to supervise someone at work? If so, how did you handle providing feedback? Are there things that you would do differently today?
- In your opinion, should employers be allowed to discipline workers for things that they post on social media? What kind of content do you think warrants discipline?

10 Unions and Collective Bargaining

In 1996, a group of Calgary investors launched WestJet Airlines. It was originally designed to provide a no-frills, low-cost alternative to Air Canada. WestJet has been a huge success, growing consistently for 20 years, becoming the second largest airline in Canada, and emerging as an international player in the industry. WestJet's growth is due partly to its low-cost business model, providing an affordable option for flyers. Many also attribute its success to its unique corporate culture.[1]

Staff, referred to as "WestJetters," are instructed to be fun and entertaining. The company established an open, friendly workplace culture. The senior executives were highly accessible to employees, often taking turns doing various jobs at the airline. The company attempted to foster a sense of employee ownership of the airline, offering profit-sharing and an employee share purchase program. That program replaced a traditional pension for workers at the company. WestJet's advertising played on this approach, boasting how employees care because they own the company.

This approach to employee relations was also designed to keep the company non-unionized, a rarity in the airline industry. Instead of unions, WestJet established informal proactive communication teams to manage employee concerns. The strategy worked, and WestJet was non-unionized for over 20 years. That started to change a few years ago. As the company became larger and set its sights on the international market, it became harder to maintain that small, family-like feel. Employees started to complain that wages and benefits were below industry averages. In 2018, the company was sold to Onex Corporation, a large investment firm, which put an end to the employee share program and replaced it with a voluntary savings plan.

After a couple of failed organizing drives, WestJet pilots certified a union in 2017 and almost went on strike in 2018 for a first agreement. Then, in 2019, WestJet's flight attendants joined the Canadian Union of Public Employees (CUPE), signing a first collective agreement in 2021. In both cases, employees cited a lack of seniority protection and safety concerns (e.g., accumulated flying hours) as key reasons for unionizing.[2] WestJet flight attendants and ground staff also subsequently unionized. In 2023, the pilots once again narrowly averted a strike when negotiating their latest agreement.

WestJet's leadership took an aggressive anti-union stance during organizing drives, sending emails to all staff claiming that they would lose millions of dollars because of union dues and framing unions as outsiders that, as then-CEO Gregg Saretsky was quoted as saying, "are opportunistically trying to grow their businesses by targeting WestJetters."[3] Saretsky blamed workers' naïveté for their interest in unionization. "There's an expression that companies get the unions they deserve; you treat your people poorly, you'll get a union to protect them. . . . We don't treat our people poorly. . . . But we've got a group of flight attendants and pilots who have only ever worked at WestJet and they have no idea what it's like out there [in unionized places]."[4]

Unionization of the company forced a major change in how it handled human resources matters. Matters formerly under exclusive management discretion, such as scheduling and timing of pay increases, were negotiated with the workers' unions. Employees gained a formal process for handling complaints (i.e., a grievance process). In addition to having to comply with Parts Two ("Health and Safety") and Three ("Standard Hours, Wages, Vacations and Holidays") of the *Canada Labour Code* (as an airline, WestJet is federally regulated), it now had to abide by the terms of Part One ("Industrial Relations"), which regulates union and management behaviour. The company had to retool its HR department to add expertise in union-management relations.

WestJet's experience moving from a non-union to a union environment highlights some of the key differences between unionized and non-unionized workplaces. Unionization introduces a new party (invited by and representative of workers) into the relationship. It also adds a new layer of legislation and regulation with which the employer must comply. More importantly, matters formerly within the sole domain of the employer become subject to negotiation. In other words, aspects of management's control over the workplace are circumscribed. Relations with employees become more formalized, particularly in managing disagreements and disputes.

The WestJet example also demonstrates that most employers oppose unionization, and many, like WestJet, go to great lengths to thwart workers' efforts to join a union. The source of an employer's enmity is concern about losing control in the workplace and, to a degree, sharing power and profit with workers and a "third party" (i.e., a union that represents the interests of the workers). Employers might also be concerned about higher labour costs because unions tend to improve workers' wages and working conditions.[5] Nevertheless, as we will discuss in this chapter, those costs can be offset by productivity and other gains.

We begin this chapter by explaining what unions are and why workers organize them. We then outline the key steps in the certification and collective bargaining processes before turning to the administration of collective agreements and how unionization affects human resources. Finally, we examine the economic impacts of unions on workplaces and in society.

What Are Unions?

A **union** is a worker-controlled organization formed to advance the interests of its members through collective representation to an employer. Unions exist because workers and employers have different interests in the workplace. In simple terms, on the one hand, employers try to capture as much of the value created by labour that they can in the form of profit. Workers, on the other hand, want to capture that surplus value in the form of better wages and improved working conditions. These differing interests can result in friction and conflict resolved by one or both parties exerting power to get what they want.

As indicated in Chapter 2, employers have significantly more power in the workplace than workers. In practical terms, employers possess most of the power because they have the legal and economic authority to hire and fire workers, determine working conditions, and direct all work that takes place in the workplace. The other reason that power is skewed toward employers is that there is almost always a surplus of workers available. This labour surplus means that there is always another worker to fill a vacancy if another worker quits or is fired. The relative inequality of power can ebb and flow, based on a range of labour market factors (e.g., labour shortages), but the balance of power almost always favours the employer.

Over time, workers have learned that, by combining their efforts (via a union), they can create a counterbalancing source of power. In this way, unions are an expression of workers' desire to assert their interests. Unions do not balance the power dynamic—employers still hold the legal and economic advantage—but they do offer workers a new avenue by which they can pursue their interests. Unions can increase workers' power because they speak for and can coordinate the actions of all workers at a workplace. This allows workers to resist an employer's demands by collectively threatening to withhold their labour when bargaining for improved conditions. If all workers in a workplace stop working (i.e., strike), then the employer pays a significant economic price for not addressing their demands. This threat pressures employers to compromise and accommodate some of the interests of workers. Although negotiations are almost always resolved without a work stoppage, the threat of a strike is what gives unions leverage to bargain for better terms and conditions of employment.

Every union develops its unique structure and internal processes, but all have some features in common. Some unions are stand-alone organizations, representing workers at one workplace. Many unions are affiliated with a provincial, national, or international union. Although unions can be large, and some employ hundreds of staff, at heart they are democratic organizations accountable to their members. Union members elect executives, who handle the day-to-day affairs of the union. All key decisions, including ratifying the collective agreement and deciding whether or not to strike, are made through a vote of the membership.

Workers choose to join unions for a variety of reasons.

- *Economic*: If workers believe that their pay, benefits, and working conditions are not adequate, then they might turn to a union to help them negotiate improvements.
- *Fairness*: Workers might perceive that the actions of their employer are in some way unfair. They also might believe that the union, through its ability to curtail management discretion, can curb some of that unfairness.
- *Affinity*: Some workers enter the workplace with predeveloped perceptions of unions and their effectiveness and/or desirability that create a pre-existing affinity for them. This affinity can emerge from their own experiences (e.g., they or family members were previously union members), or the role of unions might align with their broader political and social worldviews.

In 2022, there were just under 5.2 million union members in Canada, approximately 30% of workers.[6] The percentage of workers covered by a collective agreement, sometimes called **union density**, has remained relatively stable during the past 25 years. Current union density, however, is down from historical highs of approximately 40% in the early 1980s. This situation is in stark contrast with that in the United States, where unionization has been dropping steadily over the past three decades and now stands at only 10.8%.[7]

There are significant provincial differences in unionization, from a high of 38.8% in Newfoundland and Labrador to a low of 22.9% in Alberta.[8] Most union members in Canada are found in the public sector, where 77.0% of workers are represented by a union. In the private sector, only 15.1% of workers are unionized. Industries with higher than average unionization include utilities (65.3%), transportation and warehousing (39.0%), education (72.9%), health care and social assistance (54.0%), and public administration (75.4%). At the low end are agriculture (2.7%), wholesale and retail trade (11.9%), finance (8.7%), and professional and scientific services (4.2%).[9]

More women are unionized than men (2.7 million versus 2.5 million) because of higher rates of unionization in the public sector, where a higher proportion of women work. Younger workers are less likely to be unionized, as are workers with lower levels of education. Small employers (under 20 employees) are significantly less unionized than large employers (over 500 employees). Workers of colour and immigrants continue to be less unionized than other workers, a factor that contributes to relative pay gaps.[10]

Labour Relations Legislation

Chapter 2 provided an overview of key elements of employment law in Canada. Labour relations add another set of rules addressing unionization and collective bargaining. For the most part, labour relations law does not replace existing employment legislation but supplements it. Employers still need to comply with occupational health and safety, workers' compensation, human rights, and other employment law. An exception is dismissal (see Chapter 9), in which common law provisions are not applicable to unionized workplaces. Unionizing also means that individual contracts of employment are replaced by a **collective agreement**. As the name implies, this contract is negotiated by and between the union and the employer and applies to all workers in the bargaining unit. The collective agreement can be changed only through the agreement of both parties—the union and the employer.

Every province, as well as the federal government, has a **labour relations act** (LRA). LRAs do not address working conditions. Instead, they establish the rules for how each party will behave when interacting, including allowing or prohibiting certain actions. The specific provisions of the LRA will vary from province to province, but all LRAs address

- workers' right to join a union;
- employers' obligation to recognize a certified union;
- the certification process;
- the bargaining process;
- dispute resolution processes, including strikes and lockouts;
- required collective agreement provisions;
- obligations and prohibited actions for employers and unions; and
- penalties for violations of the LRA.

The purpose of labour relations law is to establish a playing field (although not a level one) on which the two parties can bargain and rules by which they must abide. The law does not dictate the content of a collective agreement beyond requiring certain minimum provisions, such as a dispute resolution mechanism and payment of dues. Rather, it leaves the parties to fashion a collective agreement that suits them.

LRAs also set up **labour relations boards** (LRBs), quasi-judicial bodies tasked with interpreting and enforcing the LRAs and resolving disputes between the parties. LRBs have sweeping powers to address issues related to unions' and employers' actions. Among other things, LRBs supervise certification and strike votes, hear and rule on complaints related to prohibited actions by a party, and interpret provisions of the act. Orders of LRBs can be enforced by the courts, essentially giving them court-like powers in the area of labour relations.

In the next sections of this chapter, we walk through some of the key provisions of LRAs. Feature Box 10.1 defines some of the key legal terms that we reference.

Feature Box 10.1 Key Labour Relations Terms

Bargaining agent: A union recognized by the LRB to represent a group of workers for the purposes of negotiating and administering a collective agreement.

Bargaining unit: A group of workers recognized by the LRB to be represented by a union for the purposes of negotiating and administering a collective agreement. A bargaining unit can consist of all or a portion of workers at a workplace or workers across multiple workplaces.

Certification: The determination that the workers in a bargaining unit have expressed their desire to be represented by a union through signing membership cards and/or a supervised vote.

Collective agreement: An employment contract between an employer and a union addressing the working conditions for workers in a bargaining unit.

Duty of fair representation: A legal obligation in the LRA requiring unions to represent all workers fairly in a bargaining unit and not to act in an arbitrary, discriminatory, capricious, or bad faith manner against workers in the unit.

Lockout: A stoppage of work initiated by an employer for the purpose of applying economic pressure on workers during negotiation of a collective agreement.

Strike: A stoppage of work initiated by workers in a bargaining unit for the purpose of applying economic pressure on an employer during negotiation of a collective agreement.

Unfair labour practice: An action or behaviour by a union or employer that contravenes the provisions of the LRA.

Unionizing a Workplace

The **certification** process consists of the steps that workers take to join a union and have that union legally recognized as their bargaining agent. There is usually an informal phase and a formal phase to the process. The informal phase, more commonly referred to as the **organizing campaign** or drive, is when workers build support for unionizing through a variety of tactics. Organizing campaigns usually begin when a small group of workers agree that their workplace should be represented by a union. These workers usually approach an existing union for assistance in building support for unionization. Sometimes, though, a union might initiate contact with workers identified as interested in unionizing, or a group of workers might form a new union on their own.

The usual next step is to hold a meeting between union representatives and the workers interested in organizing the workplace. This information meeting is usually held off-hours at a location away from the workplace. For the union, the purpose of the meeting is to gauge the level of support among workers for unionizing, assess the prospects of achieving certification, and identify leaders within the workplace. If the union determines that there is sufficient support, then it will form an organizing committee made up of workers in the workplace with support from the union to lead the organizing campaign. This committee will make decisions about campaign strategy and organize the campaign.

At this point, organizing campaigns can take many different directions that depend on the characteristics of the workers and the workplace. Regardless of the different tactics taken, organizing campaigns have one primary task: contacting every worker to discuss the merits of joining the union and persuading the workers to sign a union card (or petition). Most often this contact occurs in one-on-one meetings in workers' homes or other non-work locations, but it can also include group meetings and other tactics. One of the goals of an organizing campaign is to avoid detection by the employer for as long as possible. Once an employer is aware that workers are organizing, often it will try to dissuade them from joining the union (see Feature Box 10.2).

Organizing approaches that maximize personal contact with individual workers increase the chance of success, especially if more than one strategy is used.[11] Incorporating workers from the workplace into the campaign (as opposed to using union staff exclusively), especially in positions of leadership, is also linked to success. Related to this, in successful campaigns, the union is more likely to make it a priority to understand thoroughly the workers' concerns and clearly communicate its commitment to the workers to address those concerns. Finally, the reaction of the employer to the campaign is also a key factor. Campaigns in which employers learn of them late or do not take any significant action to stop them are more likely to succeed.[12]

The formal phase begins when the union files an **application for certification** with the LRB. The application legally informs the LRB (and the employer) that a group of workers wishes to be represented by a trade union. An application must identify the union and employer covered by it, describe the desired bargaining unit, and demonstrate sufficient membership support. That support can be in the form of signed union cards or a petition from workers in the proposed bargaining unit. The number of cards/signatures must meet a minimum threshold of support to be valid. This threshold varies by jurisdiction but ranges between 35% and 45% of the workers in the proposed bargaining unit.

The LRB assesses certification applications to determine whether the bargaining unit is appropriate and whether the union has adequate evidence of member support. Appropriateness requires consideration of whether the workers share a community of interest and would create a viable bargaining unit. The LRB can reject or amend the proposed bargaining unit. Once the unit description is determined, the LRB confirms that the minimum support threshold has been met. If so, then it will order a board-supervised **representation vote**, a secret ballot yes/

no vote asking all workers in the proposed unit whether they support being represented by the union. In some jurisdictions, if the union can demonstrate majority (or supermajority) support, then the LRB issues an **automatic certification** (sometimes called card-check certification) granting the union the right to represent the bargaining unit without the need for a certification vote.

The period between the ordering of a representation vote and the actual vote is an intense time in an organizing campaign. Typically, both the union and the employer openly campaign to persuade workers to vote for or against the union. Under LRAs, employers have the right to express themselves to workers during this period within certain limitations. The employer can express its opinion on the prospect of a union as long as it does not use coercion, intimidation, threats, or promises or unduly influence workers to act against their beliefs. Unions are also prohibited from engaging in any of those activities. As one might expect, determining when and if an employer or a union has crossed the line can be difficult.

Violating the rules on organizing campaigns is an example of an **unfair labour practice** (ULP). If a party complains that the other party is engaging in a ULP, then the LRB will hold a hearing. Both sides make their cases and present evidence. The LRB decides whether a ULP occurred and will issue an order that might include imposing a remedy. Remedies can range from issuing a cease-and-desist order (requiring the party to stop doing what it was doing) to ordering a new vote to (in some jurisdictions) granting an automatic certification.

The period between the application and the vote is a risky time for unions and their supporters. Even with the limits imposed by the LRA, employers hold significant power in the workplace, and their actions often create a "chilling effect" among workers concerned about the repercussions of a yes vote. Many employers are aggressive in their efforts to prevent unionization (again see Box 10.2). Research has shown that, the longer the vote is delayed, the more likely the union will lose the vote.[13] If a majority of the workers who voted indicate that they support the union, then the LRB will issue a formal certification, and the union will become the legal bargaining agent for the workers in the bargaining unit. At this point, the parties turn their attention to the next step of the labour relations process: collective bargaining.

Feature Box 10.2 Union Busting

Employers often seek to thwart union-organizing drives because unionization is associated with higher wages and less employer discretion. Many employers see this as an impediment to their ability to maximize profits. Some organizations hire professional union busters to help them defeat a union organizing drive.

In the following excerpt from *Confessions of a Union Buster*, author Martin Jay Levitt, a former union buster who became disillusioned with the work, talks about some of his strategies in thwarting organizing campaigns:

> I refined the Sheridan specialty called "counter-organizing drives," battling non-union employees as they struggled to win union representation. The enemy was the collective spirit. I got hold of that spirit while it was still a seedling; I poisoned it, choked it, bludgeoned it if I had to, anything to be sure it would never blossom into a united work force, the dreaded foe of any corporate tyrant.
>
> For my campaigns I identified two key targets: the rank-and-file workers and their immediate supervisors. The supervisors served as my front line. . . . I knew that people who didn't feel threatened wouldn't fight. So, through hours of seminars, rallies and one-on-one encounters, I taught the supervisors to despise and fear the union. I persuaded them that a union organizing drive was a personal attack on them, a referendum on their leadership skills, and an attempt to humiliate them. I was friendly, even jovial at times, but always unforgiving as I compelled each supervisor to feel he was somehow to blame for the union push and consequently obliged to defeat it.[14]

Levitt focuses here on how he convinced managers to become active union busters among their employees. Elsewhere in the book, he discusses tactics to undermine support for a union among workers. Relentless communications with employees framing the union in a bad light is a key action. Supervisors are directed to target "soft" supporters to sway them against the union. Union opponents among workers are used as "spies" to relay information to management and feed misinformation to fellow workers. The employer might hold mandatory meetings with workers (called captive audience meetings) to present its perspective forcefully to groups of workers. All of these tactics are designed to undermine support for the union in the lead-up to a representation vote.

In his book, Levitt says that union busters save their most focused efforts to target the strongest union supporters:

> To stop a union proponent—a "pusher" in the anti-union lexicon—the buster will go anywhere, not just to the lunchroom, but into the bedroom if necessary. . . . My team and I routinely pried into workers' police records, personnel files, credit histories, medical records, and family lives in search of a weakness that we could use to discredit union activists. Once in a while, a worker is impeccable. So, some consultants resort to lies.[15]

Another tactic targeting union supporters is to find reasons to reprimand or fire them, which has the dual effect of removing a union organizer from the workplace and putting a chill on other workers thinking of getting involved. Firing workers for union activity is an unfair labour practice, but the hearing is often weeks or months after the representation vote takes place, making remedies effectively meaningless.

Union busters are often outside consultants, like Levitt, hired to wage a counter-campaign against either a fledgling union or an established union that the employer wants weakened or removed. Nevertheless, the tactics that they use are often incorporated by employers directly, without the use of consultants. Some of the actions described by Levitt are at the extreme end, but many are common tactics used by employers to avoid unionization. Union busting is a stark example of how employers use their power to pursue their interests in the workplace.

Collective Bargaining

Once a union is certified, the employer and the union begin negotiations on a collective agreement for the new bargaining unit. Once a collective agreement is signed, it operates for a fixed period. When the agreement expires, the parties renegotiate its terms. The collective bargaining process typically entails a series of stages as set out in Figure 10.1. These stages look the same whether negotiating a first agreement or updating an existing agreement. First agreements tend to be more difficult to negotiate

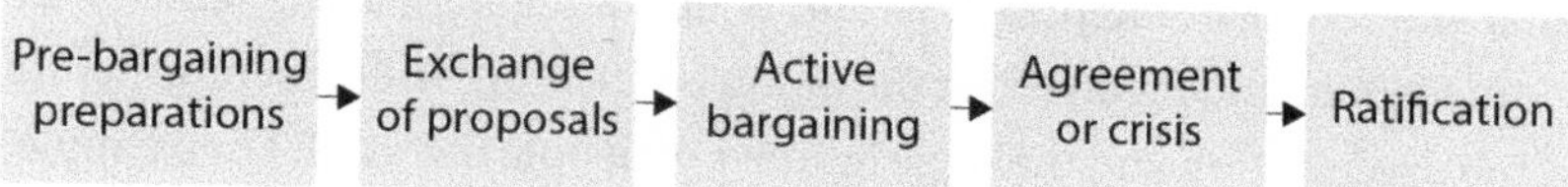

Figure 10.1 Bargaining process

since every provision is new. In contrast, when negotiating changes to an agreement, much of the contract language previously agreed does not need to be reconsidered.

The first stage of bargaining takes place before the parties meet. At the pre-bargaining stage, the parties determine which issues they wish to bargain on and develop an initial set of proposals. They also develop an overall bargaining strategy, establishing the key goals that they wish to achieve and how they will achieve them. In developing the strategy, the parties prioritize the issues to determine which are essential. Identifying one's bargaining priorities is important because, during negotiations, there will be a need to revise one's proposals or drop certain proposals to increase the likelihood of achieving the essential goals. Part of the process of establishing proposals includes conducting research to support the demands. Research can include finding economic or financial data, compiling evidence to demonstrate a problem (e.g., the number of workers taking sick days), or polling to assess union members' opinions.

This is also the stage at which the parties determine who will represent them at the bargaining table. For the employer, the bargaining team usually comprises a handful of managers, possibly representing different sections of the organization, and sometimes representatives from the HR department. There might also be an outside consultant, such as a labour lawyer, to assist the employer. For the union, the bargaining team typically will consist of rank-and-file members, again often representing different groups of workers, assisted by a union staff member with some expertise in bargaining. Both parties need to appoint a lead negotiator, who acts as the chief spokesperson and chair of the team's meetings.

Although it is common to speak about the union and the employer as if they are monolithic groups, in fact the members of each group will have a range of interests. During the pre-bargaining stage, the parties will engage in **intra-organizational bargaining** by which they determine their side's bargaining priorities and issues. Such bargaining tends to be more obvious and involved for the union because of the democratic nature of the organization and the large number of people involved. For example, within a union, younger workers might want a pay increase, whereas older workers might prioritize improvements in the pension plan. The negotiating team needs to balance various interests and perspectives to ensure that the final proposal has legitimacy.

The employer's side might also engage in some degree of intra-organizational bargaining, but the hierarchical and private nature of most employers means that such bargaining is less obvious and protracted. At this stage, the bargaining team might also work to manage expectations among key constituents about bargaining outcomes by communicating what to expect. Finally, it is common for the parties to meet informally during this stage to establish the protocols and procedures that will govern the bargaining process. Establishing the ground rules early helps the process to proceed more smoothly.

The next stage entails a meeting in which the parties exchange their initial proposals, often called **opening offers**. Typically, the chief negotiators present their proposals and explain the rationale behind the demands. It is common at this stage for the parties to have widely different proposals, each emphasizing different issues and, on common issues, having divergent positions. The purpose of this stage is to establish the scope of bargaining (i.e., what will be at issue) and the negotiating range (i.e., the outside bounds of what will be bargained). Once the bargaining scope and range are established, each side can re-evaluate its position and adjust its strategy accordingly. At this stage, the negotiators can also start to identify which issues are priorities for the other side, which will also shape the negotiation dynamics.

Once the opening offers are tabled, the two parties enter the third stage of **active bargaining**. In this stage, they adjust their proposals to make them more palatable to the other side while still holding to their own priorities. This back-and-forth process can appear to be somewhat chaotic as each party attempts to determine where agreement can be found with the other side on each issue being negotiated. This can take the form of discussion and the exchange of proposals on specific issues designed to identify the **zone of agreement**. That zone is the space where both parties can live with the outcome, even if it is less than ideal.

Figure 10.2 is an example of the zone of agreement. Imagine that the parties are negotiating the basic hourly pay of a group of cleaners. Each party will have an ideal outcome in mind (which might or might not be the same as its opening proposal). Each party will also have a bottom line beyond which it is not prepared to agree. Where each side's bottom-line overlaps comprises the zone of agreement. In Figure 10.2, the zone of settlement is between $18 and $21 per hour. If there is no overlap, then no settlement is currently possible. As bargaining proceeds and each side considers the consequences of not reaching agreement, unions and employers often adjust their bottom lines, and zones of settlement can appear.

The parties rarely openly communicate their bottom lines. Instead, it is common for them to inch toward a position with which both can live, thereby discovering the zone of agreement. Since there are usually multiple items up for negotiation, teams can also engage in exchanges ("we'll agree to X if you agree to Y" or "we'll drop our demands on A if you agree to B"). This behaviour is sometimes referred to as "log rolling."

This back-and-forth type of bargaining is called distributive, or positional, bargaining. In **distributive bargaining**, the parties are engaged in a conflict over the distribution of finite resources. They are focused on their own interests and how best to advance them, even if it is at the

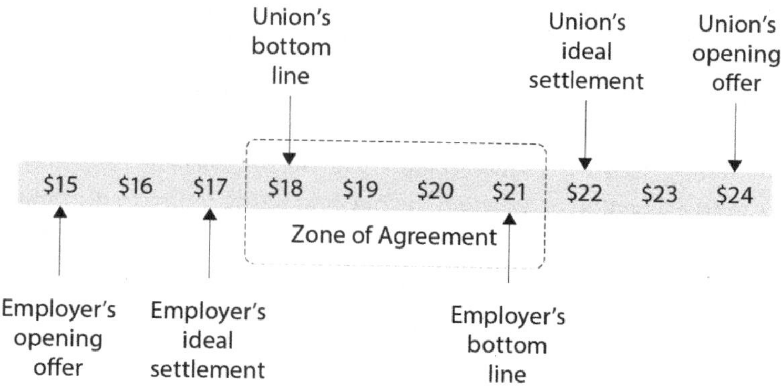

Figure 10.2 Bargaining positions and the zone of agreement

expense of the other party. This type of bargaining might strike some as adversarial and divisive, and to a degree it is. An alternative form of bargaining attempts to reduce the adversarial aspects. It is called **integrative bargaining**, commonly referred to as principle-based, interest-based, or mutual-gains bargaining. Feature Box 10.3 discusses integrative bargaining.

Feature Box 10.3 Integrative versus Distributive Bargaining

Integrative bargaining is an approach to negotiations that aims to find common interests and create win-win solutions through mutual trust and problem solving. The integrative bargaining process looks quite different from that of traditional bargaining. The parties identify problems and agree to find solutions together. Information is shared openly, and the parties work informally to explore possible solutions that would be mutually satisfactory. There is less focus on gaining advantage over the other party. This approach is often called mutual-gains bargaining because it assumes that, through this process, both parties can achieve positive outcomes.

Many advocates of integrative bargaining argue that it is more efficient and builds a healthier relationship between the parties over the long term.[16] They argue that distributive bargaining wastes time with posturing and the need to guess what the other party's position is and that it entrenches negative attitudes about the other side. Integrative bargaining has become a popular alternative in many HR circles but is not without its own issues.

First, it tends to work better when the parties' interests are naturally aligned. When there is a legitimate conflict of interests, as is often the case in labour relations, assumptions about win-win can break down. Specifically, integrative bargaining is not well suited to resolving monetary issues. The finite monetary resources available inevitably lead to a question of "dividing the pie" and thus a return to distributive bargaining. Since most bargaining issues in labour relations are monetary to some degree (e.g., vacations, dental coverage, and processes of discipline have costs for the employer), integrative bargaining might not be very useful.[17]

Second, integrative bargaining tends to entrench existing power dynamics. It is more effective for the party that holds greater bargaining power since it is better placed to determine the terms of the discussion. For this reason, unions tend to view it suspiciously, whereas employers are usually the party to suggest using it.

Third, the parties must have (or spend time developing) a considerable level of mutual trust to feel comfortable sharing priorities and information (required for integrative bargaining to succeed). This level of trust is rare, hard to develop, and hard to maintain given the conflicting interests of the parties.

Fourth, in practice distributive bargaining can incorporate elements of integrative bargaining when the parties recognize that there is a legitimate mutual interest. The so-called win-win issues are often the first ones settled and can be achieved without rancour or adversarial positioning. Integrative bargaining's ability to incorporate distributive approaches when needed is less certain.

Meetings at this stage will alternate between bargaining sessions in which the two parties meet, to make arguments and present counterproposals, and private sessions, sometimes called "caucusing," in which each party meets independently to discuss strategy and decide how to respond to proposals from the other side. The joint sessions are often "staged" affairs with clear plans and tight scripts, whereas much of the real discussion and work happens in the caucuses. Depending on the complexity of the bargaining and how far apart the parties are, this stage can be completed quickly, over a couple of meetings, or extend across many months. In fact, moving quickly or slowly can be a part of a team's bargaining strategy since timing can affect issues of bargaining power (see below).

Eventually, the back-and-forth process gets to a point where the parties are confronted with a choice. Either they are able to make some final concessions to find an agreement, or they declare that they have reached an impasse and proceed to a dispute resolution mechanism, either a work stoppage (i.e., a strike and/or lockout) or some form of mediation/arbitration. (We will discuss dispute resolution more fully in the next section.) This can be a difficult choice for each side to make, and the decision will turn on whether the bargaining process sufficiently narrowed the gap between the parties that they are within the zone of agreement regarding the main items of contention. If this is the case, then they will weigh the costs of any alternative to agreement, identify the final items on which they are prepared to change their positions, and find a way to reach a settlement. This process usually involves both parties deciding that an imperfect settlement is preferable to either more bargaining or a dispute.

If one or both parties are not in the zone of agreement, then they will not be willing to make that final calculation. In this case, either one party must move its position to fit within the other's zone (offering significant concessions that it did not wish to make), or bargaining reaches an impasse, the point at which one party believes, or both of them believe, that further bargaining will not lead to an agreement. In practice, it is often the threat of a strike or lockout (and its associated costs) that leads the parties to shift their positions enough to find a settlement. Often this occurs at the 11th hour when a work stoppage is looming. The calculations that the parties make at the crisis/settlement stage are heavily influenced by their respective **bargaining power.** Such power is the perceived or actual ability of one party to get the other party to agree to its terms. It affects all stages of collective bargaining but tends to come to the fore at the crisis stage, for this is when the parties need to act in some fashion. Feature Box 10.4 discusses bargaining power in more detail.

Feature Box 10.4 The Importance of Bargaining Power

Bargaining power is the ability of one party to impose costs on the other party if it does not agree to a proposed settlement. Costs can be many things. For example, employers can impose costs on workers, such as lost wages and benefits or even job loss. And workers can impose costs on employers, such as lost profits because of disrupted production, reduced productivity, or a poor reputation among consumers, the community, or potential workers. The capacity of each party to impose economic costs on the other is a central factor in its bargaining power.

A union's bargaining power rests mostly on its ability to mobilize its members in support of its demands in ways that disrupt production and reduce productivity. Unions can engage in work slowdowns, overtime refusals, "sick-ins," and ultimately strikes to disrupt production and/or reduce productivity. These activities give unions their bargaining power, both because they can impose actual costs on employers and because of employers' fear of these costs (if an employer believes that the union is capable of disrupting operations, then that perception can be enough to increase union bargaining power).

Conversely, an employer positioned to withstand a dispute holds a great deal of bargaining power. Creating stockpiles of products, hiring replacement workers, or shifting production to other facilities are all ways by which employers can increase bargaining power because they can suspend operations and let workers experience life without regular paycheques. The ability to place workers' employment under threat over the longer term (e.g., by layoffs and plant closures) also increases an employer's bargaining power. Workers' fear of these consequences is often enough to increase an employer's bargaining power.

Several other factors shape a party's bargaining power.

- Economic conditions influence bargaining power by shifting the context of the negotiations. An economic downturn can increase an employer's bargaining power since workers have fewer alternative job opportunities and there are more unemployed workers available to be replacement workers.
- Legislation and government policy can provide an advantage to one party or another. For example, a law banning replacement workers during a strike will weaken an employer's power because it makes continuing production during a strike more difficult.
- Public opinion can affect the parties' positions by threatening their reputations and social capital. It is more difficult to maintain a position if the public has antipathy toward it. For example, a health-care crisis can reduce a hospital employer's bargaining power by making it hard for the employer to refuse demands for wage increases by nurses.

Bargaining power influences all stages of the bargaining process. It will shape which demands go into the opening proposal. It will affect bargaining strategy. And, ultimately, it will determine how much a party is willing to move to achieve a settlement.

The decisions made at the crisis/settlement stage are determined by the parties' answers to whether the available settlement is better or worse than the likely outcome of proceeding with a dispute and whether the dispute will improve prospects for a more acceptable settlement. Answering these questions requires that the negotiating team has a clear understanding of its own bargaining power and of the other side's willingness to engage in a dispute. It can be a difficult calculation, and often the stakes are high. It is not surprising that over 90% of all collective agreements in Canada are settled without a strike or lockout.[18]

The final stage in collective bargaining is formal ratification of the agreement. Under the LRA, both negotiating teams must present the settlement, at this point called a tentative agreement, to their respective organizations for ratification. For the union, this usually means holding a ratification vote of bargaining unit members. For the employer, depending on its structure, ratification might require a vote by the board of directors or simply approval by the head of the organization. If either party rejects the tentative agreement, then the negotiating teams must return to the table to continue negotiations to find an acceptable agreement. If both parties ratify the tentative agreement, then representatives for each side will sign the new collective agreement, bringing it into legal effect.

Dispute Resolution

If the parties are unable to reach a settlement during collective bargaining, then they will turn to a dispute resolution mechanism. There are two types of dispute resolution: (1) having a third party decide any outstanding issues and (2) imposing costs on the other party through a strike or lockout in the hope that it changes its final position and negotiates an end to the dispute.

Using a neutral third party can take three forms.

- *Conciliation* sees a third party evaluate the parties' positions and why resolution is not possible. The third party does not get involved in the bargaining process but merely discusses the impasse with both sides. The conciliator issues a report recommending a possible avenue to settlement. It is often viewed as a first step in resolving an impasse. In many Canadian jurisdictions, conciliation is a mandatory step before strike/lockout action can be taken. However, its recommendations are not binding on the parties.

- *Mediation* differs from conciliation by having the neutral third party actively engage in the bargaining process by meeting jointly and separately with the parties and/or observing bargaining sessions. The mediator will recommend possible terms of settlement. These recommendations are not binding on the parties. Usually, mediation is a voluntary process in which one of the parties requests a mediator. In some circumstances, the government can order mediation, and in some jurisdictions it is a mandatory requirement before a strike or lockout. Although a mediator's recommendations are not binding, they can be persuasive in the process and lead parties to shift their positions.
- *Interest arbitration,* like mediation, inserts the third party into the bargaining process. However, unlike a mediator, the arbitrator is empowered to impose some or all of the terms of the settlement between the parties. Arbitration rulings are binding on the parties. They must agree mutually to move to arbitration, although in some circumstances the government will impose it on the parties. Given that the rulings are binding, the stakes are high when parties use arbitration to resolve their dispute.

Some hybrid forms of third-party resolution incorporate elements of the three types. One common one is mediation-arbitration, in which the third party begins the process as a mediator and, if mediation fails, then becomes an arbitrator and chooses the settlement terms.

There are multiple reasons that the parties might select third-party intervention to resolve an impasse. One or both might be unwilling to engage in a labour dispute and see intervention as a way out. More often third parties, especially mediators, are used as a delay tactic or to "corner" the other side through a favourable finding. Arbitration is rarely used voluntarily and then usually when one party has significantly higher bargaining power and the weaker side fears further escalation.

The other dispute resolution method is a work stoppage. A **strike** occurs when the workers in a bargaining unit refuse to perform all or part of their regular duties or refuse to go to work. A **lockout** is when the employer refuses workers access to part or all of the workplace so that workers cannot perform their jobs. A key element of the definitions is "part or all." A strike/lockout need not be a complete cessation of work. Workers who slow down the pace of work or have a "sick-out" (collectively calling in "sick") and employers who deny workers the opportunity to do aspects of work are both engaging in a work stoppage.

The purpose of a strike or lockout is to increase the pressure on the other side to accept certain proposals by attaching costs to refusing them (i.e., lost profits or wages). In practice, both sides bear economic costs during a strike or lockout, and a resolution is reached when one or both decide that the costs have become too high to justify further action.

Strikes/lockouts are heavily regulated in Canada. They can occur legally only when a collective agreement has expired. Before a strike or lockout takes place, the parties must go through a series of steps. The first step is the mandatory conciliation or mediation discussed above. The second step is that the union must acquire a mandate to strike via a secret ballot strike vote of its members (employers must complete a similar authorization to impose a lockout). If a strike is authorized, then in most jurisdictions the party must give notice of strike or lockout action to the other party (and often the government).

Actions during a strike or lockout are similarly controlled. In most strikes, the workers set up a **picket line** along which they walk around the perimeter of the workplace usually wearing or carrying signs. The purpose of a picket line is twofold. First, it is to create visibility for the strike, informing the public that there is a dispute happening at the workplace. Second, it is to prevent or slow traffic into and out of the workplace. This second purpose is key to creating economic costs as the striking workers attempt to prevent other workers, managers, deliveries, and needed items from entering or exiting the workplace and thus interfering with production and productivity.

During a work stoppage, pay and benefits are suspended by the employer. The workers instead receive **strike pay** from the union, aimed at lessening the economic costs to the striking workers. Strike pay is usually a fraction of the workers' regular pay. In return for strike pay, workers are expected to engage in activities related to the strike, such as taking turns on the picket line or providing other types of support.

One contentious issue during strikes is the use of **replacement workers** (often called "scabs" by union supporters). Employers often hire new workers during the work stoppage to keep production going and thus lessen the financial impact of the strike. Striking workers often strongly oppose the use of replacement workers. Bringing in replacement workers can result in violence on the picket line, which is why some jurisdictions ban the use of replacement workers.

A strike or lockout continues until the parties can come to an agreement to end the dispute. Most of the time, this occurs when the parties negotiate a settlement, but sometimes workers return to work without a deal in place. There are also times when the government issues a **back-to-work order**, legislation directing an end to the work stoppage and often determining the terms of the agreement or establishing arbitration. Governments issue back-to-work orders when they believe that public safety or public interest is at risk. Normally, governments use this tool to order an end to public sector strikes or strikes in economically sensitive industries (e.g., rail transport, seaports, mail). Governments have been using back-to-work orders more often recently.[19]

Not all strikes are legal. Sometimes workers act of their own accord outside the legal processes for strikes. These **wildcat strikes** are not directed by the union and can occur spontaneously in response to a perceived grievance or injustice. Wildcat strikes are controversial because, though they are illegal, they can also be effective in getting an employer's attention and causing changes because often an employer is unable to prepare for or cope with such a strike. Sometimes workers who participate in a wildcat strike face penalties in the form of a fine or discipline.

Collective Agreement Terms and Administration

At the conclusion of bargaining, both parties ratify the new collective agreement (generally through a vote). After ratification, the new collective agreement governs the employment relationship. Aside from a few legislative requirements for some form of dispute resolution, a union recognition clause, a no-strike/lockout commitment, and union security provisions (see Feature Box 10.5 for an explanation of union security), the content of a collective agreement is determined by the two parties. The scope of the issues in the agreement and how those issues are resolved vary greatly as a result.

Feature Box 10.5 Union Security Provisions

Under the applicable LRA, a union has an obligation to represent all workers in a bargaining unit regardless of whether they join the union or pay dues. This situation can give rise to a **free-rider problem** since someone gains an economic benefit from something without having to pay for it. In response, the courts have long recognized that, in exchange for the union obligation to represent all workers, it is reasonable to expect all workers, whether members of the union or not, to pay dues to the union to fund its operations. Consequently, all governments today require collective agreements to include some form of union security provision ensuring that the union receives dues from workers. Union security can take several forms.

- *Agency shop*: An agency shop requires the employer to deduct union dues from the paycheques of all workers in the bargaining unit and to remit the money to the union. This requirement is sometimes called the "Rand Formula" after the arbitrator who first established the principle in 1946. Governments require this provision, as a minimum, to be included in collective agreements. Workers do not have to join the union but are required to pay dues.
- *Open shop*: Increasingly rare in Canada because of legislation but more common in the United States, an open shop allows workers to decide if they wish to join the union and pay dues. This requires ongoing efforts by the union to persuade workers to agree to pay dues.
- *Union shop*: In a union shop, workers must join the union and pay dues as a condition of employment.
- *Hiring hall/closed shop*: In a hiring hall model (sometimes called a **closed shop**), the employer agrees to hire only from a pool of union members. This form is common in the construction industry, in which workers move from worksite to worksite frequently and the union is the source of constancy in the employment relationship.

The only time that workers can evade a union security clause is if they hold legitimate religious objections to unions. This belief is common among Seventh Day Adventists. Typically, the free-rider problem is avoided by having these workers make payments equivalent to the union dues to a charity.

In the United States, many states have passed so-called right-to-work laws that prohibit the establishment of mandatory union dues, making all workplaces effectively open shop. In Canada, the Alberta government recently passed a law that moves in that direction, mandating payment of only a portion of union dues dedicated to representational activities (i.e., bargaining, administration of the collective agreement) and requiring workers to "opt in" to the portion of dues that goes to fund charitable giving, political activity, advertising, and other non-core union functions.

In practice, most collective agreements cover similar issues. These agreements also tend to be long and at times complicated. The reason is the concept of **residual rights**. They are a function of the legal principle that management's authority in all work-related matters is intact unless explicitly curtailed in the collective agreement. In other words, if an issue is not addressed in the agreement, then the employer has an unfettered ability to act as it wishes. This incentivizes unions to address as many items in the agreement as possible.

Broadly speaking, clauses in collective agreements can be divided into two groups: **substantive rights** and **procedural rights**. Substantive rights tend to focus on the terms and conditions of employment (e.g., wages, benefits). Procedural rights address process and curtail the ability of management to act unilaterally (e.g., setting out procedures for discipline). Feature Box 10.6 lists some common substantive and procedural issues found in collective agreements.

Feature Box 10.6 Substantive and Procedural Rights

All collective agreements contain clauses that address substantive and procedural issues. Both types of clause are important. The need to address substantive issues is self-evident since they are the core of the employment relationship. What many overlook, however, is that, without addressing procedural issues, it can be difficult for unions to enforce substantive clauses and to create accountability for management's actions in general. So, the procedural rights can be seen as building a base on which substantive rights can be enforced. Some examples might clarify this point.

The following are some substantive clauses.

- Salaries and salary grids
- Overtime premiums
- Vacation leave provisions
- Illness, bereavement, and other leaves
- Health and dental plan provisions
- Travel allowances/per diems
- OHS protections

And here are some procedural clauses.

- Grievance procedures
- Seniority-based job security and promotion provisions
- Disciplinary procedures
- Right to union representation at disciplinary meetings
- Probationary periods
- A mechanism by which dues are collected and remitted to the union (called a **dues check-off**)
- Time off to conduct union business
- Layoff protection
- Joint labour-management committee

As these examples show, the substantive clauses affect what happens to workers on the job—how they are paid, when they get time off, et cetera. Nevertheless, the procedural clauses allow the union to be effective at its job. Without a grievance procedure, there would be no formal avenue for the union to seek redress for unpaid overtime. Although the substantive clauses are often the high-profile issues in a dispute, negotiations on the procedural issues often can be the most contentious because both parties recognize their importance, and they involve the giving over of managerial power.

Once the agreement is in force, it must be administered and enforced. In practice, the employer is charged with implementing the agreement (e.g., making required payments, assigning shifts according to seniority). If the employer interprets a clause differently from the union (or simply ignores or contravenes the clause), then a dispute can arise. Every collective agreement contains a process for resolving such disputes. The exact structure of the process will differ according to what the parties negotiate, but all start and end the same way. Dispute resolution is triggered by launching a grievance and, if not resolved earlier, ended by a grievance arbitration decision.

Grievances and Rights Arbitration

A **grievance** is a formal allegation that one or more clauses of the collective agreement have been violated. Either party can file a grievance, although in practice unions file most grievances since employers have more control over the day-to-day operations of the workplace. Not every action or inaction perceived by one party to be unfair or inappropriate is a ground for a grievance. The offending incident must relate directly to provisions in the collective agreement. There are four general types of grievance, outlined in Feature Box 10.7.

Feature Box 10.7 Types of Grievance

Individual grievances occur when the employer acts (or does not act) in a manner that negatively affects a specific individual worker. An example is the imposition of discipline against a worker with which the worker and the union disagree.

Group grievances occur when the employer's actions affect several workers in the same manner. An example is laying off a group of workers without abiding by the seniority provisions in the agreement.

Continuing grievances occur when the alleged violation of the agreement results not from a single incident or incidents but is part of an ongoing practice. An example is when the employer regularly refuses to allow a union representative to be present at disciplinary hearings when the collective agreement states that one should be present.

Policy grievances occur when the employer's (in)action can affect all workers in the bargaining unit. This differs from a group grievance in that the effect of the employer's (in)action might not have been experienced by any workers but there is the potential for harm. A key element is that the harm could affect everyone, not just a group of workers. An example is if the employer does not provide sufficient security measures to prevent robberies, which could affect any employee at any time.

The grievance process begins when a worker, group of workers, or the union makes a complaint about a violation of the agreement to an immediate supervisor or manager. The affected person or group is the **griever**. The complaint can be oral or written. A shop floor union representative, often called a shop steward, might or might not participate in the filing. The collective agreement will usually specify a timeline for the supervisor to consider and respond to the grievance.

If the grievance is not resolved at that first step, then the union can file a formal grievance. Here the nature of the grievance is formalized in writing, indicating dates, a description of the incident, the names of parties involved (including witnesses), the relevant provisions of the agreement, and the desired remedy. Both parties will conduct their own investigations and meet to discuss the facts and determine whether a resolution is possible.

At this point, grievance procedures can differ widely. Some are streamlined and have only one or two steps, whereas others can have multiple steps for possible resolution, each increasing in formality and level of management. During this process, a couple of concepts are important to remember. First, filing a grievance does not require the employer to change its actions immediately. This reality means that a worker might object to an employer's decision or direction but need to continue to abide by it until the grievance is resolved. This concept is commonly referred to as **work now, grieve later**, to reflect the fact that a grievance is a post-incident remedy.

Second, beyond the initial complaint, the grievance is "owned" by the union, not the individual worker. This means that, as the grievance advances through the process, it is the union, usually in consultation with the worker, that decides whether to continue to pursue it or not. The effect is that the union might choose to discontinue a grievance even if the worker is not yet satisfied with the outcome. This right to control the grievance process is balanced by a union's duty of fair representation, discussed earlier in this chapter, which means that the union must fairly consider the worker's interests. If the parties exhaust the grievance process stipulated in the collective agreement, then the final step is usually to take the matter to arbitration.

If an issue remains unresolved, then the union usually has the option to advance the grievance to arbitration. **Grievance arbitration** (sometimes called rights arbitration) entails the appointment of a neutral third party to adjudicate the dispute and render a decision, including any necessary remedy. The arbitrator's decision becomes binding on both parties. The arbitrator has many of the powers of a judge, including the ability to compel the attendance of witnesses and the production of documents. The arbitration process is quite formal, and often both parties will engage lawyers for assistance. The arbitrator will preside over a hearing at which the parties present their cases, submit evidence, and examine witnesses. The arbitrator will consider the evidence, refer to **jurisprudence** (i.e., previous arbitration awards and court decisions relevant to the grievance), and render a decision. The award will outline the facts, explain the arbitrator's decision, and, when required, identify a remedy and instructions for implementing it. The award can be released many weeks or months after the hearing. Arbitrator awards can be appealed only to the courts (called a judicial review) for a narrow range of reasons, typically an error of fact or law.

Given their formality, arbitrations are expensive and time consuming. The parties normally split the costs of the arbitrator in addition to paying for their own legal and staff representation. Hearings are often scheduled many months (and occasionally years) after the initial incident and can last many days in complicated cases. The highly legal nature of the process also excludes rank-and-file workers, requiring reliance on lawyers and trained professionals. Given these shortcomings, many have criticized arbitrations for not effectively addressing workers' concerns and for sapping unions and employers of resources that could be used elsewhere. For these reasons, some unions and employers have agreed to alternatives to traditional arbitration to reduce delays and costs. Feature Box 10.8 summarizes some alternatives.

Feature Box 10.8 Alternatives to Grievance Arbitration

Because of the costs and lengthy delays of traditional grievance arbitration, some parties have sought alternative ways to resolve disputes. There are three basic alternatives.

Expedited arbitration: In some jurisdictions, the parties can agree to enter expedited arbitration, which streamlines the process by eliminating some of the formal aspects, providing strict timelines for the hearing and award release, and minimizing the use of lawyers. Expedited arbitrations are not considered precedent setting (meaning that they cannot be used in future cases).

Grievance mediation: Some jurisdictions allow the parties to utilize government mediation services (usually reserved for bargaining) for grievances. The mediators cannot issue a formal award binding on the parties, but they can use mediation techniques to assist the parties to come to a resolution.

Mediation-arbitration (med-arb): This is a hybrid model of resolution in which the arbitrator begins the process acting as a mediator and engaging the parties in a more informal mediation process. If this process is unsuccessful, then the mediator acts as an arbitrator. This process allows for an earlier resolution by reducing the need for formal hearings.

Results from these alternatives are mixed. Although often they shorten the amount of time needed to reach a decision, which is good for the griever, the overall impacts have been disappointing. Mediation options rarely resolve the dispute since usually only the most contentious grievances end up in arbitration. These alternatives do not address a major reason for delay: namely, the full schedules of the lawyers and arbitrators involved in the process, which can add weeks and months to hearing schedules.

Sometimes union members will address wrongs in the workplace through direct action. Direct action is behaviour that places pressure on the employer to resolve an issue immediately. The most obvious form of direct action is the wildcat strike (discussed above), in which workers put down their tools and stop production until the employer meets their demands. Other tactics include sick-outs, slowdowns, and marching as a group to confront the boss. These tactics require an organized and mobilized union membership and are not without the risk that workers might be disciplined or terminated. The utility of these tactics to workers is that they offer immediate resolution. These tactics can also shift power in the workplace by making supervisors or managers reluctant to repeat the experience and thus more responsive to future complaints.

Impacts of Unions

Opinions about unions are often strongly held and mixed. Many people perceive unions as unnecessary intrusions into the employment relationship, interfering with the management of an organization. They also fear that unionization will drive up labour costs and make it harder for managers to manage. A commonly articulated fear is that unions protect "lazy" workers. Yet many people recognize that a union acts as an important countervailing force to management's power and control in the workplace. They also believe that improving wages and working conditions for workers is good for society and the economy.

The reality is that most people do not know much about unions. Unions are in the public eye only during confrontations or disputes, giving most people a distorted sense of what they do. There are many misconceptions about what happens when an organization is unionized. For example, unions cannot protect so-called lazy workers from legitimate management of their performance. All that unions can negotiate is a process for discipline ensuring that all workers are treated fairly. If a worker performs poorly and the employer follows the proper process of discipline, then there is little that the union can do to prevent termination.

So let us spend a bit of time looking at the impacts of unions. Research confirms that unions, on average, do increase wages and benefits. Unionized workers in Canada earn approximately $5 more per hour than non-unionized workers ($28.87 to $23.57).[20] For women, this advantage increases to $7 per hour. The union effect on wages is also stronger for workers of colour and vulnerable workers.[21] Overall, unions tend to make wage structures more equitable in workplaces, bringing up lower incomes to shrink the difference between top and bottom. Economic benefits to workers extend beyond union members. International research has shown that higher levels of unionization are associated with lower levels of inequality and low pay (they pull up the lowest-paid workers).[22] It has also found that union density leads to smaller gender and racial pay gaps.[23]

The union effect on non-wage benefits (e.g., health benefits, pensions) is even stronger. Unionized workers are more than 50% more likely to have medical and dental coverage than non-unionized workers.[24] One of the biggest differences is in pension coverage. A large majority of unionized workers have pension plans (and most of them are defined-benefit pensions) compared with fewer than one-third of non-unionized workers.[25] Unionized workers have more job stability and security, in part a factor of their disproportionate presence in the public sector and among large employers. Unions also tend to make workplaces safer. Although unionized workplaces are subject to more safety complaints and inspections, overall injury rates and severity are lower.[26] Most researchers attribute this effect to unions' capacity to educate and train workers on their safety rights.

What about their impacts on business? Although unionization does seem to affect employers' profits negatively, much of that effect is countered by lower turnover and higher productivity at unionized firms. Unions also increase employers' potential labour pool by compelling higher-quality working conditions attractive to job seekers.[27] Unionized organizations are no more likely to close or go bankrupt than non-unionized employers.[28] In terms of broader economic impacts, there is no statistical relationship between levels of unionization and economic and employment performance in advanced industrial countries.[29] Overall, unions can win tangible gains both for their members and for other workers. They do affect employers' profits but provide other secondary benefits that can outweigh those costs.

Conclusion

As WestJet experienced, the presence of a union in a workplace can profoundly change an organization's approach to human resources. New sets of rules come into play, and the employer has to deal with an additional party when addressing employment issues. Many employers, as WestJet did, chafe at the prospect of unionization and work to prevent it. From the perspective of HR management, unionization changes the dynamics of managing workers, but unionization itself can be well managed by HR practitioners. Much of the animosity and conflict that can emerge with unionization stems from an employer's reluctance to build a respectful relationship with the union. Understanding the structures and processes of labour relations and navigating those processes in good faith can go a long way toward ensuring that the presence of a union can be a net positive, even for the employer.

EXERCISES

KEY TERMS

Define the following terms.

- Active bargaining
- Application for certification
- Arbitration
- Automatic certification
- Back-to-work order
- Bargaining power
- Bargaining unit
- Certification
- Closed shop
- Collective agreement
- Distributive bargaining
- Dues check-off
- Duty of fair representation
- Free-rider problem
- Grievance
- Grievance arbitration
- Griever
- Integrative bargaining
- Intra-organizational bargaining
- Jurisprudence
- Labour relations act
- Labour relations board
- Lockout
- Mediation
- Open shop
- Opening offer
- Organizing drive

- Picket line
- Procedural rights
- Replacement workers
- Representation vote
- Residual rights
- Strike
- Strike pay
- Substantive rights
- Unfair labour practice
- Union
- Union density
- Union shop
- Wildcat strike
- Work now, grieve later
- Zone of agreement

DISCUSSION QUESTIONS

Discuss the following questions.

- What motivates workers to join a union?
- What are some of the tactics that employers use to thwart a union drive? Why do they employ them?
- What are the key steps in the bargaining process?
- What is the difference between integrative and distributive bargaining, and when might a party prefer one over the other?
- What are the goals of the parties when they move to a strike or lockout? What is the alternative to a strike/lockout?
- What is the function of a picket line?
- Which mechanisms do unions and employers have to resolve disagreements over the application of the collective agreement?

ACTIVITIES

Complete the following activities.

- Go to Unifor's national website, www.unifor.org, and find its constitution. Outline the organizational structures of the union, including the roles of members in the operation of the national union and its locals and how democratic accountability is achieved.
- Identify a strike/lockout that recently occurred in your area. Search media reports about it. Identify the parties' positions on key issues at the beginning. Find the final settlement. How does it differ? Which events and dynamics shaped the final outcome?
- Search the labour relations legislation for your jurisdiction. What are its provisions regarding certification vote timelines and the use of replacement workers during strikes/lockouts? Analyze how these provisions might affect an organizing drive or strike.

SELF-REFLECTION QUESTIONS

Write self-reflections of 200 to 500 words on the following questions.

- Do you or a family member have experience with being a member of a union? What was your/their experience? How might it differ from being in a non-unionized workplace?
- Think about media portrayals of unions and their actions. How do they differ from the actions and processes outlined in this chapter?
- In your opinion, why do employers oppose unionization? Are their concerns reasonable given the evidence?
- In your opinion, are there better options for resolving disputes regarding the interpretation of the collective agreement than grievance arbitration?

11 Practicing Human Resource Management

Human resource management often entails solving problems so that the work of the organization can proceed. Some problems are common and easy to resolve. For example, when a worker quits, HR practitioners often assist with processing that worker's exit as well as hiring a replacement. Although every departure or hiring is unique, the work involved is mostly straightforward, and often an organization has an established way to handle these events.

Other HR problems can be more complex. They can involve unique or complicated circumstances and require difficult decisions and trade-offs. This is where the technical approach to human resource management needs to be leavened with a political analysis that considers conflicting interests, power, and intersecting identity factors.

In this chapter, we offer a series of short cases illustrating some complex problems that HR practitioners can be asked to solve. These cases are loosely based on real-world problems encountered by HR practitioners. They are designed to make visible the thought processes and strategies that experienced practitioners can use (often unconsciously) when solving problems. We close the chapter with advice on how HR practitioners can cope with being asked to do unethical or illegal things.

Hiring Bias at ABC Cars & Trucks

ABC Cars & Trucks is a large, locally owned dealership in a medium-sized city with approximately 45 employees, including eight mechanics. It sells and services a major car brand. The owner resides in the community but is semi-retired and has turned over day-to-day operations to a general manager. There is a significant level of staff turnover in the service division, particularly among mechanics, often lured away by higher wages in the oil and gas industry. On average, ABC hires four new mechanics per year. Hiring is normally done by the general manager and the manager of the relevant area. As the organization's sole HR practitioner, you attend the hiring meetings to take notes and answer questions. You also report directly to the general manager and handle all HR tasks except payroll and benefits (outsourced to a payroll agency).

The most recent advertisement for an automotive mechanic yielded 10 applicants, including (unusually) two qualified women. The general manager and service manager winnowed the list down to four applicants to interview, all men. One of the women who applied called your office this morning and left a message wondering why she was not short-listed. She indicated that she suspects she was not interviewed because she is a woman and that such behaviour is discriminatory. A quick review of hiring records shows that approximately 5% of applicants for mechanic positions (roughly 10 of 200) over the past five years have been women, but no women have been short-listed for an interview. Overall, employment at ABC is highly gendered, with all mechanics, sales staff, and managers being men, whereas women hold most of the (lower-paying) support and administrative positions.

This phone call seems to require some action since your job description includes ensuring that ABC Cars & Trucks is compliant with relevant laws and that employment issues are resolved discreetly so as not to damage ABC's reputation in the community. Your first instinct is to call the applicant back. But you are not sure what purpose that would serve or even what the issue is. Feature Box 11.1 outlines some basic steps to take when confronted with a difficult employment-related issue.

Feature Box 11.1 Issue Analysis Framing and Checklist

When faced with what seems like a thorny HR problem, it is often useful to spend some time thinking carefully through the answers to four questions. Although the questions are set out in a specific order, answering them might require moving back and forth through them until you are satisfied with all four answers.

1. What is the issue?
2. How will the issue affect the organization and the people involved?
3. What ways can the issue be resolved?
4. Which of these options is the best one?

The most important question to answer is the first. What is the issue that you must resolve? It is often possible to frame a problem in several ways. How you frame the issue shapes the options available to you and how you can proceed. For example, imagine that a worker in your organization is seriously injured on the job. Your job is to investigate what happened.

You might frame this task as "the worker likely did something wrong, and I need to find out what that was so we can prevent it in the future." Naturally, this framing would lead you to focus on the worker's behaviour. As noted in Chapter 2, focusing on the proximate cause of the incident tends to obscure structural factors that contributed to the injury and, consequently, yields fewer effective controls. For example, if your conclusion is that Kelly cut their arm because they reached across the saw, a reasonable control might be a rule that workers should not reach across the saw.

An alternative framing of the issue is that "I need to identify behavioural and structural factors that contributed to this injury." Looking for the root cause of the injury yields a full understanding of why the injury occurred and thus which changes are necessary to prevent future incidents. Continuing with the saw example, if you look at the structural contributions, you might find that Kelly reached across the saw because the wood is stacked on the other side. Moving the wood so that the worker does not have to reach across the saw to do the job is a more effective control than an administrative rule because moving the wood eliminates the hazard.

Framing is often driven by who is affected by the issue, what their interests are, and how much power they have in the organization and society. Continuing with our example, focusing on a worker's behaviour shifts responsibility for the injury onto the worker. This framing benefits the supervisor and organization by helping them to avoid reputational and legal consequences of operating unsafely. In contrast, a root cause analysis is good for workers because it will eliminate the hazard. In the short term, it might impose costs on the supervisor and organization. These costs can be ameliorated in the long term because there will be fewer injuries. This analysis suggests that there can be a political dimension to the framing decision (i.e., conflicting interests) that HR practitioners must consider and navigate.

In applying the issues analysis checklist in Feature Box 11.1 to the situation at ABC Cars & Trucks, you find several intertwined issues.

- The general manager and/or service manager are sexist (perhaps unconsciously) in their selection practices.
- The company discriminates against women.
- Raising this issue with your direct supervisor (the general manager) might have negative consequences for you (including possible firing).

Unpacking the situation and writing down the different issues helps us to think carefully through the situation. It also helps us to identify who is affected and in what ways. In this case, those affected include the following:

- prospective women workers who might be denied jobs for which they are qualified;
- the general manager and service manager, who might face discipline or termination as well as harm to their personal reputations, both inside and outside the organization;
- to the degree that sexism extends beyond the hiring process, women workers who might be discriminated against in other ways;
- the company, which might miss out on hiring qualified workers;
- the company, which might also face both legal and reputational harms for allowing discrimination against women, perhaps making it harder to fill future vacancies and driving away customers; and

- you as an HR practitioner who might be implicated, albeit innocently, in potentially discriminatory hiring practices, causing you to face reputational harm or even employment termination for exposing the misconduct of the general manager and service manager.

Thinking the issues through, you conclude the following.

- The behaviour of the general manager and service manager is sexist in its effect. It is harder to draw conclusions about their intentions. This could just be an example of similar-to-me bias (see Chapter 6).
- Regardless of their intentions, both direct discrimination and indirect discrimination on the basis of gender are prohibited (see Chapter 2). Repeatedly failing to interview and hire qualified women suggests that discrimination is occurring. It can have legal, financial, and reputational costs.
- It is likely that the general manager will be discomforted by the implicit criticism of his behaviour. He might also fear consequences should the owner of the business be made aware of his behaviour. Your contract of employment allows the general manager to fire you without cause in exchange for six months of notice or pay in lieu (see Chapter 9).

Given all of these factors, probably the optimal framing of this issue is that

- there has been an accusation of gender-based discrimination in the hiring process;
- a cursory examination of records suggests that there might be some basis for this accusation;
- this accusation poses significant organizational risk; and
- addressing this issue will require navigating some interpersonal politics.

The potentially serious consequences of this allegation mean that you are obligated to take some action to protect the interests of ABC Cars & Trucks. The most pressing issue is the potential for organizational harm if the caller files a human rights complaint, goes to the media, or simply complains to her friends and family members. In the short term, there are several ways in which this issue can be resolved.

- Take no action and hope that the applicant loses interest.
- Offer the applicant an interview. This might satisfy her and undercut her claim of discrimination. If she is not the successful candidate, however, this approach can increase her dissatisfaction and heighten the risk of reputational harm.
- Redo the selection process in a way that gives the applicant an equal chance at being selected for an interview and the job.
- Offer the applicant a payment to pre-empt her complaint of discrimination in exchange for a non-disclosure agreement.

A complicating factor here is that the decision about how to proceed likely belongs to the general manager (your boss and one of the accused). This places him in a potential conflict of interest (i.e., his personal interest in avoiding consequences can conflict with his organizational duty to take action). Essentially, you have two options here.

- Figure out a tactful way to introduce the issue to the general manager and get him to take action to address the pressing aspect of the issue. For example, you might identify the risk, his potential conflict of interest, and suggest a solution that you could implement to address the problem. This approach is most likely to preserve your relationship with your boss and generate a measured response, but there is no guarantee of that.
- On the pretext that the conflict of interest and risk are significant, you could contact the owner directly and lay out the issue and recommend solutions to both the immediate issue and the underlying problem. This approach is riskier for you: the owner might not appreciate you end-running your boss, and your boss is unlikely to be happy to be end-run.

It is also possible for you to exercise these options sequentially, starting with the boss and, if you are unsuccessful with him, escalating matters to the owner. In the longer term, there are several potential solutions to address the issue of gender bias in hiring.

- Implicit bias training can help individuals to identify and correct implicit biases that shape their decisions (e.g., sexist attitudes resulting in women's applications being discarded). This can result in more women being short-listed and hired. The evidence that such training can change behaviour, however, is limited.[1]

- Gender-blind hiring processes remove information (e.g., names) that can be used to infer gender and other personal characteristics. This should result in more women being short-listed for interviews. The efficacy of this approach appears to be limited by the tendency of managers to infer characteristics from other clues on resumés.[2]
- Hiring quotas seek to compel the hiring of workers in proportion to their representation in the workforce or society. For example, approximately 5% of automotive mechanics are women. An organization might then mandate interviews and/or hirings to include a similar percentage of women. Quotas can stigmatize new hires (e.g., "you were hired because of your gender, not your skill") and do not necessarily result in long-term changes in representation because hires might leave hostile workplaces.
- Eliminating those with known biases from responsibility for hiring might reduce bias in hiring if those who replace them are less biased. Removing duties can cause hard feelings and result in managers claiming constructive dismissal (see Chapter 9). An alternative is to ensure that hiring committees are representative of the general population (e.g., gender balanced).

There is no perfect solution to this problem. You might prioritize containing the immediate risk (e.g., reputational harm) to the organization. This could entail identifying to the general manager the risk posed by the caller and proposing to mitigate it by offering her a financial settlement in exchange for a non-disclosure agreement. This reduces both the immediate organizational risk and the personal risk to the general manager as well as signals to him that you are his ally. The general manager's resulting goodwill might then be used to generate buy-in to the implementation of gender-blind applicant screening and gender-balanced hiring committees to eliminate the risk of future complaints via a process that both is and appears to be unbiased.

It is notable that this approach offers no real justice to the worker(s) who might have been discriminated against. That fact (rightly) might sit uneasily with many people. But the role of an HR practitioner is to advance the interests of the employer. Sometimes that requires countenancing (or just politely ignoring) bad behaviour by powerful organizational actors to achieve the best outcome possible for the organization.

If this approach is not effective (e.g., the general manager refuses to act), then you can choose either to escalate the issue to the owner or to take no further action (i.e., hope that the issue goes away). In either case, savvy HR practitioners will carefully document their efforts to address the problem and record the general manager's reluctance to take action on the issue. Although this paper trail will not necessarily prevent future problems (e.g., retaliation by the general manager or a human rights complaint), a clear paper trail documenting his behaviour can be useful if you need to defend the organization or pursue legal action yourself for being wrongfully dismissed.

Pay Raises at ABC Marketing & Advertising

ABC Marketing & Advertising is a mid-sized national media company that specializes in creating print and online advertisements for major brands. The company employs approximately 100 non-unionized workers in a large urban centre. You are the compensation specialist in the three-person HR shop, and you report directly to the managing partner. You often work with department managers to set compensation and administer benefits. ABC has adopted a differentiation business strategy based on carefully cultivated client relationships, high levels of client servicing, and creative advertising campaigns (see Chapter 1). Account staff, who bring in clients, maintain their loyalty, and pitch new advertising ideas and campaigns, are central to this strategy, whereas the work of everyone else is focused on supporting them.

As a result, the organization has developed a two-tier HR strategy (see Chapter 4). ABC Marketing & Advertising emphasizes retaining high-performing accounts staff through competitive compensation because their personal relationships with clients are central to the company's business strategy. This HR strategy incentivizes accounts staff to maximize the revenue that they generate each year. In practice, this means that they are paid a modest base salary and receive the standard benefits package.

Most of their income is earned through a generous commission on overall revenue from the accounts that they manage. Performance-based pay via commissions is an industry-standard practice that incentivizes the recruitment and retention of clients (see Chapter 8). Earned commissions can double, triple, or even quadruple the base salary provided to the accounts staff. There are significant differences in their annual commission earnings based on the sizes of the accounts that they handle and the rate of commission that they receive. New accounts staff are generally hired through word of mouth and based on their ability to bring in new clients with whom they have pre-existing relationships.

Other workers, whose work is less directly connected to revenue generation, are compensated with a base salary plus benefits. Every employment contract at ABC Marketing & Advertising includes a requirement that workers keep their compensation and benefits package confidential or face discipline. In theory, this policy is designed to limit conflict among workers over compensation. In practice, the company uses it to make it harder for workers to argue that they deserve a raise by comparing their performance and compensation with those of their co-workers.

Over the past five years, existing clients have begun shifting to online advertising and away from traditional print (e.g., newspapers, magazines, billboards), and new clients are almost entirely interested in online advertising. It is cheaper for clients than print advertising, and this has reduced the revenue generated by each account. Consequently, accounts staff commissions have declined by an average of 5% per year over five years, and this decline is accelerating. These accounts continue to require the same amount of effort to maintain, so accounts staff cannot just add additional clients to make up the difference in commissions.

A number of newer accounts staff have been discussing declining commissions and appear to have nominated Ashok Kumar to approach their manager about them. They indicate that they would like their income stabilized at the level that it was five years earlier and suggest increasing either their commission rates or their base salaries. Their manager immediately comes to your office and says that she feels like she is being ganged up on and pressured. From what you can tell, the workers' request was made very civilly. She suggests that the accounts staff have clearly violated the policy on discussing their compensation and wants to know if she can terminate Kumar as a lesson to the other workers. A few hours later the managing partner sends you an email indicating that he would like you to brief the partners on this situation and propose a way to resolve "this issue." He does not specify what the issue is, and your past experience suggests that asking him for clarification will be both unpleasant and unsuccessful ("You're the HR person; figure it out").

You decide to spend some time discussing the matter with managers as well as some employees with whom you are friendly. You then sit down to apply the issues analysis checklist (see Feature Box 11.1) to this problem. You begin by trying to decide how to frame the issue. As is often the case with thorny HR problems, several intertwined issues have different impacts on different groups.

- A change in the industry is eroding the revenue of ABC Marketing & Advertising. This suggests that the business strategy adopted by the company might no longer be viable. Declining revenue is also threatening the organization's ability to retain revenue-producing staff, suggesting that the compensation plan might require adjustment. Other staff are watching the accounts staff's demand and might seek salary adjustments of their own if the accounts staff are successful.
- The manager of the accounts staff believes that her authority has been undermined. She might also be worried that her unit's performance will suffer (because of either worker attrition or declining effort) and thereby raise questions about her management skills.
- The accounts staff see the pay system as unfair because their income is declining for reasons unrelated to their performance. They are quietly discussing what to do if their concerns are not taken seriously (see Feature Box 11.2).

Feature Box 11.2 Exit, Voice, Loyalty, and Neglect

Human resource management focuses our attention on organizational strategies. But it is important for HR practitioners to remember that workers also have strategies. Their responses to changes in the wage-effort bargain (see Chapter 1) and unionization (see Chapter 10) are examples of their adoption of a strategy to make their lives better. When making decisions, effective HR practitioners give some thought to how workers might respond and why they might act that way. This can help organizations to avoid unnecessary conflicts with workers. This is the utility of treating human resources as both a technical and a political activity.

In 1970, Albert Hirschman posited a model of behaviour when an organization acts in a way that no longer meets the needs of its members.[3] This model has been extended over time and is now called the *exit-voice-loyalty-neglect (EVLN) model*. It identifies four possible worker responses to HR policies, changes, and issues (see Figure 11.1).

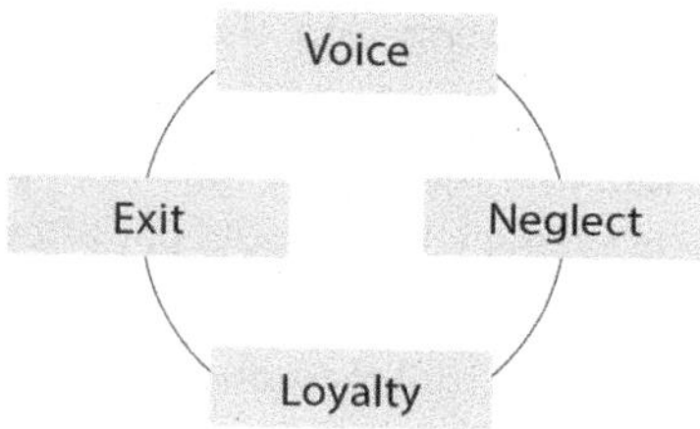

Figure 11.1 Exit-voice-loyalty-neglect model

Exit sees workers leave the organization. Quitting entails costs for workers, which vary depending on a job's wage rate and the state of the labour market (tight or loose). For example, workers in low-wage work during an economic boom might quit with little provocation because a comparable job is easy to find. Exit also entails costs for organizations, particularly if the worker is important for achieving organizational goals or there is a spate of workers quitting that disrupts production.

Voice entails trying to remedy the situation. This occurs most often by workers who communicate their concerns to organizational decision makers in the hope of a resolution. Communication can be formal (e.g., a request, complaint, or grievance) or informal (e.g., grousing or backtalking a supervisor). If this approach is not successful, then workers might increase the intensity of their communication or adopt different approaches (e.g., legal action, unionizing) before abandoning this strategy.

Loyalty sees workers deciding to accept an unsatisfactory situation and continue to contribute to the organization. This might be in the hope that a remedy will be available later or that they will at least be rewarded for their loyalty. It might also reflect a cost-benefit analysis that suggests staying with the organization and remaining quiet is the best option. How much workers need their jobs and the expected response to any voice effort will influence how attractive workers find loyalty.

Neglect is an alternative to loyalty; workers remain with the organization but perform in a perfunctory manner (this is often called presenteeism or quiet quitting). Less commonly, workers might take actions contrary to the organization's interests to express their discontent (e.g., absenteeism, malingering, theft, sabotage).

Once HR practitioners have identified workers' potential responses to a specific decision, they must assess each risk to determine the responses to which organizations should pay attention. HR practitioners can do this assessment in their heads, but it is often useful to do so on paper. The risk assessment tool for workplace hazards (see Figure 2.2) can be modified to assess the risk of various responses by workers.

Risk = Probability x Consequences x Frequency

- Probability: The likelihood that the workers' response will have a negative effect on organizational performance.

  ☐ Rare (1) ☐ Possible (2) ☐ Probable (3) ☐ Likely (4)

- Consequence: The severity of the impact on organizational performance caused by the workers' response.

  ☐ Negligible (1) ☐ Marginal (2) ☐ Significant (3) ☐ Catastrophic (4)

- Frequency: The frequency with which workers will exhibit the response.

  ☐ Rare (1) ☐ Occasional (2) ☐ Frequent (3) ☐ Continuous (4)

For example, a worker who exits because the organization allows her boss to harass her might be assessed as follows.

- Probability of quitting: Probable (3) because she has complained and is experiencing anxiety.
- Consequence: Marginal (2) because it will be reasonably easy to replace her.
- Exposure: Rare (1) because the harassment appears to be isolated and no other workers are affected.

Using this tool, HR practitioners can quantify this risk as 3 x 2 x 1 = 6 and compare it with the risk associated with other workers' potential responses to determine which risks to focus on. For example, they might assess the risk associated with this worker filing a human rights complaint (a more intense form of voice) as much higher (because of the consequences of reputational harm to the organization). It is also worth keeping in mind that workers' potential responses are not mutually exclusive (i.e., a worker can quit and file a human rights complaint).

Once HR practitioners have prioritized which potential risks to address, there are basically three options. An organization can decide to take no action (i.e., accept the potential harm). An organization can take some action fully or partially to accommodate workers' interests or demands in the hope that the workers will be satisfied enough that the organization can avoid the negative consequence. Finally, an organization can pre-emptively terminate a worker's employment (see Chapter 9) and thereby potentially reduce the risk that it faces (although, in cases such as harassment, this action can exacerbate the issue).

In theory, an organization's response should be driven by a cost-benefit analysis. In practice, things are more complex. Sometimes it is hard to assess accurately the level of organizational risk and/or the cost and effectiveness of attenuating it. Some risk-mitigation strategies can give rise to other risks (e.g., acceding to a salary demand might trigger a spate of such demands). Finally, decision makers can select a response based on non-rational factors, such as anger, fear, compassion, or competitiveness.

You decide that the compensation plan adopted by ABC Marketing & Advertising for its accounts staff no longer motivates them to seek new clients (they all have full client lists), and declining commissions is causing dissatisfaction, which can result in attrition. This poses a significant risk of future client loss if accounts staff quit and then use their relationships with their clients to woo them to a different agency. You see three main options to address this risk that you decide to present to the managing partner.

- *Status quo*: ABC Marketing & Advertising should take no action and let the accounts staff decide how they want to proceed. The key risk with this option is that the staff will exit the company and seek to take their clients with them. The likelihood of this outcome is not clear.
- *Compensation change*: The compensation of accounts staff could be altered to address declining commissions. The options include a one-time payment or short-term increase in their commission rates to fully or partially to offset their decline in income. The cost of this option is modest, but it does not address the underlying and seemingly systemic problem of declining accounts revenue. Alternatively, accounts staff could be offered a fixed salary, and the company could use performance management techniques (e.g., sales targets) to maintain revenue levels. Such a contractual change would require the agreement of the workers or their termination without cause and the hiring of new accounts staff (see Chapter 9).
- *Fire Kumar*: The company could fire Kumar for violating the compensation confidentiality clause in his contract. This would make it difficult for him to get another job. This action could be combined with status quo or change compensation options in the hope that his firing will discourage further demands by the accounts staff. This approach might alienate the remaining staff and trigger neglect and/or exit behaviours.

A key risk that you believe you need to address is the possibility that accounts staff will quit and take their clients with them at a low cost. An additional risk is that changing the compensation of accounts staff will cause other staff to make their own demands for wage increases. You also note the need to deal with the manager's hurt feelings but decide to set that issue aside. How you handle the manager might depend on which option the management group prefers.

Maternity Leaves in the County of Fair Haven

The County of Fair Haven provides municipal services to a sprawling rural region. You are an HR practitioner employed by the county. It hires approximately 25 employees per year in entry-level administrative positions. These workers are not unionized and work a standard 8:30 to 4:30 work day in one of the county's two main offices. The average age of these new hires is 25 (typically postsecondary graduates with one to two years of work experience), and approximately 56% of new hires are women. About half of newly hired women take parental leave within three years of being hired, necessitating the hiring of cover-off employees and redistribution of some tasks.

The chief administrative officer (CAO) of the county has expressed frustration with the cost and work associated with accommodating parental leaves. After three relatively new hires announced the previous week that they were pregnant, the CAO directs you to "do something about this problem." You are expected to provide a memo to the county's management team in response to this request by the end of the week. Although the CAO does not give you any direction on how to proceed, his past comments suggest that he would prefer not to hire young women because of the inconvenience posed by accommodating parental leaves and childcare demands (e.g., sick children, medical appointments).

As you sit down to draft the memo, you worry that the CAO and management team expect you to find a way for them to avoid hiring young women. You decide to apply the issues analysis checklist (see Feature Box 11.1) to this problem, beginning by determining the issue. As is often the case with thorny HR problems, several intertwined issues have different impacts on different groups.

- There are financial and administrative costs associated with employing workers who have (or will have) families. These costs include additional hiring, training, and overtime to manage parental leaves and other absences related to social reproductive responsibilities (see Feature Box 1.3). Accommodating workers' family responsibilities is also administratively burdensome to managers. The cost and irritation of doing so do not rise to the level of undue hardship (Chapter 2), but minimizing organizational costs associated with workers' family responsibilities is a reasonable action for the county to take.
- The CAO has attributed these costs primarily to young women. Your data suggest that family-related responsibilities affect workers

of all genders and ages. Parental leaves, however, are the highest and most visible cost. A negligible number of men employed by the county use parental leaves, so clearly this is a gendered issue. Any recommendation that results in a negative effect for an identifiable group runs the risk of being found discriminatory (see Chapter 2).

- Discriminating against young women entails financial and reputational risks for the county, which can affect its ability to attract and retain qualified workers. If the county faces accusations of discrimination, then the CAO might be directed by the elected county council to fix the problem. Doing so might include firing the staff member responsible for the discriminatory policy or practice. You do not wish to get fired for cause (see Chapter 9).

You decide that the issue to tackle is reducing the financial and administrative costs associated with accommodating workers' family responsibilities by proposing changes to job design, HR planning, and training. You decide to address parental leave first because it is the issue with the highest cost and the one that the CAO has flagged as problematic. There are various options available to you.

- *Job design*: Examining the job descriptions and specifications for entry-level jobs, you note that there is substantial overlap in requirements, duties, and working conditions (see Chapter 3). This suggests that it might be possible to have existing employees cover parental leaves via job rotation and/or job enlargement.
- *HR planning*: Although the timing of specific leaves is unpredictable, in each of the past three years approximately seven staff were absent on parental leave at any one time. Slightly increasing the staffing complement to account for this level of absence (see Chapter 4) combined with job rotation or enlargement would reduce or even eliminate the need to hire temporary employees.
- *Training*: For job rotation or enlargement to be effective, it is necessary to cross-train staff (see Chapter 7). Additional training would increase costs slightly, in terms of both additional training and lost productivity. But it would save the cost associated with training temporary workers and provide greater organizational flexibility should there be some sort of unexpected shock to the organization.

Overall, this set of options reduces the administrative costs associated with the parental leave, is likely financially neutral, and avoids placing the organization in legal jeopardy. These changes are likely to have a mixed impact on workers. Some workers will appreciate the opportunity to move from position to position in the organization. The new skills will make them more employable and better able to compete on more senior jobs. Other workers will not appreciate having to learn new skills and develop new work relationships and might see it as an increase in their workloads. It is hard to tell how this will affect overall rates of staff turnover or demands for wage increases, so it is difficult to assess meaningfully the risk of this option for the organization.

Complicating things is that some entry-level positions are viewed by workers as inherently better than others because of the working conditions and duties. For example, working in the public library is more pleasant than answering questions and accepting appeals about property tax assessments. Workers can be incentivized by job rotation to perform better in good jobs and worse in bad jobs in the hope of influencing where they are placed in the future. This dynamic can negatively affect performance in some departments, but it is hard to assess the risk that it can pose. It is possible that further job redesign might improve the quality of some of these jobs.

Worker Underperforming

Kelly Moody is a 54-year-old snowplow driver. Two years ago, the small city where Kelly lives decided to contract out snow removal. They were laid off by the city and then hired by Plow King, the company that won the contract. Plow King pays Kelly 20% less than the city did and does not offer a pension plan. Their performance with Plow King has been satisfactory. This winter, however, homeowners in neighbourhoods where Kelly is clearing snow are complaining to the city that their driveways are partially blocked.

The city has been referring these complaints to Plow King for remediation. This usually entails dispatching a small bobcat crew to remove the windrows. Many of the windrows that have led to complaints are very small (less than six inches high) and pose no real barrier. A small number of windrows are larger and impede or simply narrow access for residents. Windrows are a common outcome of snow clearing and usually cleaned up by the operator. A small number of citizen complaints are common. There has been an increase in complaints this year, and Kelly has received the most complaints of the 15 operators.

Kelly's supervisor has told them to ensure that there are no windrows left. This direction has improved but not resolved the problem. The general manager is concerned that continued complaints will mean that Plow King's contract with the city will not be renewed. The supervisor wants to suspend or terminate Kelly's employment over these performance issues. You are the only HR practitioner employed by Plow King, and the general manager has directed you to resolve "Kelly's performance problem" immediately.

Since the general manager is framing this as a performance problem, you decide to start by assessing its cause(s) using the process set out in Figure 9.2 (go back to refer to this process). You begin by determining whether the expectations of windrow removal have been made clear to Kelly. The supervisor provides you with a list of three dates when Kelly was verbally instructed to remove all windrows. The supervisor also sent Kelly two text messages with the same directions. Given the context of the text messages and the supervisor's recollections of the verbal instructions, you are satisfied that the expectation has been clearly communicated.

Reviewing Kelly's HR file also suggested that they do have the ability to clear windrows. Kelly has more than 30 years of experience operating a snowplow and two satisfactory performance assessments, which include a supervisor's observation of their work. There are no references to inadequate windrow clearing. The administrative data that you can find about complaints from past years are incomplete, so you set the data aside as not valid or reliable.

Kelly has the same equipment as every other snowplow operator, and this equipment has not changed over time, so you are satisfied that they have the resources necessary to clear windrows. With this basic background research done, you decide to interview Kelly and arrange to meet them in a coffee shop during the lunch break. Your interview yields four salient pieces of information.

- The time required to plow a given area depends, in part, on the amount of snow that has fallen, the condition of the snow (e.g., loose or compacted), and the presence of obstructions (e.g., parked cars, traffic, stacked snow). Poor plowing conditions historically required operators to work overtime, for which they received overtime pay.
- This year operators were directed not to put in for overtime. It is not clear who made this decision, but Kelly says that all operators were given this direction by their respective supervisors. Some operators continue to work overtime but not record it. Kelly has reduced the number of passes made down each street to complete the work in the allotted time.
- Kelly harbours some resentment about the reduction in pay and loss of benefits following contracting out of snow removal by the city. This resentment has been intensified by the loss of overtime pay.
- Kelly is deeply resentful of being chastened for the declining quality of work. Their supervisor has repeatedly refused to address the impact of the overtime ban on the quality of the plowing.

Following the interview, you are not necessarily sure that this is a performance problem. You decide to use the issues analysis checklist in Feature Box 11.1. That analysis yields three potential ways to frame the problem.

- *Resource shortage*: The decision to eliminate overtime has put plow operators in a difficult situation. To complete the job, they must either self-exploit (i.e., work without wages) or trade quality for speed.
- *Dissatisfaction with compensation*: Kelly is dissatisfied with both the overall compensation mix and the loss of overtime pay, and this might be affecting their performance.
- *Insubordination*: Kelly might be complying maliciously with the supervisor's directive to complete the task within a fixed amount of time by lowering the quality of the work.

Each framing suggests different pathways to a fix. Allowing operators to claim overtime is likely to resolve the problem of poor quality (and thus attenuate the risk of contract loss) and bring Plow King into compliance with the law on overtime premiums (see Chapter 2). It would also, however, increase labour costs and thereby reduce profitability. Since the overtime ban externalizes some labour costs to the workers (i.e., some continue to work without pay), it might be cheaper for the company simply to let workers like Kelly, unwilling to self-exploit, quit.

Alternatively, if Kelly's dissatisfaction with the compensation package is causing them to reduce the amount of effort expended on the job, then altering the compensation structure might induce greater effort and thereby address the concerns about quality. Compensation could be linked explicitly with meeting certain quality benchmarks, although how to set and assess them is unclear. Altering the compensation structure would require the agreement of the workers (see Chapter 9) and likely increase labour costs.

Finally, there is obviously friction between Kelly and their supervisor. The reinstatement of overtime or a change in Kelly's compensation might be an opportunity to assist them to resolve their differences. Alternatively, the employment of one or the other could be terminated with notice. Mediation or termination alone would not solve the root problem that operators have not been allocated adequate time to meet performance standards. That said, terminating Kelly (unhappy with the job) might allow Plow King to hire a different plow operator who would be prepared to work uncompensated overtime.

Disability Accommodation and Harassment

You are an HR practitioner in the provincial government. Your manager has directed you to place a long-term employee (Brian) into a vacant, unionized position rather than running the usual job competition. The collective agreement allows you to do this in "exceptional circumstances" as long as you provide notice and explanation to the union. The job that you have been directed to put Brian into will see him work in a unit with 20 other unionized staff members and one non-unionized manager, most of whom are women.

You looked at his personnel file to confirm that Brian has the KSAs required for the position (he does) and discovered an extensive record of performance and disciplinary issues. His performance has varied over time from unsatisfactory to marginally satisfactory. Over the past 15 years, two of his past managers attempted to dismiss him (using progressive discipline) for poor performance. A combination of slight performance improvements and medical notes frustrated these efforts to terminate him. Instead, Brian has been issued a series of verbal and written reprimands.

The only active medical note in the file indicates that he has post-traumatic stress disorder (PTSD) following a non-work-related car accident five years ago. The psychologist indicates that the PTSD can compromise Brian's judgment in social situations and ability to focus on tasks. Since the accident, Brian has received additional written warnings for excessive absenteeism, poor job performance, and inappropriate behaviour in the workplace (specifically leering at and repeatedly asking out female co-workers).

At present, he is suspended from work without pay after being accused of harassing another government employee (in a different department) during his lunch hour at an offsite location. Noting Brian's government identification card hanging around his neck, the victim of the alleged harassment complained to her manager. During the investigation of this incident, it was discovered that Brian had also kept extensive notes about the performance and errors of his then manager, perhaps in retaliation for past verbal discipline that she had meted out.

After consultation with legal counsel, it was decided that the latest incident did not justify termination. Reading between the lines, it appears that there is concern that the union would grieve such a termination as discriminatory, arguing that Brian's behaviour was the result of his PTSD. Instead, it was determined that Brian should receive a written reprimand and be moved to a comparable job in a different office. This is how his file found its way to you.

You are very concerned that Brian's previous behaviour is placing 20 employees at risk of harassment, which would violate the organization's obligation to identify and control hazards (see Chapter 2). Your past experience is that your own manager expects you to obey orders and not push back. You have a good working relationship with the manager of the unit into which Brian is to be transferred. You are fairly sure that the manager of this unit does not know about his past behaviour. You are concerned that placing Brian into her unit and not telling her about his past will damage your relationship with the manager. So what do you do?

You could focus on a number of potential issues, but after some reflection the most compelling one, both personally and organizationally, is that placing Brian in the new unit places the workers in that unit at risk. There is also the need to comply with your manager's directions to place Brian into a job and not discriminate against him on the basis of his PTSD.

You can think of three ways to approach this situation.

- You can place Brian into the unit and not disclose his past behavioural issues. This complies with your manager's direction. But it creates a real risk that Brian will harass one or more of the workers in that unit. In addition to the potential harm caused to the worker(s) whom he might harass, if human resources fails to flag this as a hazard and control it, then there can be legal risk (the union also represents these workers) as well as distrust between line managers and HR personnel.
- You can propose the placement to the unit manager and tell her your concerns about Brian so that she can take steps to protect her staff. She will almost certainly resist his placement, and that will anger your boss, who will see this as an effort to thwart his clear direction to place Brian in the unit.
- You can call the unit manager and tell her that you have been directed to place a worker into the vacant position in her unit. You can then ask her if she wants to review the worker's personnel file first. This is the manager's right but one rarely exercised. This review will likely forewarn the unit manager of Brian's issues and give you an opportunity to discuss the manager's options. These options might include the unit manager resisting the placement or implementing a performance management plan (see Chapter 9). Some performance management options might include requiring Brian to complete training or serving him with a letter of behavioural expectations.

None of these options is ideal. In the end, you decide that the third option is the best one. It allows you to give the receiving manager an informal heads up but leaves the final decision about resisting the placement to her.

Union Drive

The Station Bar and Grill is a family-operated restaurant and bar. It is the largest eatery in your small urban centre and employs approximately 10 servers, 10 kitchen staff, four assistant managers, and one general manager (also the owner). You report to the general manager and handle all administrative functions, including accounting and human resources.

All serving and kitchen staff are paid the minimum wage. All tips are pooled. Any costs (e.g., dine and dash, breakage) are deducted from the tip pool, and the remainder is distributed evenly among all staff working that shift, including the assistant and general managers. Staff are resentful of using tips to cover losses and sharing tips with managers (already better compensated). The Station does not currently offer any paid sick leave for its employees. Staff are entitled to unpaid time off for illness, but many go to work when sick because they cannot afford to lose their wages.

The servers are mostly female. In your observation, they are all both young and attractive and required to wear tight-fitting outfits. Over time, servers have reported significant sexual harassment by customers and, occasionally, the assistant managers. As far as you know, the general manager has not taken any effective action to address this issue. Overall, morale seems to be low, and there has been a slight uptick in staff turnover during the past year.

On your way home on Tuesday, you note that local union organizer Sean O'Brien is handing out leaflets to servers and cooks arriving for the evening shift. O'Brien seems to be quite friendly with several of the cooks and a few of the servers. You are worried that the Guild of Restaurant and Casino Employees is organizing a union among your workers, and you immediately call the general manager. He is very upset by this news and tells you to prevent the guild from organizing the Station at all costs.

You know that there is some worker dissatisfaction at the Station. You also know that dissatisfied workers can exhibit loyalty, voice, neglect, or exit behaviours (see Feature Box 11.2). The heightened turnover might be a sign of exit behaviour. Unionization is a form of voice and often reflects workers' desire for better wages and working conditions. In thinking back on your conversations with the general manager, he has expressed negative views about unions. His specific worries about unionization are that it will trigger significant cost increases and interfere with the operation of the restaurant. His family worked very hard to create a successful business, and he is very resistant to anyone—workers, the government, a union—interfering in its operation.

Basically, you see two ways to approach this issue. First, you could recommend that the manager take some action to pressure the workers into giving up on the union. For example, he could threaten to close the business if the workers join a union, or he could threaten to (or actually) fire some of the workers whom you saw talking to O'Brien. Based on your experience, you expect that this approach would dissuade the workers from pursuing unionization. But you also know that it entails some risks. The union might file a complaint with the labour board that the Station engaged in unfair labour practices by interfering with the workers' right to join a union (see Chapter 10). The workers might also go to the press and damage the Station's reputation, or, since comparable jobs are easy enough to find, they might quit in protest, possibly all at once.

The second option is to propose addressing the concerns that you believe are driving the workers toward the union. This could include

- ending the practice of covering losses from the tip jar;
- no longer requiring tips to be split with managers;
- introducing a small number of paid sick days, giving managers the discretion to ask for medical evidence of illness (to prevent abuse);
- allowing servers to choose their own working attire;
- implementing a zero-tolerance policy on sexual harassment by customers or staff (including a process for complaints); and
- investigating past complaints about one of the assistant managers.

These changes might be enough to cause the workers to lose interest in joining the union. There will be some small costs associated with these changes, but you suspect that they will be offset by savings on hiring and training costs. The major risk here is that the workers will learn that they can effect change through cooperation and might make future demands. You think that this risk is relatively low. This second option is clearly better for the organization because it has much lower risk attached to it. It also entails meaningful improvements in the workers' wages and working conditions.

It is not clear that the general manager will be interested in increased upfront costs or in accommodating the interests of the workers. One way to frame the second option to him is as an opportunity to implement minor and low-cost operational changes that will maintain the Station's long-standing reputation as a good, family-operated employer. This framing will fit with his view that his family runs a fair workplace and thus will make these changes more palatable to him. You expect that these changes, as a bonus, will keep the union out of the workplace by undermining the key benefits that unionization might offer. This is an example of how attending to the psychological needs of decision makers can increase the likelihood that they will adopt a recommendation.

The Conflicted Roles of HR Practitioners

The cases presented above highlight that HR practitioners sometimes can find themselves in difficult positions while doing their job. Although most HR departments and practitioners abide by both contractual obligations and legal requirements, sometimes organizations or organizational decision makers can find advantage in acting otherwise. These instances can place them into positions that are tricky to navigate. For example, an organization might wish to get rid of a worker without providing a reasonable period of notice or pay in lieu. To avoid such a cost, the employer might fire the worker wrongfully (perhaps with a small amount of money in lieu of notice) and rely on the high cost of legal action to pressure the worker into accepting the employer's terms.

This demand by an organization places an HR practitioner in a tough spot. An HR employee can face significant pressure to participate in this activity and close ranks with the employer, regardless of whether or not such behaviour causes personal discomfort. The HR employee might even be tasked with breaking the news to the worker and handling that worker's subsequent phone calls and workplace appearances. As this HR practitioner, do you go along with the employer's demands? And what does this say about the employer's commitment to its workers (including you)?

Such moral dilemmas occur frequently in human resource management. There is often contractual ambiguity or room for discretion in handling HR matters. What if an employee misses a deadline by one day for opting-in to an employment benefit? Do you overlook this and process the worker's request anyway? Do you hold the worker to the policy? On what basis do you make this decision? Would you risk arguing with your boss to do right by a worker?

Savvy HR practitioners can use several strategies to protect themselves (and their employers) when placed in such difficult circumstances. As discussed in Feature Box 11.1, one strategy is to ensure that the "real" problem or issue at hand has been identified. This is important because often there are multiple ways to look at an issue. How an issue is framed can shape how an organization responds and the options available to it. Often carefully examining an issue to identify the real problem can productively change the options available to remedy the issue. For example, is recurring tardiness the result of a worker's flaunting of a supervisor's authority? Or does it reflect the limitations of public transit and could be eliminated through a slight variation in start and end times? How tardiness is framed shapes the potential solutions. In figuring out the real problem, it is important to recognize that frustration can affect the perspectives of those closest to the issue.

A second useful strategy is to identify the risks associated with the problem, the issue, or the resolution. Sometimes difficult situations emerge when those involved do not recognize the risks associated with particular actions or behaviours. Identifying the potential legal, reputational, or other risks associated with a decision can (re)focus discussion and cause decision makers to reassess how they wish to proceed. For example, many employers are keen to implement random drug testing in their workplaces. Sometimes this reflects an earnest belief that testing will improve safety. In other cases, it reflects a moral position that drug use is wrong. In either case, identifying the legal and reputational risks of such a decision can induce (if you will pardon the pun) sober second thoughts. The challenge here is tactfully to frame a risk assessment so as not to alienate the decision maker (or others).

A third useful strategy is to document the process. Maintaining a complete record of difficult situations is helpful in a number of ways. If there are questions about what happened, then a written record can be an important and credible source of information for the employer. Furthermore, the process of documenting decisions can cause decision makers to reflect on the consequences of their decisions should the written record ever be reviewed. This is sometimes called the *observer effect:* that is, writing things down often makes decision makers think more carefully about their actions because writing things down makes those decisions visible to others. If a decision maker decides to proceed in a questionable manner, then documentation records that the decision maker was apprised of the risks associated with the decision. This is referred to colloquially as CYA (cover your ass) paperwork and ensures that, if something bad happens, then the decision maker is not able to deflect blame onto you or your department.

Conclusion

The purpose of human resource management is to achieve organizational goals. The role of an HR practitioner is to facilitate achieving those goals in a legally and ethically grounded manner. That is not always easy. Organizational decision makers might wish to act in ways not anchored in law and ethics. Even if legal, some actions will disproportionately harm certain actors. This means that there are often unavoidable trade-offs and compromises in the day-to-day work of an HR practitioner.

Furthermore, employers and employees have conflicting interests. An HR practitioner can feel "caught in the middle" wanting to ensure decent working conditions for employees but needing to be responsible and accountable to the employer. Although HR practitioners might feel that they are caught in the middle, their role in the organization puts them on the side of the employer. The result can be situations in which practitioners might feel awkward and uncomfortable but have an obligation to resolve them.

That is why the practice of human resource management requires combining our technical knowledge of it with a political analysis of differing interests and goals. Navigating difficult situations requires understanding what motivates people and where their interests lie. With that understanding, the technical knowledge can be utilized in as responsible a fashion as possible and in a manner that protects the practitioner.

Notes

Chapter 1: Introduction to the Practice of Human Resource Management

1 C. Perkel, Medical officer hid relationships with fraudster during his hiring as CFO, *National Post*, January 31, 2020, https://nationalpost.com/pmn/news-pmn/canada-news-pmn/medical-officer-hid-relationship-with-fraudster-during-his-hiring-as-cfo; Canadian Press, Barker hid relationship with fraudster during hiring as CFO: Report, *Sault Star*, February 3, 2020, https://www.saultstar.com/news/local-news/barker-hid-relationship-with-fraudster-during-hiring-as-cfo-report.

2 P. Collins & S. Bilge, *Intersectionality* (2nd ed.) (Polity Press, 2002).

3 D. Doorey, *The law of work: Common law and the regulation of work* (2nd ed.) (Emond, 2020).

4 D. Broad & G. Hunter, Work, welfare, and the new economy, in N. Pupo & M. Thomas (Eds.), *Interrogating the new economy: Restructuring work in the 21st century* (pp. 21–42) (University of Toronto Press, 2010).

5 M. Yates, *Naming the system: Inequality and work in the global economy* (Monthly Review Press, 2003).

6 I. Bakker, Social reproduction and the constitution of a gendered political economy, *New Political Economy, 12*(4) (2007), 541–556.

7 H. Drost & R. Hird, *Introduction to the Canadian labour market* (2nd ed.) (Nelson, 2005).

8 L. Vosko, *Precarious employment: Understanding labour market insecurity in Canada* (McGill-Queen's University Press, 2006).

9 F. Fong, *Navigating precarious employment in Canada: Who is really at risk?* (Chartered Professional Accountants of Canada, 2018).

10 M. Porter, *Competitive advantage: Creating and sustaining superior performance* (Free Press, 1985).

11 D. Kaushik & U. Mukherjee, High-performance work system: A systematic review of literature, *International Journal of Organizational Analysis, 30*(6) (2022), 1624–1643.

12 D. Bowen & C. Ostroff, Understanding HRM-firm performance linkages: The role of the "strength" of the HRM system, *Academy of Management Review, 29*(2) (2004), 203–221.

13 J. Storey, Human resource management today: An assessment, in J. Storey (Ed.), *Human resource management: A critical text* (2nd ed.) (pp. 3–20) (Nelson, 2009).

14 J. Delery & D. Doty, Modes of theorizing in strategic human resource management: Test of universalistic, contingency and configurational performance predictions, *Academy of Management Journal, 39*(4) (1996), 802–815.

15 K. Anderson et al., The effect of SHRM practices on perceived firm financial performance: Some initial evidence from Australia, *Asia Pacific Journal of Human Resources, 45*(2) (2007), 168–179.

16 L. Harris & E. Ogbonna, Strategic human resource management, market orientation, and organizational performance, *Journal of Business Research, 51*(2) (2001), 157–166.

17 V. Haines et al., The influence of human resource management practices on employee voluntary turnover rates in the Canadian non governmental sector, *Industrial & Labor Relations Review, 63*(2) (2010), 228–246.

Chapter 2: Employment Law

1 *British Columbia (Public Service Employee Relations Commission) v. British Columbia Government Service Employees' Union*, [1999] 3 SCR 3.

2 M. Emara, Where are they now?, March 19, 2020, https://supremeadvocacy.ca/2020/03/19/where-are-they-now/.

3 D. Doorey, *The law of work: Common law and the regulation of work* (2nd ed.) (Emond, 2020).

4 Ibid.

5 *Canadian Charter of Rights and Freedoms*, Part I of the *Constitution Act, 1982*, being Schedule B to the *Canada Act 1982* (UK), 1982, c. 11, https://laws-lois.justice.gc.ca/eng/const/page-15.html.

6 *Vriend v. Alberta*, [1998] 1 SCR 493.

7 *Saskatchewan Federation of Labour v. Saskatchewan*, [2015] 1 SCR 245.

8 K. Mirchandani & S. Bromfield, Roundabout wage theft: The limits of regulatory protections for Ontario workers in precarious jobs, *Journal of Labour and Society, 22* (2019), 661–677.

9 N. Narwa, International student wins $16k in unpaid wages after going public with labour fight, *CBC News*, February 28, 2022, https://www.cbc.ca/news/canada/toronto/brampton-student-wins-labour-dispute-1.6364821.

10 J. Foster et al., Fear factory: Retaliation and rights claiming in Alberta, Canada, *Journal of Workplace Rights, 8*(2) (2018), 1–12.

11 J. Foster & B. Barnetson, *Health and safety in Canadian workplaces* (Athabasca University Press, 2016).

12 Ibid.

13 Association of Workers' Compensation Boards of Canada, *National work injury, disease and fatality statistics* (Author, 2019), http://awcbc.org/wp-content/uploads/2020/01/National-Work-Injury-Disease-and-Fatality-Statistics-2016-2018.pdf.

14 B. Barnetson et al., Estimating underclaiming of compensable workplace injuries in Alberta, Canada, *Canadian Public Policy, 44*(4) (2018), 400–410.

15 B. Barnetson & J. Matsunaga-Turnbull, *Safer by design: How Alberta can improve workplace safety* (Parkland Institute & Alberta Workers' Health Centre, 2018), https://d3n8a8pro7vhmx.cloudfront.net/parklandinstitute/pages/1569/attachments/original/1524676203/saferbydesign.pdf?1524676203.

16 W. Meredith, *Final report* (Author, 1913), http://awcbc.org/wp-content/uploads/2013/12/meredith_report.pdf.

17 B. Barnetson *The political economy of workplace injury in Canada* (Athabasca University Press, 2010).

18 Prism Economics and Analysis, *Claims suppression in the Manitoba Workers' Compensation System: A research report* (Author, 2013), https://www.wcb.mb.ca/sites/default/files/Manitoba%20WCB%20Claim%20Suppression%20Report%20-%20Final-1.pdf.

19 E. MacEachen et al., A deliberation on "hurt versus harm" logic in early return-to-work policy, *Policy and Practice in Health and Safety, 5*(2) (2007), 41–62.

20 *Canada (Attorney General) v. Johnstone*, 2014 FCA 110 (CanLII).

21 *Streeter v. HR Technologies*, 2009 HRTO 841.

22 Doorey, *The law of work.*

Chapter 3: Workflow, Job Analysis, and Job Design

1 E. Basker, Change at the checkout: Tracing the impact of a process innovation, *Journal of Industrial Economics, 63*(2) (2015), 339–370.

2 E. Basker & T. Simcoe, Upstream, downstream: Diffusion and economic impacts of the universal product code, January 18, 2018, https://voxeu.org/article/how-barcode-changed-retailing.

3 H. Tuller, Grocery store clerks, *Healthday News*, December 31, 2020, https://perma.cc/WCE4-4DKD.

4 A. Sagan, Metro to double number of stores with self-checkouts amid labour crunch, *BNN Bloomberg*, November 20, 2019, https://www.bnnbloomberg.ca/metro-quarterly-same-store-sales-rise-for-food-pharmacy-1.1350969.

5 S. Harris, Why some stores have pulled their self-checkout machines, *CBC News*, February 10, 2019, https://www.cbc.ca/news/business/canadian-tire-self-checkout-cashiers-automation-1.5011981.

6 C. Gilligan, *In a different voice: Psychological theory and women's development* (Harvard University Press, 1982).

7 A. Hochschild, *The managed heart* (University of California Press, 1983).

8 A. Warton, The affective consequences of service work: Managing emotions on the job, *Work and Occupations, 20*(2) (1993), 205–232.

9 K. Pugliesi, The consequences of emotional labour: Effects on work stress, job satisfaction, and well being, *Motivation and Emotion, 23*(2) (1999), 125–154.

10 R. Hackman & G. Oldham, Motivation through the design of work: Test of a theory, *Organizational Behaviour and Human Performance, 16* (1976), 250–279.

11 Ibid.

12 Y. Fried & G. Ferris, The validity of the job characteristics model: A review and meta-analysis, *Personnel Psychology, 40* (1987), 287–322.

13 Ibid.; S. Behson et al., The importance of the critical psychology states in the job characteristics model: A meta-analytic and structural equations modeling examination, *Current Research in Social Psychology, 5*(12) (2000), 170–189.

14 M. Adria & A. Woudstra, Who's on the line? Managing student interactions in distance education using a one-window approach, *Open Learning, 16*(3) (2001), 249–261.

15 A. Kondra et al., Call centres in distance education, in T. Anderson (Ed.), *The theory and practice of online learning* (pp. 367–396) (Athabasca University Press, 2008).

16 S. Zhang et al., A work-life conflict perspective on telework, *Transportation Research Part A: Policy and Practice, 141* (2020), 51–68, https://doi.org/10.1016/j.tra.2020.09.007.
17 T. Tan & S. Netessine, When does the devil make work?: An empirical study of the impact of workload on worker productivity, *Management Science, 60*(6) (2014), 1574–1593.
18 B. Barnetson, *Canada's labour market training system* (Athabasca University Press, 2018).

Chapter 4: Human Resource Strategy and Planning

1 K. Zarzour, Almost 100 registered nurse positions to be cut at Southlake Hospital, *Yorkregion.com*, September 22, 2020, https://www.yorkregion.com/news-story/10206713-almost-100-registered-nurse-positions-to-be-cut-at-southlake-hospital/.
2 M. Porter, *Competitive advantage: Creating and sustaining superior performance* (Free Press, 1985).
3 M. Armstrong & A. Baron, *Strategic HRM: The key to improved business performance* (Chartered Institute of Personnel and Development, 2002).
4 P. Wright et al., Current approaches to HR strategies: Inside-out versus outside-in, *Human Resource Planning, 27* (4) (2004), 36–46.
5 P. Wright & S. Snell, Towards a unifying framework for exploring fit and flexibility in strategic human resource management, *Academy of Management Review, 23*(4) (1998), 756–772.
6 Porter, *Competitive advantage.*
7 D. Mills, Planning with people in mind, *Harvard Business Review*, July–August 1985, 97–105.
8 Ibid.
9 N. Taleb, *The black swan: The impact of the highly improbable* (Random House, 2010).
10 M. Hawkesworth, *Theoretical issues in policy analysis* (Oxford University Press, 1988).
11 Government of Canada, Labour force characteristics by province, monthly, seasonally adjusted, Table: 14-10-0287-03, 2021, https://www150.statcan.gc.ca/t1/tbl1/en/tv.action?pid=1410028703.
12 Government of Canada, Job bank, 2021, https://www.jobbank.gc.ca/marketreport/outlook-occupation/21460/ca.
13 Government of Canada, Canadian occupational projection system, 2019, https://open.canada.ca/data/en/dataset/e80851b8-de68-43bd-a85c-c72e1b3a3890.

14 Government of Alberta, Alberta's occupational outlook, 2019, https://open.alberta.ca/publications/albertas-occupational-outlook.

15 Canada, Construction Sector Council, *The state of women in construction in Canada* (Author, 2010).

16 J. Foster & B. Barnetson, Who's on secondary? The impact of temporary foreign workers on Alberta construction employment patterns, *Labour/Le Travail, 80* (2017), 27–53.

17 H. O'Neill & J. Lenn, Voices of survivors: Words that CEOs should hear, *Academy of Management Executives, 9*(4) (1995), 23–33.

18 P. Dolan et al., It ain't what you do, it's the way that you do it: Characteristics of procedural justice and their importance in social decision-making, *Journal of Economic Behaviour & Organization, 64*(1) (2007), 157–170.

19 A. Hale, 2020 sunshine list: CAO tops list of Newmarket's 186 top-earning public sector employees, *Newmarket Today*, March 23, 2021, https://www.newmarkettoday.ca/local-news/2020-sunshine-list-cao-tops-list-of-newmarkets-186-top-earning-public-sector-employees-3567841.

20 E. Payne, Desperate hospitals seek nurses, offer signing bonuses, *Healthing.ca*, https://www.healthing.ca/partners/healthcare-professionals/desperate-hospitals-seek-nurses-offer-signing-bonuses.

Chapter 5: Recruitment

1 J. Dastin, Amazon scraps secret AI recruiting tool that showed bias against women, *Technology News*, October 9, 2018, https://www.reuters.com/article/us-amazon-com-jobs-automation-insight/amazon-scraps-secret-ai-recruiting-tool-that-showed-bias-against-women-idUSKCN1MK08G.

2 Job seekers line up for part-time work at Saddledome job fair, *Global News*, August 22, 2016, https://globalnews.ca/news/2896020/calgary-job-seekers-expected-to-pack-saddledome-job-fair/.

3 A. Saxena, Workforce diversity: A key to improve productivity, *Procedia Economics and Finance, 11* (2014), 76–85, https://doi.org/10.1016/S2212-5671(14)00178-6.

4 W. T. Self et al., Balancing fairness and efficiency: The impact of identity-blind and identity-conscious accountability on applicant screening (R. E. Tractenberg, Ed.), *PLOS ONE, 10*(12) (2015), e0145208, https://doi.org/10.1371/journal.pone.0145208.

5 F. Dobbin & A. Kalev, Why diversity programs fail, *Harvard Business Review*, July/August (2016), 52–60.

6 S. Hawkins, The long arc of diversity bends towards equality: Deconstructing the progressive critique of workplace diversity efforts, *University of Maryland Law Journal of Race, Religion, Gender and Class, 16*(1) (2016), 61–116.

7 S. Cheng et al., Challenging diversity training myths, *Organizational Dynamics, 48*(4) (2019), 100678, https://doi.org/10.1016/j.orgdyn.2018.09.001; Hawkins, The long arc of diversity.

8 N. Tiku, Three years of misery inside Google, the happiest company in tech, *Wired Magazine*, August 13, 2019, https://www.wired.com/story/inside-google-three-years-misery-happiest-company-tech/.

9 A. Blakemore & D. Hoffman, Seniority rules and productivity: An empirical test, *Economica, 56* (1989), 359–371; F. Belloc & M.D'Antoni, The elusive effect of employment protection on labor turnover, *Structural Change and Economic Dynamics, 54* (2020), 11–25, https://doi.org/10.1016/j.strueco.2020.04.001; P.Böckerman et al., Seniority rules, worker mobility and wages: Evidence from multi-country linked employer-employee data, *Labour Economics, 51* (2018), 48–62, https://doi.org/10.1016/j.labeco.2017.11.006.

10 K. Matos et al., Toxic leadership and the masculinity contest culture: How "win or die" cultures breed abusive leadership: Toxic leadership, *Journal of Social Issues, 74*(3) (2018), 500–528, https://doi.org/10.1111/josi.12284; T. Jana et al., *Erasing institutional bias: How to create systemic change for organizational inclusion*, (Oakland: Berrett-Koehler Publishers, Incorporated, 2018).

11 Randstad Canada, Is technology helping or hindering the job search process?, November 11, 2019, https://www.randstad.ca/employers/workplace-insights/workplace-innovation/infographic-is-technology-helping-or-hindering-the-job-search-process/.

12 Top Draw Inc., Online advertising costs in 2021, March 26, 2021, https://www.topdraw.com/insights/is-online-advertising-expensive/.

13 Statistics Canada, Job vacancies, third quarter 2019, *The Daily* (Statistics Canada), December 17, 2019; Statistics Canada, Table 14-10-0328-08 (2023).

14 A. Smith, Searching for work in the digital era, *Pew Research Center* (blog), November 19, 2015, https://www.pewresearch.org/internet/2015/11/19/searching-for-work-in-the-digital-era/; L. Adler, New survey reveals 85% of all jobs are filled via networking, *Linkedin.com* (blog), February 29, 2016, https://www.linkedin.com/pulse/new-survey-reveals-85-all-jobs-filled-via-networking-lou-adler.

15 B. Barnetson, *Canada's labour market training system* (Athabasca University Press, 2018).

16 J. Lauret, Amazon's sexist recruiting tool: How did it go so wrong?, *Becoming Human,* August 16, 2019, https://becominghuman.ai/amazons-sexist-ai-recruiting-tool-how-did-it-go-so-wrong-e3d14816d98e.

Chapter 6: Selection

1 L.A. Harris, *Rebuilding the foundation: External review into systemic racism and oppression at the Canadian Museum for Human Rights,* (Canadian Museum for Human rights, 2020).

2 M. Bertrand & S. Mullainathan, Are Emily and Greg more employable than Lakisha and Jamal? A field experiment on labor market discrimination, *The American Economic Review, 94*(4) (2004), 991–1013; S. K. Kang et al., Whitened résumés: Race and self-presentation in the labor market, *Administrative Science Quarterly, 61*(3) (2016), 469–502, https://doi.org/10.1177/0001839216639577.

3 M. S. Cole et al., Interaction of recruiter and applicant gender in resume evaluation: A field study, *Sex Roles, 51*(9–10) (2004), 597–608, https://doi.org/10.1007/s11199-004-5469-1.

4 E. Derous & R. Pepermans, Gender discrimination in hiring: Intersectional effects with ethnicity and cognitive job demands, *Archives of Scientific Psychology, 7*(1) (2019), 40–49, https://doi.org/10.1037/arc0000061.

5 W. T. Self et al., Balancing fairness and efficiency: The impact of identity-blind and identity-conscious accountability on applicant screening (R. E. Tractenberg, Ed.), *PLOS ONE, 10*(12) (2015), e0145208, https://doi.org/10.1371/journal.pone.0145208.

6 G. S. Jelf, A narrative review of post-1989 employment interview research, *Journal of Business and Psychology, 14*(1) (1999), 25–58, https://doi.org/10.1023/A:1022954316857.

7 M. A. McDaniel et al., The validity of employment interviews: A comprehensive review and meta-analysis, *Journal of Applied Psychology, 79*(4) (1994), 599–616, https://doi.org/10.1037/0021-9010.79.4.599.

8 G. J. Sears & P. M. Rowe, A personality-based similar-to-me effect in the employment interview: Conscientiousness, affect versus competence-mediated interpretations, and the role of job relevance, *Canadian Journal of Behavioural Science, 35*(1) (2003), 13–24, https://doi.org/10.1037/h0087182.

9 J. Levashina et al., The structured employment interview: Narrative and quantitative review of the research literature, *Personnel Psychology, 67*(1) (2014), 241–293, https://doi.org/10.1111/peps.12052.

10 R. A. Posthuma et al., Beyond employment interview validity: A comprehensive narrative review of recent research and trends over time,

Personnel Psychology, 55(1) (2002), 1–81, https://doi.org/10.1111/j.1744-6570.2002.tb00103.x.

11 S. Macdonald, Work-place alcohol and other drug testing: A review of the scientific evidence, *Drug and Alcohol Review, 1693* (1997), 251–259; J. Hoffman & C. Larison, Drug use, workplace accidents and employee turnover, *Journal of Drug Issues, 28*(2) (1999), 341–364; J. Beach et al., *Final report: A literature review of the role of alcohol and drugs in contributing to work-related injury* (University of Alberta, 2006); K. Pidd & M. Roche, How effective is drug testing as a workplace safety strategy? A systematic review of the evidence, *Accident Analysis & Prevention, 71* (2014), 154–165; W. Biasutto et al., Systematic review of cannabis use and risk of occupational injury, *Substance Use & Misuse, 55*(11) (2020), 1733–1745.

12 D. Doorey, *The law of work: Common law and the regulation of work* (2nd ed.) (Emond, 2020).

13 V. Catano et al., *Recruitment and selection in Canada* (TopHat, 2016).

14 L. M. Hough & A. Furnham, Use of personality variables in work settings, in I. B. Weiner (Ed.), *Handbook of psychology* (wei1207) (John Wiley & Sons, 2003), https://doi.org/10.1002/0471264385.wei1207.

15 B. Puplampu et al., Reference taking in employee selection: Predication or verification, *IFE PsychologIA*, (1) (2003), 1–11. https://doi.org/10.4314/ifep.v11i1.23435

16 CareerBuilder, More than half of employers have found content on social media that caused them NOT to hire a candidate, according to recent CareerBuilder survey, August 9, 2018, https://press.careerbuilder.com/2018-08-09-More-Than-Half-of-Employers-Have-Found-Content-on-Social-Media-That-Caused-Them-NOT-to-Hire-a-Candidate-According-to-Recent-CareerBuilder-Survey.

17 *HBR* Editors, Stop screening job candidates' social media, *Harvard Business Review*, September/October (2021), https://hbr.org/2021/09/stop-screening-job-candidates-social-media.

18 L. Zhang et al., What's on job seekers' social media sites? A content analysis and effects of structure on recruiter judgments and predictive validity, *Journal of Applied Psychology, 105*(12) (2020), 1530–1546, https://doi.org/10.1037/apl0000490.

Chapter 7: Orientation and Training

1 D. Bilefsky, "I'm speaking out": Calgary firefighters allege decades of racism, *New York Times*, February 12, 2021, https://www.nytimes.com/2021/02/11/world/canada/calgary-firefighters-racism.html.

2 A. Toy, Calgary fire chief Dongworth admits to racism problem in CFD, outlines plan, *Global News*, February 10, 2021, https://globalnews.ca/news/7633673/calgary-fire-chief-racism-problem-plan/.

3 S. Cotsman & C. Hall, *Learning cultures lead the way: Learning and development outlook* (14th ed.) (Conference Board of Canada, 2018).

4 B. Barnetson, *Canada's labour market training system* (Athabasca University Press, 2018).

5 E. Vallance, Hiding the hidden curriculum: An interpretation of the language of justification in nineteenth-century educational reform, *Curriculum Theory Network, 4*(1) (1973–1974) 5–21.

6 J. Anyon, Social class and the hidden curriculum of work, *Journal of Education, 162*(1) (1980), 67–92.

7 A. Saks & R. Haccoun, *Managing performance through training and development* (8th ed.) (Nelson, 2019).

8 T. Sitzmann, A meta-analytic examination of the instructional effectiveness of computer-based simulation games, *Personnel Psychology, 64* (2011), 489–528.

9 R. Gagne et al., *Principles of instructional design* (5th ed.) (Wadsworth, 2005).

10 K. Bezrukova et al., A meta-analytical integration of over 40 years of research on diversity training evaluation, *Psychological Bulletin, 142*(11) (2016), 1227–1274.

11 K. Kraiger, Decision-based evaluation, in K. Kraiger (Ed.), *Creating, implementing and managing effective training and development* (pp. 331–375) (Jossey-Bass, 2001).

12 A. Saks & L. Burke, An investigation into the relationship between training evaluation and the transfer of training, *International Journal of Training and Development, 16*(2) (2012), 118–127.

13 K. Wallace, Creating an effective new employee orientation program, *Library Leadership and Management, 23*(4) (2009), 168–176.

14 H. Klein et al., Specific onboarding practices for the socialization of new employees, *International Journal of Selection and Assessment, 23*(3) (2015), 263–283.

15 M. Meyer & L. Bartels, The impact of onboarding levels on perceived utility, organizational commitment, organizational support, and job satisfaction, *Journal of Organizational Psychology, 17*(5) (2017), 10–27.

16 Toy, Calgary fire chief Dongworth.

Chapter 8: Wages and Benefits

1 A. Makhoul & Caledon Institute of Social Policy, *The living wage learning initiative*, Caledon Institute of Social Policy, Ottawa, 2005, https://www.deslibris.ca/ID/200725.

2 Statistics Canada, Table 14-10-0064-01 Labour force survey, 2023.

3 S. Block et al., *Canada's colour coded income inequality*, 2019, http://www.deslibris.ca/ID/10102903.

4 Conference Board of Canada, Income of people with disabilities, April 2017, https://www.conferenceboard.ca/hcp/provincial/society/disability-income.aspx.

5 J. French, U of A academics vote to accept pay raise for female professors, *Edmonton Journal*, April 16, 2019, https://edmontonjournal.com/news/local-news/u-of-a-academics-vote-to-accept-pay-raise-for-female-professors.

6 Salaries are derived from occupational profiles located on alis.alberta.ca.

7 M. Wayland, Scandal at Nissan deepens as CEO Saikawa resigns after admitting he was improperly overpaid, *CNBC News*, September 9, 2019, https://www.cnbc.com/2019/09/09/nissan-ceo-saikawa-to-step-down-on-september-16.html.

8 L. Mishel & J. Wolfe, CEO compensation has grown 940% since 1978, Economic Policy Institute, Washington, DC, August 14, 2019.

9 D. Macdonald, *Breakfast of champions: CEO pay in 2021*, 2023, https://policyalternatives.ca/newsroom/news-releases/canadian-ceo-pay-soars-new-all-time-high-due-inflation-report.

10 Mishel & Wolfe, CEO compensation.

11 J. Colombo, "Why has the U.S. CEO-to-worker pay ratio increased so much?," *Forbes Magazine*, August 31, 2019, https://www.forbes.com/sites/jessecolombo/2019/08/31/why-has-the-u-s-ceo-to-worker-pay-ratio-increased-so-much/?sh=67c4ca3f455e; X. Gabaix & A. Landier, Why has CEO pay increased so much?, *The Quarterly Journal of Economics, 123*(1) (2008), 49–100.

12 Mishel & Wolfe, CEO compensation.

13 J. E. Stiglitz, *The price of inequality* (W. W. Norton & Company, 2013).

14 G. Pransky et al., "Under-reporting of work-related disorders in the workplace: A case study and review of the literature," *Ergonomics, 42*(1) (1999), 171–182, https://doi.org/10.1080/001401399185874.

15 R. Tranjan, *Towards an inclusive economy syncing EI to the reality of low-wage work*, 2019, https://www.policyalternatives.ca/publications/reports/towards-inclusive-economy.

16 B. Barnetson, *The political economy of workplace injury in Canada* (Athabasca University Press, 2010).
17 S. Smith, Survey reveals majority of workers would rather work from home, *EHS Today*, August 19, 2013, https://www.ehstoday.com/health/article/21915844/survey-reveals-majority-of-workers-would-rather-work-from-home; A. Powell & L. Craig, Gender differences in working at home and time use patterns: Evidence from Australia, *Work, Employment & Society, 29*(4) (2015), 571–589, https://doi.org/10.1177/0950017014568140.
18 C. Sullivan & S. Lewis, Home-based telework, gender, and the synchronization of work and family: Perspectives of teleworkers and their co-residents, *Gender, Work & Organization, 8*(2) (2001), 123–145, https://doi.org/10.1111/1468-0432.00125.
19 K. Mirchandani, "'The best of both worlds' and 'cutting my own throat': Contradictory images of home-based work," *Qualitative Sociology, 23*(2) (2000), 159–182, https://doi.org/10.1023/A:1005448415689.
20 Employers see significant ROI in EFAPs, *Canadian HR Reporter*, November 18, 2014, https://www.hrreporter.com/news/hr-news/employers-see-significant-roi-in-efaps/280447.
21 T. Donalson, *Trends report 2016* (Chestnut Global Partners, 2016).
22 C. Lieberman, What wellness programs don't do for workers, *Harvard Business Review*, August 14, 2019, https://hbr.org/2019/08/what-wellness-programs-dont-do-for-workers.
23 US Centers for Medicare & Medicaid Services, Wellness programs, https://www.healthcare.gov/glossary/wellness-programs/.
24 F. Gathright, The business case for wellness programs, *Corporate Wellness Magazine* (blog), 2015, https://www.corporatewellnessmagazine.com/article/the-business-case-for-wellness-programs.
25 L. Solow, The scourge of worker wellness programs, *The New Republic*, September 2, 2019, https://newrepublic.com/article/154890/scourge-worker-wellness-programs.
26 H. De La Torre & R. Goetzel, How to design a corporate wellness plan that actually works, *Harvard Business Review*, March 16, 2016, https://hbr.org/2016/03/how-to-design-a-corporate-wellness-plan-that-actually-works.
27 J. Reif et al., Effects of a workplace wellness program on employee health, health beliefs, and medical use: A randomized clinical trial, *JAMA Internal Medicine, 180*(7) (2020), 952–960, https://doi.org/10.1001/jamainternmed.2020.1321.
28 Z. Song & K. Baicker, Effect of a workplace wellness program on employee health and economic outcomes: A randomized clinical trial, *JAMA, 321*(15) (2019), 1500, https://doi.org/10.1001/jama.2019.3307.

29 D. Jones et al., What do workplace wellness programs do? Evidence from the Illinois Workplace Wellness Study, National Bureau of Economic Research, Cambridge, MA, January 2018, https://doi.org/10.3386/w24229.
30 Statistics Canada, Pension plans in Canada, as of January 1, 2019, *The Daily*, August 13, 2020, https://www150.statcan.gc.ca/n1/daily-quotidien/200813/dq200813b-eng.htm.

Chapter 9: Performance Management, Discipline, and Termination

1 *Babcock v. C. & R. Weickert Enterprises Ltd.*, No. CanLII 3112 (NSCA) (Nova Scotia Court of Appeal, January 4, 1993).
2 H. Pickford & G. Joy, *Organizational citizenship behaviours: Definitions and dimensions*, Mutuality in Business Briefing 1, 2016, https://static1.squarespace.com/static/5e53b5bc158dd15abab915d4/t/5ecba1e3b4f8de1f777681e7/1590403557180/Literature+Reviews+-+Organizational+Citizenship+Behaviours+Definitions+and+Dimensions.pdf.
3 J. Foster & B. Barnetson, *Health and safety in Canadian workplaces* (Athabasca University Press, 2016).
4 Canadian Centre for Occupational Health and Safety, Bullying in the workplace, December 1, 2016, https://www.ccohs.ca/oshanswers/psychosocial/bullying.html.
5 M. Ironside & R. Seifert, Tackling bullying in the workplace: The collective dimension, in S. Einarsen et al. (Eds.), *Bullying and emotional abuse in the workplace: International perspectives in research and practice* (pp. 383–398) (Taylor & Francis, 2003).
6 D. Beale & H. Hoel, Workplace bullying and the employment relationship: Exploring questions of prevention, control and context, *Work, Employment & Society, 25*(1) (2011), 5–18, https://doi.org/10.1177/0950017010389228.
7 K. L. Stone, From queen bees and wannabes to worker bees: Why gender considerations should inform the emerging law of workplace bullying, *New York University Annual Survey of American Law, 65*(1) (2009), 35–86.
8 J. L. Raver & L. H. Nishii, Once, twice, or three times as harmful? Ethnic harassment, gender harassment, and generalized workplace harassment, *Journal of Applied Psychology, 95*(2) (2010), 236–254, https://doi.org/10.1037/a0018377.
9 D. V. Day et al., Advances in leader and leadership development: A review of 25 years of research and theory, *The Leadership Quarterly, 25*(1) (2014), 63–82, https://doi.org/10.1016/j.leaqua.2013.11.004.

10 J. Ghorpade, Managing Five paradoxes of 360-degree feedback, *Academy of Management Perspectives, 14*(1) (2000), 140–150, https://doi.org/10.5465/ame.2000.2909846.

11 B.e I. J. M. van der Heijden & A. H. J. Nijhof, The value of subjectivity: Problems and prospects for 360-degree appraisal systems, *The International Journal of Human Resource Management, 15*(3) (2004), 493–511, https://doi.org/10.1080/0958519042000181223.

12 L. R. James et al., Estimating within-group interrater reliability with and without response bias, *Journal of Applied Psychology, 69*(1) (1984), 85–98, https://doi.org/10.1037/0021-9010.69.1.85.

13 S. E. Scullen et al., Understanding the latent structure of job performance ratings, *Journal of Applied Psychology, 85*(6) (2000), 956–970, https://doi.org/10.1037/0021-9010.85.6.956.

14 A. Benson et al., Promotions and the Peter Principle*, *The Quarterly Journal of Economics, 134*(4) (2019), 2085–2134, https://doi.org/10.1093/qje/qjz022.

15 C. W. Sherif, Bias in psychology, *Feminism & Psychology, 8*(1) (1998), 58–75, https://doi.org/10.1177/0959353598081005.

16 T. J. Maurer & M. A. Taylor, Is sex by itself enough? An exploration of gender bias issues in performance appraisal, *Organizational Behavior and Human Decision Processes, 60*(2) (1994), 231–251, https://doi.org/10.1006/obhd.1994.1082.

17 *Toronto (City) v. Toronto Professional Fire Fighters' Association, Local 3888*, 2014 CanLII 76886 (ON LA) (2014), https://www.canlii.org/en/on/onla/doc/2014/2014canlii76886/2014canlii76886.html.

18 D. J. Doorey, *The law of work* (2nd ed.) (Emond Publishing, 2020), p. 139.

19 Ibid.

Chapter 10: Unions and Collective Bargaining

1 B. Martin et al., A tale of two airlines: Westjet and Canada 3000, *Journal of the International Academy for Case Studies, 11*(1) (2005), 97–106.

2 J. Sangster & J. Smith, Canadian travellers should welcome unionization at WestJet, *CBC News Online*, August 20, 2018, https://www.cbc.ca/news/opinion/westjet-union-1.4790795.

3 I. Bickis, WestJet CEO ramps up anti-union campaign, *CTV News*, July 13, 2017, https://www.ctvnews.ca/business/westjet-ceo-ramps-up-anti-union-campaign-1.3500741.

4 K. Owram, Losing the "WestJet effect": How the once-scrappy upstart carrier's culture is changing as it expands globally, *Financial Post*, October 2,

2015, https://financialpost.com/transportation/losing-the-westjet-effect-how-the-once-scrappy-upstart-carriers-culture-is-changing-as-it-expands-globally.

5 Canadian Labour Congress, The union advantage in Canadian communities, 2012.

6 Statistics Canada, Table 14-10-0070-01 Union status by industry, 2023, https://www150.statcan.gc.ca/t1/tbl1/en/tv.action?pid=1410007001.

7 US Bureau for Labor Statistics, Union members summary, January 22, 2021, https://www.bls.gov/news.release/union2.nro.htm.

8 Statistics Canada, Table 14-10-0129-01 Union status by geography, 2023, https://www150.statcan.gc.ca/t1/tbl1/en/tv.action?pid=1410012901

9 Statistics Canada, Table 14-10-0070-01 Union status by industry.

10 J. G. Reitz & A. Verma, Immigration, race, and labor: Unionization and wages in the Canadian labor market, *Industrial Relations, 43*(4) (2004), 835–854.

11 R. Milkman & K. Voss (Eds.), *Rebuilding labor: Organizing and organizers in the new union movement* (Cornell University Press, 2004).

12 S. Slinn, An analysis of the effects on parties' unionization decisions of the choice of union representation procedure: The strategic dynamic certification model, *Osgoode Hall Law Journal, 43*(4) (2005), 407–450.

13 Ibid.

14 M. J. Levitt & T. Conrow, *Confessions of a Union Buster* (Crown Publishers, 1993), p. 2.

15 Ibid., p. 3.

16 R. Fisher et al., *Getting to yes: Negotiating an agreement without giving in* (2nd ed.) (: Random House Business Books, 1999).

17 C. Heckscher & L. Hall, Mutual gains and beyond: Two levels of intervention, *Negotiation Journal, 10* (1994), 235–248.

18 Employment and Social Development Canada, *Collective bargaining trends in Canada, 1984–2014* (Government of Canada, 2015).

19 L. Panitch & D. Swartz, *From consent to coercion: The assault on trade union freedoms* (University of Toronto Press, 2003).

20 Statistics Canada, CANSIM Table 282–0074, 2015.

21 Jackson & Thomas, *Work and labour in Canada* (Canadian Scholars Press, 2017).

22 Organization for Economic Cooperation and Development (OECD), Earnings inequality, low paid employment and earnings mobility, in *OECD employment outlook* (pp. 59–108) (OECD, 1996).

23 OECD, Can collective bargaining help close the gender way gap for women in non-standard jobs?, July 2020; R. Milkman & S. Luce, The state of the

unions 2015: A profile of organized labor in New York City, New York State and the United States, Joseph S. Murphy Institute for Worker Education and Labor Studies, New York, September 2015.

24 Jackson & Thomas, *Work and labour in Canada.*

25 Ibid.

26 B. Barnetson, Making it home: Alberta workplace injuries and the union safety dividend, Parkland Institute, Edmonton, September 2013.

27 H. Doucouliagos et al., *The economics of trade unions: A study of a research field and its findings* (Routledge, Taylor & Francis Group, 2017).

28 R. B. Freeman & M. Kleiner, Do unions make enterprises insolvent?, *Industrial & Labor Relations Review, 52*(4) (1999), 510–527.

29 T. Aidt & Z. Tzannatos, Unions and collective bargaining: Economic effects in a global environment, The World Bank, Washington, DC, 2003.

Chapter 11: The Practice of Human Resource Management

1 K. Armstrong, The bias of crowds: Beyond diversity training, 2021, Association for Psychological Science, https://www.psychologicalscience.org/observer/bias-of-crowds.

2 M. Foley & S. Williamson, Does anonymising job applications reduce gender bias? Understanding managers' perspectives, *Gender in Management, 33*(8) (2018), 623–635.

3 A. Hirschman, *Exit, voice, and loyalty: Responses to decline in forms, organizations, and states* (Harvard University Press, 1970).

Index

Figures and tables are indicated by page numbers in *italics*.

H

I

J

K

L

M

N

O

P

S

U

V

W